DRAQUALIAN SILK

DRAQUALIAN SILK

A COLLECTOR'S & BIBLIOGRAPHICAL GUIDE TO THE BOOKS OF WILLIAM MALTESE, 1969-2010

by

WILLIAM MALTESE

Edited by Robert Reginald

THE BORGO PRESS

An Imprint of Wildside Press LLC

MMX

BIBLIOGRAPHIES OF MODERN AUTHORS

ISSN 0749-470X

Number Nineteen

CONTENTS

Foreword: "Bon Appétit!" by Drewey Wayne Gunn...................... 7
Introduction: "A Mighty Fine Looking Baby" 10
About This Book.. 34

A Chronological Bibliography of Books by William Maltese 36

Pseudonym and Title Index.. 279
Publisher, Title, and Author Index... 287
Title and Author Index... 295

About the Author 303

DEDICATION

For Those Men and Women—
Oh, So Very Many—Who Sacrificed
Themselves on the Pyre of Their Art,
And Live Now Only in Their Words.

And to the Memory of My Dear Mother.

"A poet could not but be gay,
In such a jocund company."

—William Wordsworth

FOREWORD

BON APPÉTIT!

In looking over this savory bibliographical collection, I realize that I am one of a very select few who have actually seen the author hard at work in the fire of inspiration. Not that I have seen him in the flesh (though I have seen much of his flesh in his website gallery "Artists 'Do' Author William Maltese"). I first encountered him via his books many years ago and have maintained a friendship via email. I haven't read even a fifth of his production; the man is as prolific as Joyce Carol Oates or John Updike. But the uniformly high quality of his novels, not to mention their aphrodisiac qualities, have made them memorable reads, whether holding the novel in both hands or only one.

That opportunity to see the creative spirit in action occurred four years ago as the result of my casting about for someone to join me in a project I envisioned. A plan to bring out a second, expanded edition of some translations I and my late partner had made of pornographic poems by the French poets Paul Verlaine and Arthur Rimbaud (the first edition appearing in 1979 as *A Lover's Cock and Other Gay Poems*) had fallen apart. Here I was with over thirty translations, a great many of them totally new, and no publisher in sight.

That's when I had one of the best inspirations ever to bless me. What about incorporating the poems into a history of the two poets' tumultuous affair, intertwining biography, poetry, and sex beyond anything that Christopher Hampton had dared in his play and film script *Total Eclipse*? Such a mix would take a very special writer, someone whose prose could approach the music of poetry *and* someone who was willing to take risks and move into scatology that might surpass the bounds of acceptable taste. Nothing less could do justice to the complex dynamics of one of the most remarkable meetings in the history of European literature. William Maltese was the obvious, indeed the inevitable choice.

He was initially hesitant. I assured him I would wrestle with the French and the history if he would take on the passion and the psychology. Yes, it would mean his reading biography. And he would have to work out how to incorporate the poems naturally into his chapters so that they became an integral part of the story and not some appendix stuck onto the narrative. At this point I think I had more confidence in his powers than William did. But he reluctantly accepted the challenge, with the proviso that if the collaboration proved unsatisfactory to either of us, we would stop, with no hard feelings.

I waited. Then arrived his first chapter, about Rimbaud's rape (or supposed rape) at the hands of soldiers during the Commune, an assault (or fantasy) that formed the basis of the famous poem «*Mon triste coeur bave à la poupe*» ("My sad heart drools at the stern"). The chapter was every bit as brilliant as I expected. William imagined a scene that would simultaneously interest and arouse readers, take them into a most believable mental world of a nineteenth-century ragamuffin from the provinces, elucidate the poem—and make it such an integral part of the chapter that one must read it rather than skipping on to the next (as I suspect many readers do with the poems Tolkien interpolated into *Lord of the Rings*).

My part in this collaboration was largely to review each chapter as it came in and occasionally correct historical or cultural errors or make suggestions. I became editor in that I assembled the chapters and worked in some poems that could stand on their own between chapters. But mostly I read in awe. It was the first (and remains the only) time that I have caught even a glimpse of the way a creative mind fashions fiction. When the whole was finally assembled, the last tweaking done, and the manuscript ready to be sent to press under the title *Ardennian Boy* (in homage to William's earlier collection *Slovakian Boy*), I reread the novel from beginning to end.

What utterly amazed me was the unity and the extraordinarily intricate structure of the work. Even though I had watched it form, chapter by chapter, I am still mystified at how William was able instinctively to compose a work of biographical fiction whose later chapters so adroitly and so subtly mirror earlier chapters in ways that all readers must feel but few could be aware of without actually diagramming the novel's progression. The book was a finalist for the Lambda Literary Award for Best LGBT Erotica the year it was published. (Simon Sheppard beat us out with an anthology of post-World War II porn.)

I am happy that William has now assembled this collection of opening paragraphs. Some excerpts work as reminders of books I have already read. Others work as enticements to make me want to order the books that I have yet to sample. But after my experience working on this one novel with him, I realize that, if these paragraphs are *amuse-bouches*, as he has partly subtitled the collection (a good Frenchman, of course, would use the coarser expression *amuse-gueule*), they serve to whet the appetite for meals whose richness and fullness will far surpass what these first bites, no matter how tasty they may be, promise even. *Bon appétit* indeed!

—Drewey Wayne Gunn
Professor Emeritus,
Texas A&M University-Kingsville

INTRODUCTION

"A MIGHTY FINE LOOKING BABY"

Let me confess to being fully aware that my being who I am, today—where I am, today—with the backlog of literary work I have to my credit, today—is, in large part, attributable to some pretty damned good luck. There is simply no denying that anyone being the right person, at the right time, in the right place, can turn keys in a helluva lot of locks, to open wide a helluva lot of doors, otherwise usually kept tightly shut and secured.

Certainly, I, personally, had nothing whatsoever to do with my having been born such a mighty fine-looking baby, Baby! Seriously, I'm not saying that just because I'm narcissistic (although, I am), or because the nurse, who may well have been blind at the time, announced to the world at my birthing…, "Miss Scarlett, I don't know nuthin' about birthin' no baby!" Oops, I seem to have become a bit confused (literally? literarily?), which does happen to me, more and more often, at this junction of my long life, hopefully to get longer (since another wished-for elongation—of a certain anatomical part—never did take place). Rather, I say so, because, that delivery-room nurse wasn't the first or only person to say I was "too pretty to be a boy," quite aside from my parents and relatives, or anyone else, who might have possibly felt obligated to say it, true or not. Nor did my attractiveness wane as I proceeded into adolescence and early manhood, unlike most of those "other" very few beautiful male babies who usually turn into ogres before their testicles drop and/or their cocks achieve full cum-spewing capabilities. Pretty much everyone said I was beautiful and that I remained so, even when I had long since come to prefer they'd say "handsome." Definitely, undeniably, there *was* a consensus!

I mean, surely not everyone would lie, 24/7, would they? Okay, maybe, they would, but I've seen enough of my pictures, from babyhood to manhood, including a few nude ones, to know that I looked pretty damned good, the whole damned way. And, I, after all, have become quite the authority on genuinely attractive young men, having written over 180 published books that always included at least one, sometimes more than one (well, maybe not in my *THE GLUTEN-FREE WAY: MY WAY*, or in my *CATALYTIC QUOTES: SOME HEARD THROUGH A TIME WARP*), but there are always exceptions to every rule, aren't there?

People can day-dreamingly spout off all they want about "looks not counting," but, take it from me—someone who knows, and who has walked the walk—they're wrong. People, for whatever their reasons, just seem to respond more favorably to beautiful people, and would have reacted differently to me, from the get-go, if I'd popped out of my mother's womb to a loudly nurse-announced: "My God, another troll!"

My beauty (hereafter referred to as my handsomeness, if just because I'm the one writing this intro, not someone else), came naturally, but what about my writing skills? I mean, surely, my over 180 books, published over four decades, as evidenced in this reference volume, and appearing in over fourteen foreign-language editions, must speak volumes (volume?) about the way I successfully put words on paper to keep readers coming back for more (as some were, likewise, coming back for more-than-words in my bedroom). While there are those, out there, in the big wide world, usually teachers of writing, who would like everyone to think that writing skills can be taught, and therefore learned, I'm convinced those pontificators are merely self-aggrandizing blowers of smoke up wannabe writers' assholes. In that, I've yet to meet a teacher who could provide more than the basics of the English language and/or the rudiments of proper grammar; although I have met teachers who have had the ability to provide inspiration and incentive; or, on the opposite side of the coin, to provide, unfounded (except in their own hyped estimation of their opinions) put-downs to crush more than one potentially burgeoning writer and writing career.

My mother did read to me a lot as a child. While she didn't like to have people read to her, she did take great enjoyment in reading aloud to others, and I was one of the chief beneficiaries. Nor did the subject matter seem to matter all that much to her, as far as her reading to me was concerned. She would just as eagerly make the time to sit down with me to read from the pages of my school history or sociology texts, as have us mutually enjoy the latest best-selling novels (some of whose sex, I was later to discover, she sometimes censored to save us both undue embarrassment). Whether the school assignment was *Silas Marner, Moby Dick, Ethan Frome, Tale of*

Two Cities, or *The Pearl,* mother would willingly, even eagerly, read it to me.

Therefore, I might attribute my mother with having played some very important part in my success as a writer. Okay, I WILL attribute my mother with having played some very important part in my success as a writer. That said...if I wasn't inherently literarily inclined, I very much doubt I would have paid her reading any more mind than would have most of my peers who actually preferred doing other things, being elsewhere, than dealing with books (even when in a school room).

For whatever the reasons, I often went exploring through the stacks of the school library, and I invariably so often selected from them books that were designated for far older students that the school librarian had to check with my parents to be sure it was okay for me to bring home the books I was bringing home. I don't remember even one such book being rejected by my mother as too adult, too difficult, or too controversial in subject matter for me to hear most of what it contained.

Even later in my life, after having long been officially designated an adult by count of years, I would return home from university, from the military, or from wherever in the world I'd just traveled, to sit with my mother, in the family's outside swing (which I haven't had the willpower to "unwrap" since she died), while she read to me from whatever she was reading at the time—which continued to cover the whole literary spectrum from biographies, histories, mysteries, westerns, romances, to true-crime.

In her later years, suffering horribly bad eyesight from Type II Diabetes, and not nearly enjoying being read to, as much as reading it herself, or to others, my mother and I reversed reading roles, although I confess to putting her to sleep more often than she ever did me.

My father was always reading some new pulp western (he was particularly fond of Louis L'Amour), and always had a book with him when he went to his job that consisted of monitoring the men and machines at the Kaiser Aluminum Rolling Mill where he advantaged long sessions, wherein the automated equipment did its thing, and the men did their things, to make his life less boring by having a book pretty much always in hand.

There was, therefore, always an appreciation of books around my house, but never in overkill, and I early developed a genuine love of reading that was full-blown long before writing ever came into the picture. In fact, my appreciation of the written word, even by people other than myself, hasn't waned to this day, and I'm continually distraught when my increasingly busy writing and speaking schedules so often preclude me from reading as much, or as often, as I'd like and once did. I remember being happy as a lark, on one round-the-world cruise—whereon my fellow passengers bemoaned long days on the seemingly endless sea—with the ship's library copy of *War and Peace* and a deck chair positioned out of the wind.

My earliest written stories were adventures inspired by the comic ("funny" though often-not-funny) books of the time, like Tarzan, Buck Rogers, Jungle Jim, and Flash Gordon. The first remembered self-penned story that I recall was my "Spider with the Human Mind" plagiarized from some radio program unheard by me but relayed by my mother as having once pretty much scared her half to death as a young girl. Another derring-do tale, title unremembered, revolved around the discovery of a giant python skeleton in a hidden cave complex in the middle of the African jungle. Any and all of which my mother took great pride in either reading back to me, and/or seemingly being appropriately thrilled or chilled in response to my reading them (zzzzzzzz) to her.

I was always getting excellent grades for composition, although I had little real knowledge of the formal rules of English grammar, always merely writing what "sounded right." Also, I became quite proficient at writing essays of the type for contests usually sponsored by the likes of patriotic groups, like the DAR, and self-delivered before an appreciative audience. My early kudos at public speaking led me to think I would find debating of interest—which, as it turned out, when tried later, I didn't.

Strangely, though, despite my early amateurish successes in writing, including my early notoriety in reading aloud, at my high-school Papyrus Club, my jaw-dropping short story of baby-sacrifice and cannibalism on the Caribbean island of Martinique—despite my whimsical attempts at *haiku* that included a fellow Papyrus club-member—*Irene-ē, in a bikini, looks like a weenie! Hot dog!*—not to mention the English teacher and *Papyrus Club* faculty supervisor who predicted, very loudly, in the presence of my fellow club members, that I was likely the only one of that bunch she ever expected "to see officially published"—I don't recall a time, all through school, when I ever seriously considered writing as something I would do as a profession.

Although I had held various prominent posts on my junior-high school newspaper, and enjoyed the experience, I didn't seriously seek out any similar journalistic pursuits while in high-school or in university, rather under the impression, at the times, that I would prefer being an astronomer, translator, career diploma, or business tycoon; the first nipped in the bud by requiring far more mathematical genius than I—yawn!—ever saw myself acquiring; the second seeing my capacity for languages progress very little beyond, *Habla usted español*, or the totally useless, *Gallia est omnis divisa in partes tres*; the third souring with my read of *The Ugly American*, which didn't make the diplomatic service nearly as romantic as I'd anticipated; only world-scorned and damned dangerous.

On the other hand, I did foresee where one or more of my friends, especially fellow Papyrus Club members, might end up in the journalistic profession, despite what our adviser had voiced about me likely being the only one of the whole bunch ever to end up seeing anything in print. For instance, Gary, a hold-over friend of mine from junior-high school, had been the editor of our j-h newspaper, had been on our high-school newspaper and year-book staffs, and, later, often hinted of his continuing desire to "be a writer," in the letters he wrote me after he'd enlisted in the Army (he skipped college); he had his heart set on, writing for the *Stars and Stripes*.

As a quick aside, here, I might insert mention of something that, while I didn't know it, at the time, would, in the end, greatly affect my future writing, and affect how my writing was accepted, and affect the general over-all life-style I've pretty much enjoyed ever since. That being my conscious decision, at a very early age— knowing full well that I was so obviously attracted to men, and they were obviously attracted to me, my having been offered the invitation, "Want some candy, sonny?" on more than one occasion—to make sure my very first sex, above and beyond playful boyhood sexual game-play of slap-ass, grab penis, circle-jerks, was with a member of the opposite sex. This had nothing whatsoever to do with my desire to research all of the bisexual aspects of sexuality that would end up part of my writing repertoire, later. It had everything to do with my calculated realization that I was pretty much surrounded, on all sides, by a predominantly heterosexual world. Already, I knew that any successful career in business would necessitate a wife as a considered social asset, and, therefore, that my upward mobility within any industry might well depend upon my not only having a wife, but actually fucking one long enough to officially join the ranks of "breeder."

For whatever the physiological reasons, I have always been able to achieve an erection with women, as well as with men. My first full-blown sexual experience, when it did occur, was well-planned, with an older woman, and saw me perform to her satisfaction (her praise certainly coming across more genuine, rather mere patronization), and had seen me do a lot of preliminary reading up on the subject beforehand, as regards foreplay and the whole mechanics of sexual intercourse. That I found the experience enjoyable (any ejaculation not without its degree of pleasure), didn't mean I was exactly experiencing lightning bolts, skyrockets, and shooting stars. Although, to be truthful, no subsequent sexual acts, with either men or women, has ever since seen me genuinely inundated by stereotypical pyrotechnics, either.

In fact, those who have joined me in bed with the foregone anticipation that sex with me is bound to be a hot-and-heavy experience, if just because of me being who I am, of what I've written, of the life-style I've led, are likely going to come away disappointed, in that my participation in any sex act, including my first one with a woman, tends to be more planned and analytical exercise than spontaneous romp in the hay. Often, I'm more interested in the methodology of whatever I do, and whatever I say, and how it affects whomever I'm with (rather as if I'm scientist; my partner a lab rat), than I'm interested in my own pleasure (the latter never of the out-of-control kind of which I'm always hearing and writing). If the dichotomy of my easily hard cock, but my less than 100% involvement in any sex act, has seen me please more than one woman who hasn't before experienced a partner capable of my well-known sexual marathons, it's only because I'm basically not all that turned on by sex for sex's sake, or by any real biological need to procreate. Orgasms for me usually result after my partners have been coaxed into one or more of their own, and, thereby, expect me to join on in; at which point I merely concentrate a bit harder than I have been, on my own satisfaction, and muster up what they expect of me (or of any man)—"Oh, baby, you're so good, so good, oh, Jesus—I'm going to cum!—so good!"

By university, I had my sights narrowed to a profession in marketing/advertising, and I'd enrolled in subject matter accordingly. If I did venture out, on one occasion, into a 101 creative-writing course, by way of an elective, I found its teacher thoroughly unlikable (the feeling mutual), and of the type who was likely so soured by her own lack of publishing success that she was none too inspiring to me or to anyone genuinely aspiring to be a writer.

At the same time, Gary, from high-school and Papyrus Club, had been frustrated in his *Stars and Stripes* journalistic aspirations by having been picked, instead, for assignment to some kind of security-sensitive job in Germany. Anyway, that's what the guy, in black suit, said when he came by to question me at university, my having been reported as someone with whom Mr. Giles was a friend. My dark-suited visitor, after some very general questions, homed in on asking about whether I knew anyone Gary knew by the name of "Sandy." I pulled out some vague recollection of this gal, a year behind us in school, who kind of had a crush on Gary in junior-high, but the suit was specific in that "this Sandy of interest" would have to be male. There had been some innuendo, from someone else interviewed, that Sandy and Gary might have been, well, involved, and while that was, well, probably fiction, not fact, it did have to be checked on. I hadn't a clue and said so. I didn't say that I knew very little about Gary's sex life because I'd never found him all that physically attractive. When suit left, I did get to thinking, and decided that, well, yes, maybe Gary was gay, but I still didn't recall him ever being close to any guy called Sandy, at least not while around me.

I did keep a journal throughout my university years, but it was merely my way of keeping a record of mundane happenings in my life in order to relay them back to my parents who insisted I write them (those the days prior to email) on a regular basis.

After my mother and father died, I came across all of my college letters to them which they'd saved. They read pretty much verbatim what I wrote in my journal. No mention in journal or letters of how I always made it a point to go down to the college locker/ shower rooms just prior and after varsity gymnastics meets to see the muscled athletes undress and dress—how I'd been approached one night on a dark university street by a star athlete who wanted to suck me off and, when I said no, pulled out his cock and masturbated to climax in front of me—how I'd been told by one fraternity member, out to recruit me (unsuccessfully), that his frat had so many gay members that there were often openly gay orgies in which even straight frat brothers joined in—of the university professor who raised my grade from a "C" to a "B" just because I obliged his request for me to pull out my cock so he could see and confirm my dick was just as big as he fantasized—of the co-ed who took great pleasure in rubbing up against me in ballroom-dancing class and giving me the boner she always readily hand-soften during the free period we both had afterwards.

Certainly, it wasn't any epiphanic, *Damn this would make an interesting story for me to write—and sell!* that had me, and a couple other college buddies, embark upon our decidedly daredevil (as seen in retrospect) South American treasure-hunting adventure, between our junior and senior years at university, spurred by a treasure map I'd found in the back of an obscure botanical text ferreted, quite by accident, from the stacks of the Washington State University Holland Library. I didn't have a clue that my resulting experiences from that devil-make-care decision would provide me the fodder not only for one but for five future novels (my Harlequin SuperRomance *LOVE'S EMERALD FLAME*, my Heritage Books *JUNGLE-QUEST INTRIGUE*, my Wildside/Borgo *BLOOD-RED RESOLUTION*, my MLR Press *SS MANN HUNT*, and my MLR Press *BEYOND MA-CHU*), and instill within me a future impulse always to try and visit any place before writing about it.

I kept no South American journal of my adventure, too occupied, at the time, with combating exhaustion, heat, humidity, bugs, and crotch-rot, to do much of anything but cope. My write-up, almost a year after our return, during test-finals week at the university, was more for the benefit of my parents, because I hadn't been able to mail them regularly from the Mato Grasso. That I submitted the story to a men's magazine, *Argosy*, was more an afterthought than anything else. Again, I wasn't thinking to make any kind of mark as a professional writer; in fact I determinedly continued onward with my plans for a career in business, complete with every intention to enlist for my military service (an honorable discharge required, in those days, to complete any career resume).

I went to South America, at that time, simply because it appealed to the same sense of adventure that had me reading *Tarzan* comic books, and had Mom reading me the books of H. Rider Haggard, Edgar Rice Burroughs, Martin and Olsa Johnson. It was the same tunnel-vision that carried me over, in later life, when, knowing better, I climbed Mt. Rainier, hiked solo The Pacific Crest Trial, and enlisted in the U.S. Army; each time, coming to wonder, often aloud, *What in the hell ever possessed me?* Actually, I was in the last phase of my Army Basic Training at Fort Ord, California, when my "Ransom of the Incas" finally appeared in print.

In no way did I enlist in the U.S. Army thinking I was, thereby, destined to receive as much insight into the world of homosexuality as turned out. Color me naïve, especially in light of my having had, by then, my degree in always-out-to-deceive advertising/marketing, but I actually believed that bullshit, at the time, that purported the Army could make "a real man" out of me—which would have proved so much more convenient in society with its heterosexual majority. What I got, instead, was Fort Ord, California, so wracked with an outbreak of meningitis that none of us new recruits could be over-taxed, over-exercised, over-exerted—where one of my platoon's officers was so obviously gay that it was openly joked about how he blackmailed several of us into jacking off for him rather than being put by him on the notoriously gay cheerleading squad for the division's football team. Every night, one of my bunk mates threw off his covers and loudly beat off, and screamed, "Good God, eat my hard prick, Dean!"—obviously hoping (and eventually succeeding) in getting a discharge. Two of my other fellow recruits openly kissed and fondled each other, more than once, until one day neither showed up for reveille. One Drill Sergeant performed regular early morning "short-arm" inspections just so—all of us *just knew* —he could make snide remarks about the one or two of us who always showed up with morning "wood."

Though I started a journal when I first enlisted, I destroyed it when my superiors started to enforce the regulation that prevented us, for security reasons, from keeping one. I suspect, though, that what I did write in it, before I destroyed it, was likely the same mundane "stuff" as I'd written in my college journal, albeit, this time from an Army grunt's perspective. Even at that point in my life, one published article under my belt, I didn't expect I was destined to make a living via my literary endeavors.

If I looked upon that first-published article of mine as more of a lark than anything else, I was lucky enough soon to have a friend in the military who was quicker to see my writing credentials as the advantage I didn't. I met Ben in the Personnel Office of Yongsan District Command, Korea (this was after the bloody "Conflict," by the way—everyone always hears I was in there and says, "You don't look that old!"; I'm not). Ben told me that that every company in the whole of Korea was anxious "to have" the college grad who opted not to go to Officers Training School. I was assigned to Yongsan District Command, at the top of the choice assignment locales, keeping me in the Korean capital city, Seoul, instead of shipped him out into the boondocks where everyone was required, regularly, to go on bivouac.

Straight-as-a-stick Ben was the one who, during my very first days at Yongsan, provided me with a get-acquainted-with tour of the base which included the toilet stalls in the Enlisted Men's Club which had recently been replaced by steel partitions after so many queers had successfully drilled Swiss Cheese holes in the previous wood to advantage sucks-off, and fucks, between stalls, without any need to open doors, or just to play Peeping Toms as regards dicks for-show on one side or the other side. At the time of my tour, some very inventive gay had already somehow managed (with blow-torch?) to put a glory-hole in one the steel panels.

It wasn't long before Ben ferreted out the regulation defining the few ways in which U.S. military personnel in Korea might receive permission to wear civilian clothes off base; every soldier feeling a need to shed his military attire when out mingling with the local civilian population; although, if caught doing so, they were hauled back to the base by the Military Police and severely disciplined. Usually, authorized civilian attire was the bailiwick only of the "spook brigade," but there was some loophole for any soldiers "performing within the local community, in some capacity wherein military attire might not be considered convenient or apropos...."

Ben's plan was that I should query some U.S. magazine (we decided upon *National Geographic*), citing my publishing history (one article with *Argosy*), and see if it would be interested in an article by me, on speculation, photographed by Ben, about Korea. Any decision by any magazine to want and see the piece would give us the excuse to fill out the necessary requests-to-wear-civilian-wear paperwork, attaching the magazine's agreement-to-take-a-look, complete with magazine letterhead, and argue that our more candid look at Korean life was best achieved by us, as well as all avoidance of denigrating our U.S. uniforms by taking them on us into inconvenient places (up a tree, up a mountain, up a trash heap, atop of bus, car, or telephone pole), sometimes necessary to snap "the perfect photo."

To my surprise, our requests were approved and resulted in the stamped "Authorized to Wear Civilian Clothes Off-Base" suddenly appearing on the backs of our passes regularly picked up and carried with us whenever we left the compound.

My continued inability to consider writing as any kind of a career is probably best illustrated by how I didn't take advantage of any of this to actually write the article, even on speculation, for *National Geographic*. It went no farther than Ben snapping a few pictures, and both us feeling damned smug every time we left base in civvies while most all of our peers had to wear their uniforms. We became even more "men of mystery" when there was a change in the commanding officer at Yongsan District Command, during which time we had certain paperwork pulled by a friend, the office clerk, so that only a few of us, excluding our new commanding officer, knew, or remembered, just why Ben and I had been singled out for special attention in the first place.

If I did write a letter to the U.S. Ambassador, asking permission to photograph the grounds of the U.S. Embassy for our article—if our new commanding officer did call us in to tell us that the Embassy had called, asking if we'd like it to send around a car (I think he actually expected us to provide some kind of explanation, then and there; we didn't, only asking him if he'd call them back and tell them we'd walk)...it wasn't because of any intention to provide supplemental photographs for any article I was writing. I had merely heard that the embassy had once been used to house the Korean Emperor's mistresses, and I thought it might be an interesting place to see. The Ambassador's wife was gracious (her husband out of the country on business), and I still have our photos as part of all those we shot but never used to any post-military-service literary advantage.

Ben continued to show me how the military was an organization open to advantageous manipulation by any successful manipulator or manipulators, filled to the brim with opportunities for all sorts of wheeling and dealing. It was definitely an environment in which the people you knew were extremely important for providing your smooth and comfortable survival. He was the first to point out that my assigned plum position of sending soldiers home and/or for reassignments, as well as arranging their transportation (via boat or plane; NO ONE wanted to go home by boat), made me a very important cog in the Korean military machine. Ben worked in finance, another key position, in that no soldier wanted his paycheck fucked with. Between the two of us, he figured—and it turned out he was right—we had the opportunity of becoming a Duumvirate with which to be reckoned.

Not long after being assigned my position of transportation clerk, I was visited by the First Sergeant of the Military Police who frankly spelled out that there had been some bad blood between base law-enforcement and the previous transportations clerk who had gotten drunk, caused a major fuss, and inadvertently not been recognized by the arresting officer; which had resulted in George (my predecessor) deciding, by way of retribution, to ship home each and every military policeman by boat. The First Sergeant hoped that I wouldn't be carrying forth the same unfair vendetta. My magnanimous response (I'm a fast learner) was that while it wouldn't be likely that I could send home *every* military policeman by plane, I certainly would provide my best effort in shipping home as many by plane as was feasible (certainly all senior NCOs) when making up my flight rosters. It was a bit of beneficence, on my part, that benefited me by, more often than not, finding MPs willing to look the other way, as far as I was concerned, like when I was often spotted wearing my "cunt" cap (soft), and not my uniform hat, even when in the former was "out of season"; I was required only once to return to my barracks to make the exchange, during which I noted the MPs name, and was visited, once again, by the First Sergeant, who explained that the mistake had resulted from the young MP only recently assigned, unaware of whom I was, and who had definitely been overly strict in upholding a regulation, that, in my case, in that instance, really hadn't any need to be upheld so rigorously.

Once, at a civilian nightclub, military police busting in, every soldier in civvies headed for the nearest exit, where most of them were muscled into containment groups, I sat calmly, eventually approached to provide my ID. When I handed over my "pass," I waited for the solider to flip it over and see where I was "authorized to wear civilian clothes off base." Instead, without bothering, he merely handed the pass back to me, and left the premises, along with his fellow law-enforcement officers and every other solider, not in uniform, in tow.

Once, Ben and I hopped a military transport to Pusan for a couple of days of fun in the sun. He ended up with too much of the latter and with a burn that literally left it difficult for him to walk. Trying to get him back to Seoul, we found the earliest return military flight was fully booked. We were accommodated, though, replacing two "bumped" soldiers, only because of our jobs. Not that Ben came away completely unscathed from the experience, despite all of the cooperation along the way. By sun burning to such a degree that he couldn't work for a couple of days, he had "damaged government property" and suffered the consequences of confinement to his billets for a week, a reduction in pay and grade, as well as the permanent withdrawal of any wear-civvies-off-post privileges.

When my scheduled promotion from E-3 to E-4 came along, my symbiotic relationship with the MP unit again turned to my advantage. Headquarters Command, Yongsan, to which I was attached, required promotion's boards. Meaning, any soldier up for promotion went before a group of his officers for a question-and-answer session wherein certain basic questions—i.e., chain of command, weapons functions, whatever—were provided with expectations of correct answers in return. I declined any such cross-examination, thereby, in effect, turning down any chance of promotion. As a result of a resulting collaboration between my Yongsan Command First Sergeant, and the First Sergeant at the MP unit, I was transferred to the MPs just long enough to receive my promotion (the MP unit not requiring promotion's boards), and was, then, transferred back to Yongsan Command; it took exactly one day.

Ben and I were such a twosome that I was later told, after discharge, by someone who had served with us, that more than a few people thought we were lovers. Nothing, however, could have been farther from the truth. Not only because I didn't find Ben in anyway physically attractive, but because he was a totally straight man who could whore with the best of them. That I even learned he had a giant cock wasn't because I ever saw it, but because one gal he took on at the local whore house suddenly showed up in my cubicle, caterwauling as to how my "friend" had wanted to fuck her ass with his giant cock, and she simply refused to let it happen. There was a resulting confrontation between the prostitute, Ben, mamma-san and pappa-san, all conducted in the presence of me and my paid whore (we'd been interrupted mid- fuck). Ben was banned. I wasn't. It was a story that made the rounds and benefited me tremendously by definitely putting me in a whore house. Equally advantageous to my real-man reputation was the time a whore and I got into a loud argument over the fact that she was trying to overcharge me (I mean, I never had all that good a time at the regular price and wasn't about to pay any more than I already was).

In that day and age, for some strange reason, all of the Army's top brass couldn't seem to wrap their collective mind around even the mere thought of bisexuality. The Army powers-that-be operated under the universal mind-set that a man was either gay, or he was straight, no hybrids in between. [By the way, publishers, when I started writing straight erotica, were pretty much of the same opinion; I could have gal-on-gal, guy-on-gal, guy-in-gal-with-gal, but, "please, nothing so unlikely as guy-on-gal-and-then-on-guy."] Anyway, if you were in the Army, at that time, and you fucked whore cunt, like I did, then, congratulations on your manhood. If you fucked your fellow soldiers, or got fucked by them, you were queer, and better watch out.

There had been a purge of Yongsan gays from Korea shortly before I got there; which had seen a boatload of homosexuals shipped back to the states for 209 discharges. Everyone knew there was likely to be another purge, up the way. In the meantime, there was the lull in-between witch-hunts, wherein no one wanted to bother with ferreting out even more queers to show the world that there were actually so many in the Army. So complete was the existing ennui that some soldiers were so blatantly "out" that a straight sergeant actually called his troops to attention, on the parade ground, to provide mock salutes to one of them who just happened to be passing by.

Meanwhile, simultaneous with laying down subterfuge by fucking Korean whore cunt, I found, and was found by—accepted, and was accepted by—the gay Army community, which provided me with invaluable first-hand life-experience for which I would be extremely grateful once I began writing gay erotica.

Don't ask me how or why I became, so early in life, such a magnet for gays out, seemingly, to draw me in, sexually and otherwise. Maybe it was my good looks…maybe it was my acceptance of how I was as attracted to men as much as the next queer on the block, although I acted on it far less frequently and with little compulsion—or, maybe, it was just sensed that I wasn't a threat and was actually not only sympathetic/empathetic to the gay life-style but had a genuine interest in exploring its ins and outs…ins and outs…ins and outs…*oh, Johnny, fuck my asshole!*…ins and outs. Whatever it was/is, it has always seen me with a lot of gay acquaintances, as well as with a lot of simply lustful queers who just want to get into my pants, or get me into theirs, willing at times even to offer up money, by way of remuneration, to make it happen.

Actually, in retrospect, I think I might have so easily become "the" shoulder to cry on for so many of Yongsan's gays in the military because I wasn't getting physically entangled within any of the myriad affairs and or "love" interests ongoing between officers and enlisted-men, officers and officers, grunts and grunts (no pun intended). I seemed, and actually was, a willing listener, decidedly interested and fascinated by this subculture, especially since I'd long known my attraction to men and their attraction to me. If there was one time, and there was, when I actually went so far as to let an officer take me back to his quarters to—show me some gold leaf; forget etchings!—get me into a chair…turn out the lights…kneel down in front of me…and actually unzip my pants…my survival instincts, as regarded making it unscathed through the Army, and out the other end, with an honorable discharge, had me up and out of there, much to my wooer's chagrin, before my penis came out and the deed was done.

After that, I remained particularly careful to keep my pants zipped and securely belted when around any man, military or associated, who might have an interest in my zipper opened, and/or my belt buckle undone so my pants could drop around my ankles. I knew a dishonorable (209) discharge wouldn't look good on any business resume, and I was in the military primarily to get the bonus points military service provided in helping a person's civilian career. This didn't, however, keep me from my ongoing role of chief confident for pretty much one and all gay Army personnel assigned Yongsan—regular officers, warrant officers, NCOs, grunts—as well as gays among the civilian personnel attached to United States Operations Mission (USOM). The base's USOM Club, a regular hangout for Yongsan's gay contingent, was where I usually ate, restaurant-style, for a tab-to-be-paid, and drank, instead of joining the straights of my peer group at the less formal Enlisted Men's Club. Korea, in general, the USOM Club, specifically, provided any kind of booze on the cheap, and accounted for my quick, easy, and extensive exposure to exotic drinks like flaming Pousse-cafés (a drink that eventually became a key aspect of my short-story "Bottoms Up" in the MLR Press anthology *MELTING THE SLOPES*).

There were regular gay orgies at one or another of the villas that could be rented at Seoul's Walker Hill Resort. They provided me with some truly eye-opening data, in-putted my brain for play-back years later in more than one of my gay novels with military themes (*BIG GUNS, THE SIEGFRIED MATING, ENLISTED MAN, E-MISSION...*). Always more voyeur than active participant, even to this very day, I paid particular attention, back then, to all of the how-to nuances, from purely technical standpoints. That I remained paranoid that I might still end up tainted merely "by association" was more than evident by how I steered clear of one particular New Year's eve party at the Emerald Villa, because I thought its scheduled happening so-well known as to be far too tempting for MP raiders to resist; I spent that New Year's eve in my bunk, sleeping the night away, and causing all sorts of gossip among party-goers (the orgy not raided) in regard to where I was, with whom I was, and what mischief we were up to.

Not all that long before the official end to my stint of service in Korea, I was warned by two commissioned officers and one NCO that the powers-that-be had, once again, decided that the "queer situation in Korea had simply become untenable"; another crackdown in the works. It was suggested to me by each of my trio of informers that my best course of action, being transportation clerk and in the inevitable position of being able to make it happen, was to transfer myself out of Yongsan early, and (yes, please, and thank-you) do the same for them.

If I'd been careful enough about not actually participating in any of the gay sexual fun and games, camouflaging gay associations with my frequent trips to the local whore house, it was still the general consensus of my messengers-suddenly-at-my-doorstep that I would, nonetheless, still be sucked in (no pun intended), as a result of the ensuing witch-hunt (warlock-hunt?) just because I was such a storehouse of information as regarded who had slept with whom, when and where, who was sleeping with whom, when and where, who wanted to sleep with whom, when and where: destined to tar-brushing by pure association.

Neither my informers nor I had so many additional days left of our normal tours of duty in Korea that I couldn't maneuver to get us reassigned and on one or more of the next flights out of there. By that time, Ben had already been reassigned to the Oakland Army Enlistment and Examination Station (AFEES), and had been insisting that I do the very same, when my time for reassignment came; the job positions, there, affording all sorts of possibilities for wheeling and dealing at a time when more and more recruits were daily being drafted into the military for service in Vietnam.

Much to Ben's chagrin, though, I ended up with reassignment orders written for the Portland, Oregon, AFEES. I made my exit from Yongsan three weeks before the shit hit the fan. I allowed myself plenty of leave before my scheduled arrival in Portland, which allowed me some time spent with Ben who took me off for a bit of fun and games that consisted of so much cunt fucking in a tent pitched in Big Sur, that I left thinking it was probably a good thing we'd end up separated by a few hundred miles; then, as now, I find sex—gay or straight—usually far more bother than it's worth, as regards pleasure derived from the time and effort expended to have at it. I went home to my parents to spend the rest of my leave celibate, except for an occasional masturbation.

The Portland AFEES was full of surprises, from the get-go; or, then again, maybe not, considering my past history. Color my immediate supervisor in personnel gay. He was an Air Force sergeant about whose proclivities I was warned, first, by Sally, a flirty civilian attached to the Portland AFEES in the capacity of an office clerk. There were lots of attached civilians. In fact, my whole plum assignment was more like my having a regular 9-to-5 civilian job than it was military duty. We even got to live in regular apartments, instead of on a military base; the nearest Army billets were inconveniently located across the Columbia River in Vancouver, Washington. I was, then, warned about SGT Máñez by Judd, a fellow AFEES E-4 who volunteered to let me sleep on his couch until I could find living accommodations of my own.

SGT Máñez got up close and personal on day three, but not for gay sex. He said if I was still looking for an apartment, there was one suddenly available in his building, and he'd be happy to take me around for a look-see. I went with him, pleased that, at least for the moment, his showing me the accommodations was all he had in mind. I liked what I saw and moved in. That night, there was a late-afternoon after-work knock at my door. Knowing that no one was likely stopping by to say hello, except SGT Máñez, I just let him knock and didn't answer. More knocking occurred the next night, and the next. Finally, he approached me at work, asked how I liked my new apartment, which I attested to finding just fine. After which, he let drop, as a casual "aside," how he'd stopped by a couple of times, but that I'd apparently been out. He wondered if I had a lover—no query as to where any such lover might be male or female. I confessed to being unattached, and apologized for not being around when he'd dropped by. I alibied that I just, often, after a day at the AFEES office, felt in the mood for a few drinks. He wondered where I went for those few drinks. I was vague and said, "Oh, around." He said he suspected we'd run into each other, "around," and left it at that.

Actually, I *had* started going out for few drinks, after work, all by my lonesome, having never had any problem with drinking and dining on my own, in fact often enjoying my company more than if I were with someone else who I might feel obligated to engage in conversation or, worse, entertain. However, I doubted very much, and was right, that the place in which I chose to do my drinking, Trader Vic's, in Portland's Benson Hotel, was somewhere I'd likely ever run into SGT Máñez or any other of my co-workers, military or otherwise, from, the Portland AFEES.

On a Monday, at the office, SGT Máñez commented that he'd been out that weekend, and the weekend before, thinking he might run into me, but he hadn't.

"Maybe next weekend?" I held out false hope. This time, though, he was ready for me.

"Why don't we make the rounds together, this Friday," he suggested, "since we're likely drinking in the same bars, anyhow, somehow just missing each other in the process?"

I agreed, because, by then, I was curious as to what gay bars he frequented, and which ones he assumed I frequented as well. "Hitting" them would be a welcome change from Trader Vic's where I'd become such a mainstay that the *maître d'* was, by then, greeting me like an old friend.

Come Friday night, I finally answered my door to a SGT Máñez's knock, although I didn't invite him in. When he asked to which bar I'd like to go, I parried that we should start out with the one he enjoyed most, and, then, if that one didn't have enough action, we could move on from there. As a result, I was introduced to the three gay bars Portland had at the time. My previous familiarity with them, although nonexistent, seemed confirmed for SGT Máñez when, quite unexpectedly, I was tapped on the back, at "The Happy Hair" to find myself greeted, like an old friend, by the maitre 'd from Trader Vic's.

I became more at ease with SGT Máñez as soon as it quickly became obvious, from his comments while cruising for tricks, that his interest in me wasn't as much sexual as it was mere delight in having found an assumed soul mate, an assumed fellow gay, in which he could confide and go bar-hopping.

This didn't mean that everyone else I met in the Portland gay community was uninterested in getting into my pants, or my getting into theirs. At first, I was as leery of any sexual involvement, there, as I'd been in Korea. I became less leery, however, as the non-secret of SGT Máñez's sexuality among the AFEES staff didn't see anyone grabbing up torches and firewood to burn him at the stake, despite his frequent forays into the examination room to see new recruits with their trousers dropped for physical examinations. There was, also, the increasing illusion, made daily more and more predominant by our complete disassociation from most of the de-rigueur bullshit associated with military life on a confined military base, that made it seem more and more as if I were truly a civilian merely performing my job in a civilian workplace. I, likewise, felt safe because of another successful bearding of my bisexually, done in Korea by frequenting prostitutes, now done via two civilian AFEES female staff—Sally one, Jill another. Before I had to contend with any build-up jealousy between them, Sally had to quit work to take care of her father, leaving me with only Jill to fuck on occasion.

I started having gay sex. Granted, I didn't pull out my dick for sucking by every Tom, Dick, and Harry, but I did end up agreeing to offer it up on a fairly regular basis to a guy, Stan, who offered me free room and board for the privilege. When I found him way too possessive, after a time, I left him for another guy, Gil, who was willing to split the rent on a really posh apartment, just so he had a place to bring his lover, a married man, during the day. It was very seldom we even met up, except coming (no pun intended) or going.

In Portland, I finished out the last of my three-year Army enlistment and was discharged at Fort Lewis, Washington, with an honorable discharge, where I learned that most of those with whom I'd gone through basic training at Fort Ord, California (shipped out initially to Europe, where I'd wanted to go) had ended up reassigned to and dead in Viet Nam.

I went to stay for awhile with Gary Giles. My fellow high-school classmate and fellow Papyrus-club member, honorably discharged after spending his whole term of military service at a top-security job in Germany, was living in Seattle, Washington, and working for an import-export firm; we'd kept in touch. I'd written ahead to tell him I'd decided to write an article about gay bars (as much a lie as my ever having intended to do a photo-essay on Korea for *National Geographic*), and I wondered if he, off-hand, knew of any gay bars in the Seattle area that I could visit by way of research. He knew all of the gay bars in Seattle and wondered when I'd first realized he was gay. I told him about the suit who visited me in college and had queried me as regarded a same-sex "Sandy." Imagine my surprise when it turned out I knew Sandy, after all. He was Gary's cousin, with whom we'd both gone to high-school, nick-named Sandy, but with whom I'd never been really close enough, I guess, to have ever heard him called anything but Hal. Gary and he had, indeed, been Biblically close, although whoever had initially dropped that fact to the security investigator apparently hadn't had anyone else to back him/her up, because Gary had gotten his Crypto clearance and handled all sorts of sensitive material a suspected queer would never have been let near with a ten-foot pole.

I liked Seattle. I liked its bars. I liked that its gays were actually dancing with each other in after-hours clubs; something I hadn't witnessed even during the full-swing orgy days in Korea. I discovered the existence of gay baths wherein all sorts of things could be seen, or joined, either in private cubby-hole rooms, or in larger and darker communal back rooms. I decided to stay in Seattle and look for a job, first taking off a month of the summer just for some additional rest and relaxation.

Gary, his friend Hank, and I moved into larger digs. During the move, I uncovered the several gay fuck-books that Gary had picked up in the xxx-materials-only back room of one Seattle magazine store. I read one book; I read two books; both titles now forgotten. I decided that I could write a far better book than either, and I proceeded to make my attempt to do just that, composing a chapter a day, usually while sunning in Volunteer Park where I could always get (and sometimes did) a blowjob in the bushes.

Gary, Hank, sometimes friends, and I, sat down nightly, with drinks, while I read my daily chapter of *FIVE ROADS TO TLEN*, my tongue-(cock-)-in-cheek gay sci-fi, about a space traveler who asked for directions from a guy who had a mouthful of dick and whose response was misinterpreted by my protagonist, with all sorts of resulting misadventures. We all giggled, laughed, had a good time, until the book was finally finished, and I decided that I'd expended enough time and effort on the project to warrant my handing it over for some publisher's look-see. Any notion of success, by way of actual publication, was pooh-poohed by both Gary and Hank. Frankly, I only persisted as a lark, without any real expectations of my first gay book ever seeing publication. I mean, I'd not published anything since "Ransom of the Inca" in *Argosy*, never published anything gay, and I still entertained no notion of my being destined for anything, career-wise, but some advertising/marketing position within some Seattle business establishment. I sent off the manuscript to Greenleaf Classics which had been the publisher of both gay books which had been my original inspiration.

I was sunbathing in Volunteer Park when Hank turned up with a letter to me from Greenleaf Classics. He undoubtedly wanted to gloat over the confirmation of his predicted rejection by Greenleaf of my *FIVE ROADS TO TLEN*, but....

Greenleaf was delighted to be able to inform me that it had made the decision to publish my book. In fact, it looked forward to seeing anything else I could send its way. It did ask, though, that in the future, I not use a typewriter with "script" font (these the days before personal computers), because script font was just so hard to read.

With the money from that first book sale, I bought approximately twenty bottles of booze, and an IBM electric commercial typewriter. On the latter, I immediately began to type *ADONIS*, a gay detective novel, that I completed so fast (two weeks), and had accepted by Greenleaf Classics so quickly, that it beat *FIVE ROADS TO TLEN* onto the bookshelves.

After that, my output was so fast and furious, Greenleaf always more than happy to oblige by buying my each and every submission, I finally began entertaining the vague inkling that I just might have a possible career in the writing business.

ADONIS was followed by *ADONIS AT ACTUM* and *ADONIS AT BOMASA*. *FIVE ROADS TO TLEN* was followed by *THE GODS OF TLEN*. *DEMON'S STALK* was followed by *DEMON'S CORONATION*. *THE YOUNG MASTER* was followed by *MASTER BLACK*. Those were all followed by *THE MANEATERS OF MALIBU*, *VALLEY OF THE DAMNED* (the very first-ever gay werewolf novel), and *BOB, CARL, TED, AND ALAN*, until....

In 1971, the first of my many heterosexual erotica novels, *STARSHIP INTERCOURSE* for Greenleaf's "A Companion Book for Adults Only" imprint, *THE GRAY FLANNEL SWAP* from Greenleaf's "A Candid Reader" imprint, THE *DOCTOR'S UNORTHODOX PRACTICE* and *FACULTY WIFE* for Greenleaf's "This is a Nitime Swapbook" imprint, *THE JAMAICAN TRADERS* for Greenleaf's "An Adult Book" imprint, *THEIR HUSANDS ARE AT WAR* for Venice Publishing, *THE SEX LAB*, *POP 'N' SWAP* and *THE SIXTY-NINERS* for Bee-Line Books, made their appearance, center-stage.

One of the smartest moves I ever made in publishing, career-wise and socially, was my decision to add straight erotica to my writing repertoire—the result of my need for variety as a spice to life that helped combat the possible boredom and monotony of writing the same old thing all of the time…my long history of sexual experiences with women, as well as with men, from which I could draw for material…my sudden need to be sure I wasn't simultaneously flooding the market with so many gay novels (I'd already resorted to multiple-pseudonyms) that my readers would think I was pumping the books out on an assembly-line basis (although I WAS pretty much pumping them out on an assembly-line basis)—and a note from Greenleaf saying it would be more than happy to "see" anything I had "heterosexual."

Writing straight erotica not only provided me with a decidedly wider reading base (more straights in the world than gays), but it—in combination with my having a college education—an honorable enlistment and discharge from the military—a comprehension of the differences between a finger and a soup bowl—as well as not looking the part of a "dirty old man"—plus my suddenly being taken under the wing of a very prominent Seattle art-world kingpin who not only loved to "mix" people but, also, loved to shock them with the likes of, "This is William Maltese, my dear friend, who writes porno"—provided me an entrée into "polite straight society" that likely would have been denied me had my straight porn not been there to fascinate and titillate straights who liked to feel themselves liberal and adventuresome.

Suddenly, I was attending "Save Venice" dinners, symphony balls, and house parties that included all of the Seattle Opera's incoming guest stars, like Maria Callas. I wined and dined with the rich and famous, with art patrons and the artists they patronized. I collected the works of William Ivey, Paul Horiuchi, Kenneth Callahan, and William Cumming. I was flown to art shows in Kobe, Japan, with stopovers in Bangkok, Hong Kong, and Bali.

I had women suddenly anxious to confide in me some of their most intimate secrets, like the hamburger-chain heiress who confessed in a whisper that she had her best orgasms when she was drunk.

I wrote my gay erotica, *DOG-COLLAR BOYS, TOO BEAUTIFUL, MALE SEX IDOL, BLACK BALLED, MOUNTAIN MEN, THE ERECTION*, without a clue that I had already become part of the now much-venerated Golden Age of Gay Fiction wherein novels were finally allowing gay protagonists to experience happy-ever-after-endings. At the same time, I read excerpts of my straight erotica, *SEX INTRIGUE*, by way of amusement for certain discerning and "feeling very naughty" members of Seattle's straight-as-a-stick society.

I met Tara Fanel. She was charming. She was a widow. She was rich. She was seventy-six. We hit it off immediately. I bemoaned that she would soon be out of my life for six months, doing something I had always wanted to do: literally sail around the world on a cruise ship." She flirted, blinked her eyelashes, and said, "Who knows but that you might just be able to do that sooner than expect, my very handsome young man." I sent her roses and chocolates. I took her to dinner. Two months later, we embarked on a cruise-ship out of Fort Everglades, Florida, that would steam us first-class, for half a year, in our thoroughly enjoyable and memorable circumnavigation of the globe.

Between dining nightly at the captain's table, listening to onboard lectures (and being hit on by one male college professor who was on board to provide several discourses on ancient South Pacific civilizations), shooting skeet, playing shuffleboard, watching first-run movies, dining on gourmet food and drinking French wine, stopping in England, South Africa, Australia, Colombia, Panama, I was busy typing away and mailing off manuscripts to my publishers from Capetown, Sydney, Cartagena, and Panama City.

Always one or two steps, physically (not to mention mentally), removed from the actual nitty-grittiness of the ongoing "Gay Literary Revolution," I remained pretty much oblivious to it, and to Greenleaf's ongoing battles with the U.S. government as regards obscenity laws, and to my fellow Greenleaf authors sucked into the fray and sometimes threatened with loss of life and limb, not to mention jail time.

After my round-the-world, there were follow-up cruises that circled the Pacific, trans-Panama-Canal-ed (more than once), "did" the Caribbean islands from Anguilla to the Virgin Islands, cruised the coastlines of Central and South America, with side trips inland to Machu Picchu, Brasilia, Iguassu Falls, Chichen Itza. There were winters spent on the beaches of Acapulco, Puerto Vallarta, Cancun, Rio. There were two trips to Egypt for climbs of the pyramids, sails by felucca down the Nile, and a three-week vacation at the Oberoi on Elephantine Island at the First Cataract.

Tara had sent me off on my very own, for a month in Italy and Greece, when she was mugged, coming out of a taxi in front of I. Magnin. Refusing to release her hold on her purse, she suffered a broken collarbone. I returned to find her looking every one of her eighty-two years. Her declining health was soon additionally complicated by a kidney stone and by an operation that succeeded but simply strained her frail body way too much for her to survive it.

By the time Tara died of complications, I had visited enough of the world, at her and others' largesse, as well as experienced enough sex, on my own, to be ready, willing, and able to "fit the bill" when approached by George Glay, Senior editor of Harlequin Books, who was on the outlook for the all-important book two to publish as additional impetus for Harlequin's impending launch of its new Super-Romance imprint that was being commissioned only from authors who had previously published mainstream romance fiction (I'd done three for Carousel in 1979-1980). George was particularly interested in my history of published straight erotica, in that the new Harlequin line was being ballyhooed as not only far longer, with more complicated plot lines and subplots, than the usual up-until-then Harlequin offerings, BUT as far hotter and considerably steamier. I holed up in hotel room, just outside the Harlequin headquarters, in Toronto, Canada, and gave Harlequin exactly what George and the other powers-that-be at that publisher wanted—my tremendously successful *LOVE'S EMERALD FLAME* that went on to be issued in over twelve foreign-language editions. It was soon followed by my *FROM THIS BELOVED HOUR*, and *LOVE'S GOLDEN FLAME*.

While the plotline of *LOVE'S EMERALD FLAME* coincided with a locale I'd visited as far back as my college days of hunting for Inca treasure, both of the other books, one set in Egypt, and one in South Africa, were about spots I'd visited and become intimately familiar with while traveling with Tara. My extensive world travels have, I think, contributed greatly to my reputation for being an author able to word-paint a locale so vividly as to make readers comment upon how it's as if they're on-the-spot. My extensive participation in, and often clinical observation of, the mating rituals of human beings, male and female, has, I think, likewise, contributed greatly to my being able to word-paint seduction and intercourse so vividly as to make readers think they're either participants or Peeping Toms and/or Peeping Tomasinas.

Lately, I've found it more than a little ironic that I seem, with only a slight variation, to have come full circle in my writing career, excluding, if we may, that one first dabbling into writing an article for a men's magazine. Having mainly honed my writing skills on my literary renditions of fucking and sucking homosexuals, during the sixties, that Golden Age of Gay Fiction having petered out (no pun intended) to where I was more "into" heterosexual mainstream, I now find that the demand of the market place has put me right back into the genre of man-man love; these days different only in that the primary readers (and writers, for that matter) aren't men but women. Many gay men are upset by this phenomenon, unable to understand it, and unable to appreciate the subtle changes this kind of marketplace brings to the genre. Women far prefer their men to be cerebral, skilled at conversation, lengthy at foreplay, caring, considerate, and tender. Gay men, in the majority, or so it has been my experience, and continues to be, far prefer their men to be rough and woolly, ready for sex at the drop of a pair of pants, wham-bam-thank-you-man and if I don't see you tomorrow morning, then, who the hell gives a flying fuck?

Personally, I see this paradigm shift merely the final emergence of what I always suspected even in the days when girl-on-girl sex was always okay in a fuck book, when guy-on-guy sex wasn't. Women, despite, what the majority of erotica readers (mainly men) thought in times past, have always likely been just as easily turned on by two men going at it than men have always been by watching two women do the same; it's only been recently, though, that women have been able to admit it, and willing to prove it, by exercising their considerable buying power. Since straight men, in reality, won't oblige by fucking and sucking each other, women have merely taken to indulging their fantasies via the current seminal explosion (no pun intended) of man-love-romance books where male characters, predominantly gay, obligingly *do* do it.

I've always said, and continue to say, "Baby, whatever rocks your boat is A-OK with me." I've adapted to the marketplace in the past, and I'll hopefully continue to adapt to the marketplace in the future, giving readers (fewer and fewer as they become, as far as *all* books, and *all* writers are concerned) whatever they want in reading material (albeit, sometimes, not). I've been around a good many years, writing a good many of those years, and I have every intention of sticking around a helluva lot longer, certainly years passed the time and date I finally finish book two hundred; whether that book be straight, or gay…or—"Yes, Virginia, there are men and women who swing both ways, and there always have been!"—bisexual.

—William Maltese
July 2010

ABOUT THIS BOOK

This book is the result of a couple of impetuses. Firstly, what with the seeming surge, lately, as regards the collecting of pulp books, many people of whom seem to be grabbing up mine (my m/f *STARSHIP INTERCOURSE* recently offered for sale at the staggering $1,000.00), I'm often approached by collectors anxious to know which of the books "out there" (considering I've written under so many pen names) are actually mine. Secondly, I'm just as often approached by people who are convinced that the first few lines viewed, upon opening a book, are the most important in drawing in the reader, and who wonder about my perspective on the subject, considering my longevity in publishing. My best answer to that has always to trot out examples of opening lines I've utilized, over the years, by way of drawing my readers in. This book allows me to trot them all out of once and save myself, in the long run, a great deal of time and effort.

I've limited the openings I've provided from my books to their first three paragraphs (whether long or short). Although originally a random choice, I've since been convinced that three paragraphs (long or short) are of ample wordage to indicate what has worked for me, in keeping me and my work around for a good many years. I do notice that in the early years of my publishing career, my opening words were often geared toward referencing authorities on the subject of human sexuality, and I suspect this is because so many of the early erotic pulps had to come with bona fides that proved them socially relevant and not merely for prurient interest. In fact, I see where I've provided the same reference material, by way of opening more than one of my books; when that occurs I have, herein, provided those three paragraphs only for the first book in which they occur; in succeeding books, I've noted the previous usage and then moved on to the first two paragraphs of original text.

I have only provided a listing of my novels and nonfiction books, written by me alone, or written, in several cases, with one other author. I have not included any of my work published as part of any anthology or short story collection, with many authors, in that such work products are basically the purview of the editors, not of the participating authors, and, thus, my contribution to any opening paragraphs to such works, especially if my work doesn't provide the lead piece, was likely miniscule at best.

I have included as many reprints of my books that I could find; these were often, after initial publication, clandestinely reissued under different titles, different author names, and even under different publisher imprints. I welcome any additions to this list that can be provided by my readers.

While this is undoubtedly likely to be the most accurate and extensive listing of my work you're liable to come across, my having tried to make a point, over the years, to keep possession of at least one of my author copies (what with the suddenly soaring prices, I wish I'd held on to more, for my retirement), I do have to admit that I'm occasionally surprised to find that I, somehow, managed to let a book slip through the cracks. That happened a few years ago when my *BLACK MASTER* was brought to my attention, and wasn't, until then, in my private collection. What's more, I vaguely remember there being a book of mine, published, I believe by Barclay House, with a title about incestuous cousins, that has seemed to elude me to this very day.

Finally, while I realize it would have been nice to include full-color graphics of all my covers, the cost of doing such would be genuinely prohibitive. Therefore, I can only recommend that those who are interested should go to my home web-page where most of the cover graphics are available for viewing, especially under "Collectibles":

http://www.williammaltese.com

A
CHRONOLOGICAL
BIBLIOGRAPHY
OF BOOKS BY

WILLIAM MALTESE

NOTE: A typical entry in this bibliography includes: item number, book title (italics), byline, place of publication, publisher (and imprint, if appropriate), year of publication, page count, stock or ISBN number, cover price, type of book (*i.e.*, mass market paperback), known reprints, notes, and the first three paragraphs of the main text of the book (or more, if the publisher has included a standard introduction or teaser), contents lists for collections, plus bibliographical data on all known reprints.

> "The readers and the hearers like my books
> But yet some writers cannot them digest;
> But what care I? for when I make a feast
> I would my guests should praise it, not the cooks."
>
> —Sir John Harington

1. *Adonis*, by William J. Lambert III

San Diego, CA: A Pleasure Reader, Greenleaf Classics, 1969, 156 pages, stock #PR244, $1.50, mass market paperback.

A prequel to *Adonis at Actum* (#2) and *Adonis at Bomasa* (#3).

Adonis Tyler is a private dick with an eye for men and a penchant for weird cases. He thought he'd seen them all, until he ran into the case of the disemboweled rat that was responsible for several deaths, and whose remains carried a seven-million dollar price tag. Tripping gaily through this sweet mystery, our daffodil detective finds himself taken back to the days of ancient Egypt and a sex-worshiping cult capable of erotic heights unknown to modern man. Follow the tangled tale of Adonis Tyler and the truncated terror as he follows its bloody trail and discovers why the ruptured rodent was so vital.

* * * * * * *

His cock swelled large against the cum-splattered hairs of his belly. The thick juices had turned the crotch of his pants damp, his thighs sticky and covered his lower belly with its thin veneer of opaque slime. He pressed the piece of the beast's guts against his groin. The piece of gut added its own slippery-red film to the outside material of the pants covering his swollen erection.

He thought of the beast, how it had finally died, how it had expired in one last great shudder than had triggered the building force of his balls, shooting his hot jism into the cramped confines of his undershorts. Yes, the beast had died, shaking and then collapsing like a formless mass of graying hair into the slippery lake that was its own guts and clotted blood. And he'd pressed his body against that cage, rubbing the bloody piece of the beast's gut against his groin. The beast had shuddered and squealed out its death. Then he, too, had shuddered. He had squealed out his passion and flooded his pants with the hot sticky discharges that erupted from the head of his engorged cock like great wads of discharging spit.

The beast's death throes had lasted for over an hour. One hour, two minutes, and three seconds, to be exact. He knew. He had timed them. He wondered if another animal's might have lasted as long as the beast's had. Could a quite ordinary animal have gone on for one hour, two minutes, and three seconds, while its inards [sic] seeped out in lakes around its feet? Probably not.

2. *Adonis at Actum,* by William J. Lambert III

San Diego, CA: A Pleasure Reader, Greenleaf Classics, 1970, 155 pages, stock #PR276, $1.50, mass market paperback.

A sequel to *Adonis* (#1) and prequel to *Adonis at Bomasa* (#3).

Adonis Tyler, gay detective, returns from the bowels of a rat to stir up the Sudan with a trip to find the King Tut beetle. Louis and the aphrodisiac hunters lead him a merry chase. They might have been imitating the Greeks, as Professor Eric Karlson, describes them in *The Homosexual Uprising, Book 1, Man*: "Homosexual and heterosexual freedom was a way of life with them. In their innocent acceptance of such wide sexual variation they were consequently unscathed by guilt...." Adonis and Louis believed that any means was justified if it resulted in finding the beetle, whose innards allowed *the society* to enjoy orgies for days on end.

* * * * * * *

It was ether. He knew the smell of ether. He remembered that time as a child when he'd been to the hospital to have his tonsils out. There had been the smell of ether then, its sickening smell. There had been the darkness. Now there was the darkness and the smell. Then there was just the darkness.

When he came back to reality, he lay naked on the bed. His wrists were tied together with rope to the head of the bed. His ankles were tied together with rope to the foot of the bed. His stomach was pressed against the sheets.

"Welcome back to reality, Mr. Tyler," a voice said.

3. *Adonis at Bomasa*, by William J. Lambert III

San Diego, CA: A Pleasure Reader, Greenleaf Classics, 1970, 156 pages, stock #PR290, $1.95, mass market paperback.

A sequel to *Adonis* (#1) and *Adonis at Actum* (#2).

Adonis Tyler, gay detective, felt so great a love for Louis that he was willing to brave the terrors and tortures of a lizard pit—wherein an aphrodisiac drove his lover to wild abandon—in order to find him. As pointed out by Erich Fromm in his book, *The Art of Loving*, "Love can inspire the wish for sexual union; in this case the physical relationship is lacking in greediness, in a wish to conquer or be conquered, but is blended with tenderness...." Remembering the sadness of their parting after their escape from a flooded tomb in Egypt, Adonis withstood another beetle-and-wine aphrodisiac, remaining faithful to his true love, who might be dead or alive following the quest for the mysterious beetle that made possible sodomistic sex for a sensual 36 hours.

* * * * * * *

His ass was split, was bleeding, numbed with the pain of the black leather-hard cock that was ravaging it. One black cock: big, animalistic, wrist-thick, charcoal-headed. It lowed into his guts. It seared the inner corridors with a fire kindled by the friction of black cock against white asshole: white anal passages, red-streaked with the leakage of ripped flesh.

He felt the slapping of the two black balls against his ass-cheeks. He felt their spongy thumping as they collided with the white mounds of his butt. He felt their bulk even though the dominant feeling he was experiencing was that of the pain erupting through his body. He tried to moan, to cry out, to voice audibly some representation of his torment, of the nauseous rumblings the black dork was churning within his guts. He tried to moan, but to moan was impossible: his ability to moan had passed, had perished with his ability to speak, his ability to feel anything save the pain of prick shoved full-depth up his hole.

His ass bled. His wrists bled, sliced by the tightness of the hemp bindings. His ankles bled; the rope twisted about them turned scarlet with his bleeding. His mouth bled. He could taste the blood, feeling the saltiness on his tongue, fulling [sic] his mouth, ballooning his cheeks, dripping in thin trickles of red out of the corner of his lips. He turned his face into the ground, feeling the dirt stick to the blood he vomited from his mouth, could taste the grittiness of the small stones, the dust, the unbroken remnants of sod, the moist mud formed of earth and his blood. His nose smelled the earth, smelled its mustiness, smelled it with its inherent visions of an opened grave, of death, of bodies laid out in state amid the acidic smell of fresh earth.

4. *Five Roads to Tlen*, by William J. Lambert III

San Diego, CA: Greenleaf Classics, 1970, 195 pages, stock #GL148, $2.95, digest-sized paperback (text bound upside down to the cover).

A prequel to *The Gods of Tlen* (#5); this was the author's first *written* book, and the first one accepted for publication.

PRELUDE

He'd said Ten. He was going to a blast on Planet Ten. But since La Mar's swollen cock was buried to its depths in Phal's throat, it had sounded strangely like he was going to a blast on the Planet Tlen. La Mar had never heard of the Planet Tlen.

"Tlen?" La Mar asked.

"Yea," Phal had replied, still not forgoing the pleasure of running his moist mouth cavity over the thick diameter of La Mar's cock.

5. *The Gods of Tlen*, by William J. Lambert III

San Diego, CA: Greenleaf Classics, 1970, 195 pages, stock #GL158, $2.95, digest-sized paperback (text bound upside down to the cover).

A sequel to *Five Roads to Tlen* (#4).

PROLOGUE

He'd said Ten; there was going to be a party on Planet Ten. But the voice, gargling around La Mar's massive cock had sounded like "Tlen"....

And so the huge-hung misguided La Mar had set out in quest of the mysterious Planet Tlen. Five roads did he traverse before he learned the true nature of his destination, and these five roads sorely tested his mettle—his ability to cast aside immediate pleasure in the hope of a more secure and long-lasting happiness.

La Mar had proved himself equal to his fivefold task, for he now sits among the gods, and he himself is truly a god. But all is not rapture in these Elysian Fields....

6. *Demon's Stalk*, by William J. Lambert III

San Diego, CA: Greenleaf Classics, 1970, 195 pages, stock #GL153, $2.95, digest-sized paperback (text bound upside down to the cover).

A prequel to *Demon's Coronation* (#13).

COLD! My God, it was cold! It was cold where the hands were positioned on his thighs, pushing them wide. It was cold! It was cold inside the mouth which had lowered itself to take his cock in, surround it in a web of cold, freezing juices. It was as if he'd stuck his cock in a freezer, in an icebox. Yet, his cock hadn't gone soft with the cold, hadn't shriveled to nonexistence as it often did when he bathed in the pond amid the woods. This was a different kind of coldness, a different kind of freezing, as different from the chill of the forest pond as day was from night, as black was from white. It was different, yet to explain the difference, to put the difference into words, would have been impossible, even if he'd wanted to express it.

The room was darkened by shadows. There were only the few embers still aglow from the Baroque fireplace. They still cast a faint glow into the room, a faded red that diffused within the darker shadows of the room. They gave little light to the shadows around the bed, except when a piece of ash broke off, tumbled away, fell upon the irons with a stream of upward drifting flicks of orange. Then there was a momentary raising of the shadows around the bed. He was able to see the body below him, the body stretched between his legs, the head sucking at his groin, the hands pushing at his thighs: The source, the reason for the cold.

It was not the first time he'd been visited in the night, not the first time he'd been brought from slumber by the icy fingers wrapped around his cock, cupping his balls, searching out the hole in his ass. It wasn't the first time he'd felt the cold engulf the head of his cock, slip down to engulf the shaft, spread down to the base, to his balls.

7. *The Gray Flannel Swap*, by Lambert Wilhelm

San Diego, CA: A Candid Reader, Greenleaf Classics, 1970, 159 pages, stock #CA1028, $1.25, mass market paperback.

Mark and Melinda and Charles and Patty had a reason for swamping beyond mere pleasure of boredom. The stakes for sleeping around, in fact, ran quite high: Membership in the exclusive Devonshire Country Club was one small factor, but by far the most important benefit was the vice-presidency of Weston & Associates. And along with that came the exclusive suburb and the big house. The method of choosing a successor to fill this vacancy was rather unique…but it only bears out David Boroff's words in his article, "Sex, The Quiet Revolution" from *Esquire*, July 1962: "Sex is the politics of the sixties—the last arena of adventure in the quasi-welfare state in which we now live." That arena, in this case, proved to be everybody's bedroom!

* * * * * * *

Mallory Weston removed the woman's panties and bra and lowered her down on the bed. She was now completely naked. Infatuated with her nakedness, his lips panting in anticipation, eyes already glazing over with pre-pictured pleasures, he began to undress himself.

Melinda's eyes took in this emerging nakedness. When his cock bounded forth from his underwear, she couldn't help sighing with her own appreciate of it. She found it hard to believe that she'd accidentally come upon a male organ which outshone Mark's. It was even a more unique experience when she realized that the huge hunk of meat was hanging between the hairy thighs of her husband's boss. Or rather the meat usually hung limp there. Now it wasn't hanging at all. It was erect and quite hard, quite anticipatory of its upcoming duties.

She smiled invitingly, stretched out her hands to welcome him as well as his cock.

8. *The Young Master*, by William J. Lambert III

San Diego, CA: Greenleaf Classics, 1970, 195 pages, stock #GL156, $2.95, digest-sized paperback (text bound upside down to the cover).

A prequel to *Master Black* (#14).

"You think you're going to stick that big nigger cock up my ass, black boy?" Jonah asked. "If you do, you're sure as hell wrong."

"Take off those britches," Jeremiah replied. His shirt and pants were torn. Segments of his black, sweat-glistening body could be seen through the tatters.

"You think you're going to scare me?" Jonah asked.

9. *The Sixty-Niners*, by William J. Lambert III

New York: An Orpheus Original, Bee-Line Books, 1971, 221 pages, stock #727-R, $2.25, mass market paperback.

JoAnn's tits were mushroomed against her ribcage. They were large and firm. Douglas took one of the nipples in his mouth, cupping the resilient flesh with his hand. His tongue swam over the circles of darkness as they rose upward, taut and firm. JoAnn gripped a handful of his hair, pushing the man's face harder into the mound of warm, glowing flesh. She guided his head up past her neck to her face. Her tongue reached out to lap at his mouth and cheek. She probed the folds of his ear, laving them wet with her spit.

Douglas' hand found her slit, gently parting the outer lips, running a finger between them. He shifted his hips to put his throbbing hardness on target. He shoved the massive head through the doorway, lubricating the expanse of him with her juices. He pressed his hips lower, feeling more of his rod slip downward into the hot and sticky hole.

"Oh god!" JoAnn mumbled, her legs raising in one spasmodic jerk to grip at his waist, her ankles locking tightly into the small of his back. "Fast, baby. Do it fast!"

* * * * * * *

—Douglas and JoAnn—

JoAnn could feel his muscular shoulders beneath his T-shirt. They were hard. She liked the feel. She liked the sensation. She left her hand there. His nearness added strangely to the woman's feeling of weakness.

"My cock," Douglas said lowly.

"What about it?" JoAnn whispered back.

"It's hard," Douglas gave a silly grin.

JoAnn laughed.

"I think we might cure that, don't you?" she said. She swallowed. For some reason her throat had gone dry. Her knees suddenly seemed even weaker, and she leaned closer to Douglas. She felt his oversized cock through the cloth of his slacks. She found his feel strangely exciting. "Why don't you get undressed?"

10. *The Sex Lab*, by W. Lambert III

New York: An Orpheus Original, Bee-Line Books, 1971, 188 pages, stock #701-T, $1.95, mass market paperback.

READY FOR MORE!

Peter moved slowly, taking long, even thrusts. His previous orgasms had almost exhausted him. Almost!

The very slow pace only seemed to give added pleasure to their coupling. Each long, steady withdrawal sent waves of almost unbearable sensations rushing through both their nerve ends. And each unbearably ecstatic sensation was repeated to a progressively more intense degree each time he shoved his tool home....

* * * * * * *

The room was dark, six people staring intently through the darkness at the twenty white rabbits focused on the screen through the dust-speckled lens of the motion-picture projector.

"Aren't they cute," Priscella Tandy said, sitting up in her chair and squinting. She needed glasses but never wore them.

The furry little creatures ambled about their cage, stopping to wiggle their noses or their tails, or possibly they stopped long enough to nibble on one of the pieces of lettuce, cabbage, or carrot scattered haphazardly about the enclosure.

11. *Pop 'n' Swap*, by William J. Lambert III

New York: A Bee-Line Book, 1971, 156 pages, stock #496-D, $1.50, mass market paperback.

ROUGH BALLS...

He moved downward toward her body as if she were a powerful magnet pulling at him, kneeling between her legs, lowering to put his penis to her labia.

She felt the roughness of his pants on her skin, feeling the stab of his metal belt buckle against her belly, feeling his tee shirt covering her breasts, feeling the smoothness of his rod's skin coursing through the waiting tunnels of her body.

* * * * * * *

PROLOGUE

Bill moved his fingers along the slope of Terri's hip, dipping down her thigh. Her flesh was warm to the touch. He traced small circles up her leg to the moist cunt, the dark pubic hairs passing through his fingers. He felt her lips upon his, her teeth biting, demanding, insistent. He thought he tasted blood where she bit his lip.

The tips of her breasts stood rigid against her nightgown. He pushed the flimsy lace over her head, her tits flowing into view, each surmounted by the dark towers that were her erecting nipples. His eyes took in the curves of her sun-goldened body. He passed his gaze over the mounds of her tits, the slightly domed surface of her belly, touching again the hairs concealing her twat.

Terri moaned something undecipherable.

12. *The Maneaters of Malibu,* by William J. Lambert III

San Diego, CA: A Pleasure Reader, Greenleaf Classics, 1971, 157 pages, stock #PR296, $1.95, mass market paperback.

The world of the young is a secret place, full of strange feelings and even stranger actions. This was so in the K-klub, a secret surfing society rife with ambitions, jealousies and intrigue. A father and son ruled with iron hands...and the members could only guess at why they had been chosen over so many others. Had they been chosen for their incomparable physiques and smooth young countenances? Or was it their acceptance—unquestioned acceptance—of the leaders' whims, even to the point of offering their bodies for all-male sex...Howard Jones examined this clique aspect among the young in his book *Crime in a Changing Society,* and found: "The first stage may be that he joins a delinquent gang. If he finds his way...into a truly criminal subculture...then his...becomes a condition for the satisfaction...also for the meeting of normal human needs." And so it was on the beach, where the young blond gods ruled supreme.

* * * * * * *

Sunlight filtered down between the slats of the boardwalk above. It was a hot summer's sun that lost none of its strength in its extra plunge to the sand beneath the pier. It cast stripes of brightness across their naked flesh. With alternating strips of sun-drenched yellow and shadow, the sleek, muscular bodies could have been tigers: jungle animals tensed for mating in a forest glen.

The voices of the beach reached to them beneath the pier. The sounds of holiday, of summer, of bronzed bodies at play, wafted to them both on waves of heat that penetrated the forest of wooden columnar supports; laughter, screams, calls of men and women at play. They heard the sounds, but did not really hear them.

Jim slid his hand along the bulging flesh, detected the solidness of the muscle and sinew which had bunched at the surface, swelling the bronzed skin to mountains of physical perfection. He reached his hands about the slim waist, pushing his arms to follow, letting both move around to the back. He felt the slight beginning rise of Roger's ass beneath his fingers; hard flesh as the rest of the body was hard flesh, hard beautiful flesh, Grecian in its perfection. He pulled Roger to him, feeling the stickiness of their combining sweat as they touched, as the two stomachs caressed, as their bulged cocks throbbed to rigid stance, dueling for superiority in the space between their forms.

13. *Demon's Coronation*, by William J. Lambert III

San Diego, CA: A Pleasure Reader, Greenleaf Classics, 1971, 159 pages, stock #PR310, $1.95, mass market paperback.

A sequel to *Demon's Stalk* (#6).

The new Hell needed a hierarchy. Jeni and Etienne and Serge had had twins and therefore had provided the Demon, Anaroth with a choice. When He chose to pit son against mother, Adrian against Jeni, the fires of Hell began to smolder. Roger Blake, Ph.D., in his book, *The Impotent Male* says: "Incestuous fantasies where the mother is the subconscious sex object often result in impotence when a man is placed in a coital situation. Some of these victims often turn to homosexuality and other abnormal outlets as a means of satisfaction, thus denying the incest-wish." When Adrian was forced to destroy his mother he had no hangups or denials to deal with, like a true queen of the higher Diety, he gaily did away with her, sending her to Limbo with one fell swoop of his all-powerful hand.

* * * * * * *

Where? When? Who? What? How? Why?
Where was he? When did he arrive? Who had brought him? What was the meaning behind the noises, the chantings, the shadows? How did he get there from the bed in which he slept, from the house in which he lived? Why was he there?
A dream?
Not a dream! Too real for a dream, though dreams were often seemingly real. Despite its fantastic façade, despite its distorted images, the grotesqueness, the scene reeked its own peculiar reality. The fingers, the hands that touched him, were real. The tongues, the mouths that licked him, were real. The sounds, the noises that jarred his hearing, were real. The sights, the gyrating images, were real. His own inability to move, to function as he desired, was real—painfully real.

14. *Master Black*, by Wm. J. Lambert III

San Diego, CA: A Pleasure Reader, Greenleaf Classics, 1971, 159 pages, stock #PR315, $1.95, mass market paperback.

A sequel to *The Young Master* (#8).

Hawkscraven was a nest of treachery. Leroy was betrayed by Plug for the white boy's body—the golden body that could unite a black empire. As Civil War rolled over the land, men's loyalties were divided, torn free. Perhaps the only thing that could survive that savage carnage was love—love between men that transcended country and race and even greed. Did Julian love the Yankee lieutenant enough to turn his back on power? Perhaps enough to lose his own life? Dr. Leland E. Glover in *Sex Life of the Modern Adult* points out that men "longing for companionship, spiritual as well as sexual,…often live together in pairs; and…consider themselves to be more-or less-married" when defining the heights of male love. Julian lied and killed for Rolf—how much more could he do?

* * * * * * *

"Can you raise the dead?"
There was thunder, lightning to welcome the sorceress to Hawkscraven, to welcome Lumba to her hovel. Yet, the night sky was clear, absent of clouds, absent even of moon.
"You want white flesh," the withered old Negress said.
Leaves in the outside trees shivered in the chill of a nonexistent breeze, rustling to a night heavy with foreboding. Lumba trembled, his glossy ebony flesh goose pimpling beneath his shirt and trousers. His lengthy black cock shriveled, the bulky foreskin slipping to swallow up the thick ham-sized head.

15. *Bob, Carl, Ted, and Alan*, by William J. Lambert III

San Diego, CA: A Pleasure Reader, Greenleaf Classics, 1971, 159 pages, stock #PR319, $1.95, mass market paperback.

Say you're Ted, sitting in a bar, having a double martini and your best friend Bob joins you and proceeds to entertain you with the previous nights [sic] happenings. Suppose he told you his husband, Carl, had a girl over and Bob walked in on them and found them, you know, screwing. Here you've known Carl since Junior High School and you never knew he had such an unhealthy interest in cunt. Suppose Bob then offered you a chance to accept happenings in your own life like he and Carl have done. *The Final Task Force on Homosexuality (Hooker Report)* states: "Homosexuality is not a unitary phenomenon, but rather represents a variety of phenomena which take in a wide spectrum of overt behaviors and psychological experiences." Would you go along with Bob? Would you go home and smash Carl's face in? Or would you go home to Alan and try hard to understand just what in the hell is going on around here???

* * * * * * *

Love!" [sic] the voice said.

Bob looked at the large, gray charcoal penis, and he loved it, actually adored it, longed to heap affection on it, bow to it, lower over it, suck on it, relieve it of its spasms of white viscous ambrosia.

"It is black, and I still love it," he marveled aloud. He [sic] wonderful that he was able to accept it despite its color, despite its preponderance. Even the ugliness of the bulbous head, cleaved off-center and into two unequal parts by the pisshole, contained its own kind of beauty, attractive in that it was not perfect.

16. *Valley of the Damned*, by William J. Lambert

San Diego, CA: A Pleasure Reader, Greenleaf Classics, 1971, 156 pages, stock #PR335, $1.95, mass market paperback.

NOTE: Generally considered to be the first gay werewolf novel.

"There was another sound to pierce the darkness: a forlorn howling that echoed and re-echoed to chill the bones. Some said there was a wolf run mad in the valley. But there were those who knew better. There were those who knew this was something other than a four-legged wild dog accustomed to tamed flesh. This wolf walked on two legs among the very people it was destined to eventually kill. Maritu had returned to the valley. His spirit had been reincarnated."

* * * * * * *

There were noises in the darkness that were not the regular sounds of a night. Oh, of course, animals had died before. Mountain lions had come down from the hills to slaughter sheep and cattle. In the winter months when snow clogged the higher ground, burying all available food beneath piles of white fluffiness, wolves had even been known to enter the village. But this was not a mountain lion with teeth buried deep in the spasming sheep's neck, reddened by the jettisoning blood from the severed jugular vein. This was not a lion whose enormous cock was buried to its knotted base up a constricting anus, its hairy scrotal bag flopping against the wool-covered flesh of the sheep's butt. This was no lion emitting its growls of enjoyment and pleasure. Nor was it winter. Even the spring had passed. There had been no wolves sighted in the lowlands for more than three months.

Though no one saw the shadowy figures in the blackness, two passion-locked silhouettes aglow with the spectral lighting supplied by a full moon, there were those who heard the guttural groanings as sheep gave up life, as its attacker gave up wads of opaque sperm. The noises of pleasure and pain wafted across the valley, penetrating the walls of standing structures with a precision of a winter wind. They were heard, but no one dared venture out into the night to search out the cause. Few had gone out of doors in this particular valley after dusk for at least five generations. Superstition dictated the night to be reserved for those creatures of the unknown who had thrived within the valley since the beginning of time. Only the day was for humans. More than one villager had dared defy the curfew to perish with no trace into the evening.

17. *Their Husbands Are at War,* by William J. Lambert III

Van Nuys, CA: A Venice Book, Venice Publishing, 1971, 185 pages, stock #VB545, $1.95, mass market paperback.

A book of supposedly nonfiction case studies.

Readers are asked to realize that in no instance is the war per se probably the entire blame for the sequences of events to be related in this book. The removal of the husband from the family unit merely acted as the key to set everything in action.

Of all the impersonal events that affect very aspect of the individual's life, including his occupational opportunities, there is probably none of whose impact can surpass that of war. In time of war, the personal wishes and choices of large numbers of men and women must be subordinated to the demands of the national institution....

In addition to the dramatic and obvious influences of war... there are important but less obvious social and psychological results.

The above two quotes are from Louis S. Levine's *Personal and Social Development.*

18. *Starship Intercourse*, by Lambert Wilhelm

San Diego, CA: A Companion Book, Greenleaf Classics, 1971, 155 pages, stock #CB702, $1.95, mass market paperback.

After twenty-five years in deep-freeze aboard their spaceship Starship 12B, Buzz and Patricia had a lot of catching up to do! And so did their fellow crew members. When these sex-crazed space travelers started swinging, they shook the stars in a frenzied space orgy! In his book, *Unmarried Love*, Dr. Eustace Chesser states: "There is no longer any necessity for intercourse to be used solely for the purpose of reproduction, nor is there any need for sexual expression to be confined solely to intercourse. For human sexuality is not limited to our genital organs. So sensitive is the human body that sexual energy can be diffused to every part capable of responding to the appropriate contact."

* * * * * * *

"Hi," he said. "Remember me?"

Patricia Riley—*Lieutenant* Patricia Riley—yawned, stretched, lazily blinked her eyes, then suddenly realized where she was.

"My God, are we there?" she asked, sitting up with a start.

"No," Buzz Shaw replied with a smile. "I just got lonely."

Patricia looked about the cabin, noticing the neatly lined suspended-animation cylinders holding the Captain and the rest of the crew. She then turned her attention back to Buzz, who was still grinning like a little school boy.

19. *Faculty Wife*, by Lambert Wilhelm

San Diego, CA: A Nitime SwapBook, Greenleaf Classics, 1971, 159 pages, stock #NS426, $1.95, mass market paperback.

Professor Bob Wilkins condemned everyone who didn't follow his outmoded pattern of life. The students who flipped around, in and out of each other's beds, the other profs that let the students have fun while they were learning, and especially his wife, Regina, who decided his bed was too cold and moved a hot, young student in to help keep it warm. As Dr. Eustace Chesser mentions in his book, *Unmarried Love*: "To feel disgust at some kinds of behavior is one thing; to condemn it as wicked is another. The act of a maniac may rightly fill us with horror, but we cannot blame him if he was unable to restrain himself. Our instincts are tamed and domesticated in order to enable us to live in an orderly community." Only when Bob learned the advantages of inter-personal relationships with his students did he stop condemning and start accepting.

* * * * * * *

Daphne Powers, leafing through the pages on the desk with one hand, unbuttoned her blouse with the other one.

It's all there," Cliff Martin said impatiently. He was naked, his horniness more than evident by the size of his cock ballooned between his thighs.

Daphne paid no attention, her eyes checking the listed questions and answers for herself. She was a senior and had been a member of her unofficial organization since her sophomore year at Caliga U. During those years, more than one man had tried to pull the wool over her eyes. Few had succeeded.

20. *The Doctor's Unorthodox Practice*, by Lambert Wilhelm

San Diego, CA: A Nitime SwapBook, Greenleaf Classics, 1971, 159 pages, stock #NS430, $1.95, mass market paperback.

In his book, *Unmarried Love*, Dr. Eustace Chesser described the circumstances that surrounded Rastiss, the Negro with a sixteen incher; Sarah, the Negress nymph; Demiann, the cantaloupe raper; Peggy, the son-seducer; Eric, the mother-lover; Sally, the housewife with a warm welcome for several husbands; Jenny, the doctor's daughter who knew more about the male anatomy than her father; Scott, the hard-up husband who ran out of neighborhood wives, and Dr. Talbot who agreed with Dr. Chesser when he wrote, "There is no longer any necessity for intercourse to be used solely for the purpose of reproduction, nor is there any need for sexual expression to be confined solely to intercourse."

* * * * * * *

Jacob fucked Angelique, feeing the inches of his prick being swallowed up by her cunt, caressed by the muscles lining her vagina. His balls drooped along the strip of brown flesh between her asshole and twat. His pubic hairs mingled with hers, his muscled belly pushed into hers, his chest mashed against Angelique's taut-nippled breast. He bit her ear, his hot gasping breaths echoing loudly in her ear. He massaged the smooth flesh of her back, his hands dropping downward to squeeze her ass-cheeks. He buried his dong deeper into her convulsing sexual abyss.

He was within her arms; they closed around him. He was between her legs; her thighs clamped along his waist, her feet locked around the small of his back. Her vaginal walls closed like a vise around his pumping dick, a vacuum sucking the meatus deeper and deeper into her juiced-up corridor. Squeezing muscles massaged his monstrous prong.

"Jesus, hard!" Angelique bellowed. "Stick me hard!"

The woman mumbled her request over and over in Jacob's ear. Each time that his prick hurriedly churned within her twat, Angelique pleaded for more.

21. *The Jamaican Traders*, by Lambert Wilhelm

San Diego, CA: An Adult Book, Greenleaf Classics, 1971, 156 pages, stock #AB1590, $1.95, mass market paperback.

When the success or failure of an important business transaction depended on Maria's swinging with a black man...Philip's beautiful wife got cold feet. Was Maria a bigot...or was there another reason for her refusal? In their book, *The Swinging Set*, William & Jerryle Breedlove state: "Intimacy clubs, of the type known today, in which sexual freedom within the group is a requirement for maintaining status, are not new in the United States. They were known to exist in the 1930's and before in some areas...." Maria made herself unavailable to the swamping couples for reasons which only she knew!

* * * * * * *

Diana literally couldn't move. She was petrified. The size of Marlow Matthew's large black cock put a baseball-sized lump in her throat and a rock in the pit of her belly. The sight of that monstrous eel also made her cunt leak. She could feel her juices bubbling from her snatch, a trail of the wetness leaking between her legs, between the crease of her ass.

"Look at what you do to this old cock of mine, Mrs. Mills," Marlow said. The thick prick was as hard as a rock and jutting up between a pair of muscular black thighs. A big black hand was wrapped about the dick, massaging the penile shaft to milk it of pre-seminal lubricant. The Negro smeared the uprisen boner with translucent slime. The mass looked like a huge piece of shiny black licorice.

Diana couldn't help looking at it. She hadn't been able to take her eyes off it from the moment the black buck had reached in his trousers and fished out the tremendous black prick. It had been flaccid when he first pulled it out, and he kept yanking out the ebony rope like a fisherman pulling in the anchor, although this particular rope seemed to have no ending. Diana was fascinated, gasping with the rest of them when the bulbous corona yanked free and came into view. Even Betty gasped, and she had admittedly seen the monster numerous times before.

22. *Dog Collar Boys*, by Lambert Wilhelm

San Francisco, CA: Parisian Press, 1972, 147 pages, stock #P216, $2.25, mass market paperback.

Stuart asked Paul about him. He was the first one Stuart had noted among all the other bodies in the bar. He was the first one who had actually focussed [sic} out of all the movement. He was sitting in one of the high bar-like stools along the wall behind the tables. Stuart and Paul were walking toward him. The dance floor was crowded witha [sic] mash of moving bodies, making passage to the back bar almost impossible. The nearest alternative route took them between the tables and the shelf attached to the wall.

"Forget it," Paul said. "And I do mean, forget it."

There was an opening in the masses, Paul taking it, plowing a way for Stuart to follow. Paul had managed to spot the table Frank was holding for them.

23. *Too Beautiful*, by Lambert Wilhelm

San Francisco, CA: Parisian Press, undated (1972?), 147 pages, stock #P230, $2.25, mass market paperback.

The bodies were glossy with the sweat of their mating. Like a finely wrought sculpture of exquisite bronze, the two seemed momentarily transfixed, enlocked, embraced for time and eternity. The only sound of their living was the wedded hissing of their breaths: all that remained of the passion which had drained their bodies of semen—splattered pearly sperm up anal passageway, drenched black sheet against pressing belly.

The reality began to make itself known again. Christopher felt himself slipping down from the heights to which he had just been thrust. But the resulting reality of spent love was not the reality of ordinary lovers. For though the ecstasy of passion was faded, the whole aura of dreaming was not yet passed. Shadows still hung like webs within the room. Indeed, it seemed as if the two had fucked within an endless void of blackness. There were no walls, roofs, no floors to be seen. Like two bodies suspended in a sea of darkness, the two had danced out their pleasure. Their cries of enjoyment had been absorbed by the total ebony like water into a sponge.

The parted, two pieces of exquisite proportions: the sword belonging the man, the sheathe belonging the boy. The penis pulled from its hole. It was long, not yet completely flaccid. It still shone with the juices of its discharges: a powerful tool befitting a powerful body.

24. *Big Guns*, by Chad Stuart

San Diego, CA: A Pleasure Reader, Greenleaf Classics, 1972, 171 pages, stock #PR384, $1.95, mass market paperback.

"My congratulations on your victory," Gunnar said. He was impressed by Pablo's looks and body. Despite the fact he was here purely on business, Gunnar was still able to appreciate a good male body when he saw one. He could see how Jeffrey would have found it not so difficult to get sexually involved with this young revolutionary leader. The fact that Pablo was so attractive had certainly made Jeffrey's job easier.

* * * * * * *

The sniper fired. There was a dull thud as the bullet passed through rough cotton cloth and into muscular chest. The man's eyes registered glassy shock at unexpected death. The impact of the slug into guts threw his body backward into a bank of damp, rain-soaked earth. His own rifle clattered to the ground and was soon covered by the lifeless corpse that slipped along wet grass to join it.

Jeffrey knew the man, had fought beside him for the past six months. Yet, Jeffrey's own eyes were so glassed that the reality of this other man's death would not fully be thrust upon his awareness for several more minutes to come. Jeffry was absorbed in the pleasures spawned by Pablo's penis working up his ass. The fact that his own life or Pablo's could just as easily be snuffed as was the wide-eyed corpse fallen but feet from them somehow made the ecstasy of the screw all the more intense. Sex was made more vibrant with the realization that this could be the last. Enjoyment was made more extreme with the knowing that at any second another bullet might echo from the foliage and deprive flesh and blood of those vital forces that made bodies more than just inanimate shells.

Jeffrey's pants had been pulled down around his knees, his legs thrown over his head to give Pablo easy access to the offered ass. Pablo had merely unzipped his fly, hoisted out his cock and balls through the gap provided by the parting metal teeth. He had spit in his hand, rubbing the spittle and dirt over his already hardened cock. He had put the blunted head of his dick to the hair-haloed anal entrance and had put all of his weight into the initial shove. His penis had slipped into the slot, guided until heavy testicles pooled on the muscle of upturned butt.

25. *Sex Intrigue*, by Lambert Wilhelm

San Francisco, CA: Parisian Press, 1972, 147 pages, stock #P505, $1.95, mass market paperback.

"Fuck me, Charles," Rhonda said, twirling in the center of the living room, letting her coat go flying to land on the couch across the room. "Fuck me right now, here on the floor."

The shapely blond sunk to the rug, immediately beginning to undo the snaps of her skirt.

"A drink first," Charles said from behind her. He already had the wire mesh off the champagne and had popped the cork.

26. *Male Sex Idol*, by William J. Lambert III

San Francisco, CA: Parisian Press, 1972, 147 pages, stock #P243, $2.25, mass market paperback.

It had happened to many people before—even to him. But never with such intensity; that feeling of having been somewhere before. Even now as he fucked, he had a premonition that he had screwed beneath these very same palms. Perhaps not with this same boy but with another. But such thoughts were impossible. He had never been to Africa before this, had never even had the desire to go there before a week ago last Thursday. What had happened to make him change his mind against another summer in Rome? The lecture? Yes, the lecture.

The groaning of the slim Arab boy beneath him brought Lamont back to the reality. Such a young boy, this youth whose butt was so eagerly offered up to the onslaught of Lamont's cock. Ten? Eleven? God, you could never really tell their age. The youth here began plying their bodies at such an early age that it was impossible to even venture a feeble guess about how old one specific male whore was. This one had hair around his cock, in the crease of his ass. As young as he was, he was almost too old for selling his body. There was such a choice of young ripe ones that puberty was the ending rather than the beginning. Lamont had seen boys yet incapable of penile erection propositioning him on the streets, making lewd gestures with their fingers to indicate the sexual arts in which they were proficient.

As Lamont pumped the almond-skinned ass, he could tell that he was not the first to plug this asshole. Lamont's exceptional beauty had allowed him access to enough virgin ass to recognize it. This was no virgin, had not been virgin for a long, long time. It was no longer even tight. Despite the expert gyrations the Arab was using to increase Lamont's desires, to attempt to cover up the used state of his anal canal, Lamont felt the present situation veguely [sic] reminiscent of the few times he had fucked cunt. Snatch was never tight enough to please him, not even the virgin holes that bled. Twat was not tight enough and neither was this particular butt.

27. *Blackballed*, by Chad Stuart

San Diego, CA: A Pleasure Reader, Greenleaf Classics, 1972, 171 pages, stock #PR350, $1.95, mass market paperback.

Five Negroes attended Weston University, but only one of them had dared to live on campus. Only one of them wanted to be the only black player on the football team. Only one of them sought admittance to an all-white fraternity. Only one of them shared a room in the dorms with a white boy. Only one of them was gay. Paul Manson had been willing to fight the white opposition on his own, even though he had been blackballed at every corner in his college career. Then Daniel Page, his sullen blond roommate, had made a strange offer and begun pulling strings. But when Paul discovered just whose strings had been pulled, he didn't know if he should hate Daniel or continue to love him.

* * * * * * *

That summer he had decided to let his hair grow. His parents hadn't been so pleased to see him sporting the beginnings of an Afro. But he was black—his cheekbones glistened almost as brightly as the black-brown of his eyes. Despite the non-Negro sharpness of his nose and the worried look of his closely pressed lips, Paul Manson was a Negro, and he had reasoned that there wouldn't be much use in trying to adopt a white hairstyle if he was going to attend Weston University.

There was more than one Negro at Weston University. There had been Negros there for six years. Paul was not the first one. When he registered at the Administration Building there were only a few uplifted eyes. The moat that circled this particular fortress actually had been bridged for quite some time. The test case for integration had come five years before when the school was a bastion of white supremacy. There had been the riots. There had even been a murder: a campus policeman killed when the Student Union Building had been bombed. The governor of the state had announced that he would personally stand on the steps of the Administration Building and bar "the black bastard's" entrance.

That had been five years ago. The Negro had been successfully enrolled even though the governor had stood on the steps. Tempers had cooled. A few more blacks were actually allowed to cross the moat.

28. *The Erection*, by Chad Stuart

San Diego, CA: A Pleasure Reader, Greenleaf Classics, 1972, 171 pages, stock #PR360, $1.95, mass market paperback.

Adrian watched them go, his body throbbing with his controlled hate. He waited until they had both disappeared amid the labyrinth of truck trailers and machinery before turning and walking off in the other direction. When he got to his trailer, he shut the door behind him. The table and bed were strewn with architectural plans and designs. A scale model of the John Ballard building sat on the coffee table: a wedding-caked monstrosity of arches, of honeycombed terraces, of bulky parapets. It was a modern Tower of Babel, a grotesque monument to one man's vanity.

* * * * * * *

What [sic] did he say?" Manning Drake asked, coming into the office, pulling the door shut behind him.

"What they all say," John Ballard said, his back to Manning, his gaze affixed on the demolition project three blocks away and ninety-two stories below. "He said that the thing couldn't be built, that it would collapse under its own weight before we reached the eightieth level."

"He's wrong!" Manning retorted. "They're all wrong."

"Of course they are," John said, turning from the window, eyeing his lover for the last two years: two whole years. It was an evidence that John Ballard was growing old that he still had the same lover after two years, especially someone as weak as Manning Drake. John was now seventy-eight with a heart condition. It would only be a matter of time before he was no more.

29. *Mountain Men*, by Chad Stuart

San Diego, CA: A Pleasure Reader, Greenleaf Classics, 1972, 171 pages, stock #PR370, $1.95, mass market paperback.

"I felt the rope leaving my hands, and I knew you were falling," Martin said. "I remember thinking you were dead. I think I was actually happy. Can you understand that? No, I doubt you can. I saw you sprawled dead in the snow, and there, it seemed, was the chance to have all I ever wanted out of life. With you dead and me on the top of the mountain, I saw our dear father forced to pay attention to me for a change. I saw everybody for once seeing me as me, and not as someone to be held up in comparison to you. Yes, I was happy, ecstatically happy for one brief moment. But then Lars said you were alive...."

* * * * * * *

Matthew Hanover placed the receiver back on the hook, absently letting his eyes wander around the room while his mind raced with its unsaid thoughts. His eyes came to rest finally on the lone picture on his desk. He smiled at the evident likeness of himself which he saw within the frame, losing the smile only when he thought again of the telephone conversation which had just ended.

"There has to be a mistake," he mumbled finally, trying to divert his thoughts by scanning several of the official-looking documents on the desk in front of him. When that didn't succeed, he reached for the buzzer on the intercom. Miss Jansen answered from the other room.

"Yes, Mr. Hanover?"

"Janey, will you get my wife on the line for me?"

"Of course," Miss Jansen replied. "And your son is waiting to see you."

"Brad?" Matthew asked anxiously.

30. *Joint Hunger*, by Chad Stuart

San Diego, CA: Adult Reading/Gay Novel, Greenleaf Classics, 1973, 172 pages, stock #GN399, $1.95, mass market paperback.

A multimillion-dollar shipment of heroin was on its way out of Greece and it was up to Tad Wilcox to stop it. He thought he could handle himself when it came to intrigue, but he hadn't counted on sensuous and charming Bryan Talbot. Tad joined Bryan in his international sex games—from the rape of an Arab boy to the consummation of their joint hungers in the temple at Delphi.

* * * * * * *

Tad Wilcox had been selected by a computer. Two particular pieces of conversation led Bryan to suspect just for whom the electronic brain had conjured this excellent specimen of manhood. The first had been "Bryan Talbot," uttered over the phone by an INARC agent in Greece shortly before his demise due to unnatural causes. The second had been just a couple of hours before. Jackson Henry, upon noting Bryan's evident interest in the youth, had leaned away from the circle of conversation he was part of, to whisper in Bryan's ear, "One of INARC's ninety-day wonders." From then on out, Bryan knew the name of the game. He was receptive to Tad's evident interest when introductions were finally made, and was only slightly amused when Tad was passed off as a university student with no mention of International Narcotics Control. Washington, D.C. was too small for even security to think Bryan would be forever oblivious to the fact that Tad Wilcox had been sent to watch him. The fact that Tad hadn't been in the room for more than a minute before he had been identified for Bryan's convenience was good indication of how firmly entrenched Bryan Talbot was in the scheme of things.

Bryan had been expecting someone, and he was only too pleased that someone had turned out to be Tad Wilcox. INARC was always quick to take up on even the flimsiest leads, and a multimillion-dollar cache of missing heroin was certainly enough to warrant the following-up of the name uttered by a half-dead man over a phone which shortly thereafter had gone dead itself.

Bryan wondered if Tad suspected why Bryan had so quickly taken to him and invited him home. Someone of Tad's evident charms had probably been used to quick conquests. However, information, even in the INARC memory files, would indicate that Bryan Talbot was not one to jump into bed with every attractive face. But then a feed-in of all the statistics on the countless men Bryan had gone to bed with had probably been digested by the electronic marvel before it sorted through the personnel files and earmarked one of them. Tad's added assurance by electronic brain that he would be attractive to Mr. Talbot probably did a lot to bolster the youth's confidence. The fact remained, though, that Bryan somehow felt that Tad knew it was a game being played between him and a very intelligent player. If Bryan was as anxious to get Tad under his watchful eye as Tad was to get Bryan under his, it would have been logical for Bryan to be as receptive to Tad's advances as he was.

31. *Making the Jock*, by Chad Stuart

San Diego, CA: Adult Reading/Gay Novel, Greenleaf Classics, 1973, 155 pages, stock #GN404, $1.95, mass market paperback.

Ty Vandermint was a champion. Young, handsome, he won public acclaim for his activities on the gymnasium floor. Meanwhile, in the locker rooms and bedrooms of the Olympic Village, he was winning private acclaim as a champion cocksman. Confident and sexually aggressive, he never dreamed that his conquest of Marco would lead to his downfall, that he would be the conquered, the loser in the dangerous game he was playing.

* * * * * * *

It was hot in the room, the muggy heat seeping between the joints of the wood, through the plaster in the walls. The sun had long ago set behind distant mountains, but it had not taken the effects of its furnacelike rays with it. Both boys on the bed had the sparse covers thrown back to reveal their sweating flesh. Elsewhere in the room, there were other sprawled bodies, few asleep, but all trying to find some way to fight off the heat. One man yawned, stretched, scratched his sweaty crotch, his fingers coming away wet with perspiration Another youth unbuttoned his shirt, took it off and put it behind his head with his pants, which were already being used for a pillow.

Marco was on the bed with Raphael. Neither was asleep. Both could see Paulo in the chair on the other side of the room. Paulo, Marco's eldest brother, was naked except for his undershorts. He had one leg thrown up over the arm of an overstuffed chair, and his head rested on the other arm. His healthy head of blue-black hair, which hung over his forehead, was plastered in damp little ringlets to the skin. The fly of his shorts was gaped slightly, and anyone bothering to look would have been able to imagine, rather than actually see, the large uncircumcised cock curled within matted pubic hairs. His eyes were shut. He wasn't asleep, however. If the heat itself hadn't been enough to keep them all awake, then the adrenalin pumping through their veins would have been sufficient to do so.

They were all in that room waiting for the morning. In the morning they would do what they had to do, what they had been planning on doing for over three months. It wouldn't be enough, but it would be a start, another one of the many things which might end up in victory in the end. None of them were naïve enough to believe that any bombing would win them this war, but it would possibly blast one more chink in the enemy's armor. Given many such chinks, any piece of armament could be expected to fall apart.

32. *Shaft Man*, by Chad Stuart

San Diego, CA: Adult Reading/Gay Novel, Greenleaf Classics, 1973, 155 pages, stock #GN406, $1.95, mass market paperback.

Christopher imagined that he was somewhere else, anywhere but trapped in a mine. He felt Truscan's body pressing down on him, erasing his fears, creating an image of an open meadow. He knew that their gaspings were using up oxygen, lessening their chances for survival, but at that moment he didn't care. At that moment, the horror of present and past reality had faded from his mind.

* * * * * * *

Christopher Mylo used his large hands to push apart the two flabby cheeks that enclosed the brown pucker that was John Myers' asshole. The boy was astraddle the man's butt, sitting on John's loose-fleshed thighs, which shifted under his weight. Christopher kept the buns propped open with one hand while, with his other, he smeared along his prick's thick shaft those translucent preseminal juices which had been beaded at his cock's meatus.

"Get it in," John insisted, jiggling his ass in impatience. He reached his hands back, yanking his asscheeks even wider apart. His tugging distorted the sphincter-ringed opening. Salt-and-pepper colored hairs nestled about the entrance, grew profusely within the crease of sweaty flesh.

Christopher, his hand fisted about his cock, leaned forward to place his cockhead to the doorway John had obligingly continued to hold open for him. The boy's cock was so large that it almost seemed impossible that the small bowel opening could yawn adequately to accept it. The glistening slit that halved the cockhead was larger than the pucker it was pressed to.

33. *G.I. Jock*, by Chad Stuart

San Diego, CA: Adult Reading/Gay Novel, Greenleaf Classics, 1973, 155 pages, stock #GN411, $1.95, mass market paperback.

Adrian pulled himself from the water, his suit wet and molding to his body as he did so. Matthew saw the ridge of cockflesh beneath the stretched material. Adrian's balls filled the pouch of the swimsuit, and his rigid cock jutted proudly upward from his testicles to the waistband of his suit. It took all of Matthew's will power to keep from reaching for that erected prick. He stood up, wanting to hurry to their room and the bed.

* * * * * * *

"Adrian?"
"Mmmmmmmm?"
Shall we go to bed now?"
Adrian's eyes fluttered open. A rather embarrassed grin formed on his lips.
"I won't be much good tonight, you know?"
"I know," Matthew replied.
Adrian made an effort to struggle to his feet. Matthew took the boy in his arms, as much for the feel of the youth's body as to give him needed support. Adrian's arms wrapped Matthew's body, his face meeting Matthew's shoulder.
"Goddamned, I'm sorry," Adrian whispered. Despite his drunkenness, he could feel the hardness of Matthew's cock against his groin, knew that his own prick wouldn't respond no matter how badly he desired it.
"It's not you fault," Matthew spoke softly.
"You're hard," Adrian said.
"You always make me hard," Matthew replied.
"You could fuck me," Adrian said, his body still clinging to Matthew for comfort and support. "You always liked to fuck me."

34. *Gaius Maximus*, by William J. Lambert III

Chatsworth, CA: A Trojan Classic, 1973, 185 pages, stock #TC280, $1.95, mass market paperback.

Gaius straddled the youth's body, sinking to put his knee on each side of the boy's thighs. When he sat, his balls pooled over those of Gerwyn. His butt resting on the youth's thighs, Gaius reached for Gerwyn's cock again, yanking it to a position perpendicular to the muscular ripples of his belly. He scooted forward a little so that his own cock was once more belly to belly with the other.

Just the thought of what he was about to do made his penis throb in anticipation. Looking down at it, he could see its crown resting below Gerwyn's penile summit. The man concentrated on his spine, willing it to relax for the bending. He consciously sucked in his belly as far as he could, began lowering his head toward his objective: the dual-tipped apex of united sexual obelisks. He did it slowly, knowing that each vertebrae had to give at its own speed and of its own accord. It had been a long time since he had dived for his own cock in this manner. It was usually easier to lie on his back, throw his legs over his head and take his prick that way. But he'd swallowed his pecker this way before and knew it could be done.

It was Gaius' tongue which made contact first. Rolled, it flicked from Gaius' mouth and delved within the crease that halved the corona. Immediately the taste flooded his taste buds. The aphrodisiac quality of the elixir allowed his spine to bend further. His lips opened, sucked in the head and an inch of neck. His jaws were stretched by the bulk. Lip-covered teeth scraped further down the shaft, his tongue wrapped the pole. He came finally to the beginnings of his own dick. He paused, sucking in his breath, wondering if he could yawn his jaws the additional amount needed to encompass the new bulk.

* * * * * * *

Gaius was really too excited about the prospects of sex with the exquisite blond youth to speak to the Druid leader, but he decided to put business ahead of pleasure. Drak Thormu had spoken few words at all since he had been captured over two years before. For him to actually ask for an audience was a novelty. Gaius would have had the old fool killed a long time ago if he could have gotten away with it. But Drak Thormu was the religious head of thousands of these barbaric masses—his religious beliefs even rampant in far away Gaul. Religion was the one thing these filthy heathen held in common. It was, therefore, bad strategy to give them any reason for uniting in a religious war. They were hard enough to subdue in their myriad competitive groupings. Besides, Gaius was more than a little curious as to what had brought the old man so far from Londinium to see the commander of the Roman forces on this particular evening when Gaius was due back in the city within the week.

Gaius, who had been ready for bed, had very little time to slip on proper dress for receiving the old religious leader, so he settled for his robe, barely managing to get it on before Drak made his entrance.

"You must excuse my abuse of protocol," Gaius smiled. "Due to the lateness of the hour, I was preparing for bed when they announced you."

35. *E-Mission*, by Chad Stuart

San Francisco, CA: RAM-10, Hamilton House Publishing, 1974, 188 pages, stock #102, $2.25, mass market paperback.

35A. Reprinted as: *Ty's Mission*, by Mitch Stone. North Hollywood, CA: Power Force Series, Arena Publications, 1984, 188 pages, stock #PF-123, $3.95, mass market paperback.

A chance photograph, snapped by a high-flying reconnaissance plane, showed evidence of a four-bunker missle [sic] complex camouflaged amid the jungle terrain near Estella...Ty Hamilton had been brought in by U.S. security to work on MISSION E because he was well versed in oil drilling operations and had been used in South American espionage circles on several occasions using a similar cover. Ty had complicated matters by bringing his lover, Brad, with him into the International Oil Co. family against his superiors' explicit instructions not to do so. But, despite the danger, Ty could not face the long, lonesome jungle night without the warmth of Brad's muscular body next to him.

* * * * * * *

Even with all ten inches of his hard cock rammed to its knotted roots up the clutching asshole, Chester O'Brien would have killed with his bare hands any man who would have dared call him a queer. It wouldn't have been the first time he had killed using only the strength God and hard work had put into his body. He had once broken a guy's spine in Uganda during a fight which Chester, luckily for him, hadn't started. A powerful uppercut, given another wildcat drill man, while searching for oil in the Middle East, had pushed the guy's jaw up into his brain.

Chester O'Brien was a big man. He stood over six-foot, three-inches, but there was nothing gangling about him. He was well put together and had a neck that thick [sic] he couldn't span it with both hands. His chest was the size of a wine-barrel, covered with the same thick red hair that ran down his belly, clustering around the base of his cock and running over onto his two trunk-like legs. It was the same russet color as the thatch of hair covering his head and beginning to form a stubble on his cheeks, neck, and chin. Some of those pubic strands were being smashed between Chester's pressing belly and Donald Miller's firm young ass.

Chester was convinced that Donald was a queer. Not that Donald physically looked the part. Quite the opposite. If he had resembled the stereotype pansy, Donald would have been safe from Chester's advances. As it was, his tightly muscled body was something else. Donald was in good shape. He had gotten that way on his college gymnastic and swim teams, and his job kept him that way. He was one of those blonds who tanned well, and the golden hue on his flesh all the way from his head to his feet let you know he wasn't afraid to expose himself to the sun. He was lithe rather than bulky, the muscle definition etched across his arms, chest, legs and belly with a seeming perfection. The little hair he did have on his body, excepting the substantial straw-tinged pubic bush clothing his belly at the base of his cock, had been bleached white by the sun. The young man's ass looked like it had been chiseled out of marble. And there was certainly nothing unmanly about his cock. It wasn't an enormous prick, but it was big enough, and matched perfectly the rest of the young man's excellent physique. Despite all this, Chester recognized a distinct dividing line between those normal people—among whom he counted himself—and a full-fledged queer who only wanted male meat rammed up his ass or a good foot of hard dick exploding a mouthful of cum down an eagerly gagging throat even if there was a woman available.

36. *Beat the Man Down*, by Chad Stuart

San Diego, CA: Adonis Classics, Greenleaf Classics, 1975, 172 pages, stock #AC106, $1.95, mass market paperback.

In our amorphous society, emotional stability is not only hard to achieve, it is also difficult to maintain. Nowhere is this truer than in the fad-mad, glitter world of rock music. Stars come and go, their popularity dictated by the fickle whim of their worshiping fans.

Augustyn is a talented young musician with all the making of a rock superstar. When an ambitious manager, Roger Vars, realizes his potential and mounts a huge promotional campaign, Augustyn is euphoric, sure that he has caught the brass ring of fame and fortune. But the pressures and demands of existing in such an amoral, carnival atmosphere gradually erode Augustyn's defenses, exposing the basic instability of his character and a dangerous potential for violence. Augustyn finds his dreams turned into a nightmare world of depravity and madness, leaving him shattered beyond repair.

BEAT THE MAN DOWN—the chronicle of a man struggling to achieve the good life, to fulfill the American dream. His story is a reminder to us all of the high price of success. A lesson to our society. A reflection on our world.

* * * * * * *

Randolph knew what to do and he did it. It was as simple as that. Paul hadn't needed to tell him. Randolph had gone through the customary pre-sex preliminaries and, upon seeing the cock begin its initial stirrings to life, he closed his mouth about the lengthening prick.

Randolph pulled back to a kneeling position between Paul's thighs, burrowing his nose and mouth into the pubic hair clustered at Paul's groin. The cock was like a magnet pulling him to it. Randolph licked the column from the leaking tip to the bulbous balls before swallowing the prick again. The man sucked up those juices leaking from the cockhead of the heavy prick. His tongue was coated with the salty oiliness.

His tastebuds [sic] drowned in the preseminal juices, his mouth filling with the continual liquid deluge as he siphoned the sexual ambrosia into his throat and belly. The fingers of both hands encircled the base of the prick, pressed flat against Paul's firm belly and pushed to somehow swell the prick to more powerful dimensions. Paul shifted his hips, thrilling to Randolph's ministrations at his crotch.

37. *Stud Maker*, by Lambert Wilhelm

San Diego, CA: Adonis Classics, Greenleaf Classics, 1975, 172 pages, stock #AC115, $2.25, mass market paperback.

Stud Maker is the story of a man who works in an industry of false illusions, pipe dreams and commercialized sex. For Vince Matthews, the male models that he sees through the lens of a camera are paragons of masculinity, models who become the fanciful stud of any gay guy's dreams. Working behind the camera, Vince creates illusions—emphasizes, probes, exploits, the best physical features of every male model; but once the work is done, reality sets in and the sojourns to the bedrooms begin.

Many gays would be envious of Vince Matthews, would be jealous of the studs he meets and makes—until they discover that Vince Matthews has been duped by the masculinity of a sordid stud and becomes a pawn in a deadly game.

The shocking story of an innocent man who becomes the bait for a blood bath.

* * * * * * *

Vince knelt between Brig's muscled thighs. Vince had a good view of his large, healthy balls drooping beneath the root of his fat and massive cock. Brig's huge cock lay flat against Brig's muscled belly and aimed at the handsome face that, head propped on a pillow, was watching the scene with great anticipation and interest.

Vince bowed his head toward Brig's blond-furred crotch. His mouth covered his balls [sic] a suction drawing in the flaccid flesh and its two large nuts. Vince had a sudden mouthful. He rolled the two testicles back and forth inside his mouth, washing the containing sac with wet-warm saliva. He concaved his cheeks around the two balls, squeezing in on them with enough pressure to give a dull ache which was a compliment rather than a detriment to Brig's pleasure. Even while the hairy sac was moved skillfully within his mouth, Vince felt the bag contracting, converting into a grapefruit-sized mass that would, at the ultimate moment of explosion, be tugged snugly to the base of the erupting cock.

Vince wasn't long satisfied with just Brig's nuts. He had other things in mind: a different type of meal. As if Brig's cock had a mind of its own, an ability to anticipate what Vince had in mind for it, the tremendous shaft throbbed with seeming excitement.

38. *Bugger Boy*, by Lambert Wilhelm

San Diego, CA: Adonis Classics, Greenleaf Classics, 1975, 157 pages, stock #AC118, $2.25, mass market paperback.

This is the story of a young man who has reached the crossroads of life. He is faced with a problem—a problem that has confronted many homophiles—to choose the road that society deems "normal" or to take the path of homosexuality and be branded as a pervert. For him, one choice is hypocritical, the other honest.

This novel is a shocking revelation of a dilemma that every gay has faced. Many people have said that today's society has learned to tolerate an individual's preference for sexual activity—laws have been passed, times have changed, mores and standards defined and redefined—and yet, such is the situation that many homophiles are still made to feel guilty about being honest about their desires and urges.

BUGGER BOY—an insight into a perplexing situation, a problem that society recognizes as having only two answers: conform or be condemned.

* * * * * * *

Ronnie wasn't old. He was actually twenty-five. It was just that Brack liked to fuck them a little younger and a little more innocent. Not that Brack was a menace to society. Christ no. By young, he certainly didn't mean some pre-adolescent whose balls hadn't yet dropped. And by innocent, he didn't mean a kid without the slightest notion that he'd like to mess around with some guy's fat prick. High-schoolers were a nice age.

Brack liked his tricks unjaded, bordering on closet case, looking for just the right young butch stud to come along and show them that there was just as much pleasure to be derived from a man-cock up their butts or mouths as they had always imagined.

Ronnie, now, was all right. As a matter of fact, out of all the guys on Brack's shift of construction workers, Ronnie was probably the only one Brack had really been all that interested in sharing his cock with. Ronnie had been a possible sexmate from the minute he'd signed on; and it didn't take Brack too long to figure out that any feelings he had about Ronnie were reciprocal.

39. *Jock Stud*, by Lambert Wilhelm

San Diego, CA: Adonis Classics, Greenleaf Classics, 1975, 172 pages, stock #AC120, $2.25, mass market paperback.

It's been said that every person has some dark passion within his soul—some hidden secret, desire, closest confidante, or even recognized by the person himself. Such a secret can be evil and sinister, or it may be trivial and trite.

In America, such dark passions are easily subverted and hidden by the complexities of everyday living. Yet sometimes dark passions surface—and another Richard Speck or Charles Manson emerges. Sometimes such passions are exposed—and another Watergate of ITT affair hits the headlines.

JOCK STUD is a dramatic representation of a wealthy man whose secret passion for young boys and his own teenage son torment him, and of a fifteen-year-old slum kid whose practical wisdom goes far beyond his years. When the two of them meet, desires are laid bare, passions nakedly exposed, until both are set free of their own unique fears.

* * * * * * *

"Pull your fuckin' pants down! Greg ordered.

Jamie obliged. He didn't remember when he'd ever seen his brother so angry. Maybe the time over on Lester Street. Greg had almost killed that punk from the Steel Chains. He'd done it with his fists, too. Pounded the poor sonofabitch into a bloody pulp so that the kid's own mother couldn't ever recognize him. But Greg wouldn't hurt Jamie like that. That's why he'd chosen this way. He was taking out his own frustrations by fucking Jamie. This was punishment only in Greg's mind, not in Jamie's. Jamie had learned long ago to look with pleasure on the run of his brother's cock in and out of his asshole. Did Greg still think that the best way to punish was to fuck? What had supposed to be degrading had evolved from that into something else a long time ago.

"Bend over the goddamn bed," Greg said. He was undoing his belt, his fingers pausing to fondle the buckle. Slowly he pulled the leather strap free of the belt loops. He knew his brother wasn't expecting this. Jamie was bent over the bed, his firm young ass ready for Greg's cock, not for Greg's belt. Greg had never hit him. Oh, he'd threatened many times, but he'd never done it. Even the first time he'd gotten furious, over that petty theft at Johnson's Department Store, Greg had fucked because he wanted to give a punishment that would leave no scars. Jamie had such a boyishly perfect body. It would have been a shame to mar it. A butt-fuck would have been enough. "See, you ain't a man just 'cause you swiped a couple of bicycle chains, you little bastard," Greg had said that first time. "What kinda man'd let himself get fucked like a woman?" There'd been no beating that time.

40. *Trucker Sucker,* by Lambert Wilhelm

San Diego, CA: Adonis Classics, Greenleaf Classics, 1975, 157 pages, stock #AC122, $2.25, mass market paperback.

For every young person there comes a time when he must confront new ideas and lifestyles, and adapt them to his own personal code. The young boy enlisting in the Army and meeting people of varied economic backgrounds from all over the country; the young man going off to college for the first time—all must face different and sometimes shocking ideas, and dealing with them is part of what makes an adult.

TRUCKER SUCKER is about a young boy, Gary, and the changes he undergoes when confronted with a new lifestyle. What starts out as an evening of casual sex with a handsome young stranger named Peter, transits into Gary's introduction to the world of bondage and discipline, a world he is both repelled by and attracted to. Now Gary must come to a decision—to take Brand up on the trucker's offer, or to leave his life unchanged.

TRUCKER SUCKER—the story of one boy groping his way to maturity, attempting to find his own niche in life, his own particular lifestyle. His story is one which holds a lesson for us all.

* * * * * * *

Peter was bound to one of the back wheels of the semi, affixed to it with a combination of snow chains and some smaller links which Brand had incorporated into the complex binding. The boy was placed with his belly against the hard rubber, his cock pressed into the tire tread, his legs wrapping the wheel as if he were in the process of fucking it dog-style. His upper body bent forward, lodged in the space between the upper curve of the tire and the bottom of the truck trailer. He was securely anchored into place, couldn't have stood straight even if he'd wanted to without hitting his head against the underbase of the truck trailer. The boy was blindfolded, was naked, was helpless and excited by it. His body was a crescent of whiteness in the glare of the car's headlights, his leg muscles taut in anticipation, his butt-cheeks hard, his belly tense, his nipples budded against the dirtied hardness of the rubber. His right cheek rested against the tire, feeling the softness of the mask's inner surface. The mask encompassed the boy's entire head except for an opening at the nose and another for the mouth. It hid completely the thick black hair, the dark-blue eyes, the dimples, the cleft of the chin. The straps were tied securely at the neck, knotted professionally in the back. His mouth was plugged with a piss gag, buckled and locked. The hollow tube inserted between his lips and preventing his mouth from closing was equipped with a sink plug.

Brad again checked the bindings that held the boy secure, satisfied with what he'd thus far achieved.

Gary watched, fascinated and unbelieving that he was actually witnessing the ritual. He would have never believed at the beginning of this evening that it would climax like this. He was frightened, but more than being afraid, he was aroused. His cock, which had but a short half-hour before been drained by the expert sucking of Peter's mouth and throat, was now painfully hard in his pants.

41. *The Meat Eaters*, by Chad Stuart

San Francisco, CA: RAM-10, Hamilton House Publishing, 1975, 188 pages, stock #111, $2.25, mass market paperback.

Finally Johnny had come into town for a long weekend. As usual, after cleaning up at the hotel, he headed for The Stallion, a bar and restaurant that was popular with both the local ranchers and the transit rodeo crowd. It was there that he saw Brand for the first time.

Johnny liked him right off, and it wasn't just because he was a new face in town. Nor was it just because the guy was stud material. His excellent physique was readily evident beneath his black T-shirt and faded jean jacket, just as his huge cock was evident through the sandpaper thinness of the faded levis [sic] wrapping his crotch and legs. Johnny could afford to be picky. He would have stood out as prime material in any group, and in Farfax, Wyoming, where there was little competition, Johnny could really do the choosing....

* * * * * * *

His name was Brand. His cock was ten inches of hard, muscle-knotted maleness that jutted up from his belly like a massive pole of human flesh. His bull-like balls dropped from the base of his hard cock and hung proudly between a pair of muscular thighs. His belly was a mass of tight ripples that wouldn't have given an inch beneath a punch from the strongest man. The black hair began on the thighs, light and fine like it was on the young man's arms. It grew thicker as it covered his lower belly, entwined about the base of the hard cock, and overflowed onto the constantly moving flesh of the testicles. It fanned upward toward the belly button, thinning out over the washboarded ripples of brawn which separated his navel from the bulging domes of his nipple-centered pectorals. A scattering of the dark hair spread into the deep cleft of the broad chest. The neck was thick, offering a solid support to the head. Brand's face possessed finely chiseled features that managed to meld into decidedly masculine contours. The lips were full, actually sensuous. The eyes were China blue and a striking contrast to the deep tan of the flesh and the blue-black tint of the brows and the lashes that shielded them. Brand's cheeks and upper lip and chin were shadowed with the faint evidence of a dark beard. His skin was satiny in the dim lighting of the hotel room. A thick thatch of hair dropped almost into his eyes. The dark thickness covered his head in a tousled, sexy way, curling over his ears and at the base of his neck.

Brand walked to Johnny and touched him.

Johnny had the clean-cut body and good looks of the stereo-typed country stud. You could have stood him in a room full of people and anyone when asked would have said that he was the typical cowboy. His hair was blond, the type of blond that was almost white from bleaching in the sun. His complexion was the kind that tanned well and did. His golden flesh extended from the top of his head to his toes, the usual white stripe at the middle having been eliminated during countless afternoons of riding horseback in the nude. His eyes were gray. His left cheek was dimpled. There was a slight cleft in his chin. His chest was well-muscled, hardened like the rest of his body by his work in the out-of-doors. He looked virtually hairless except for the pubic thatch that clustered around the uprisen thick-ness of his hard-on, but that was merely an illusion. There was, in fact, a veneering of fair and exceedingly fine hair that covered most of his legs, chest and belly. They could only be detected at certain moments and within certain light. His belly was hard and flat, scal-loped with the horizontal run of muscular ridges. His legs were solid from hours of gripping a horse and saddle between his thighs. His cock was large and topped by a fist-sized head. His hands were also large, their callouses [sic] rough when they touched bare flesh.

42. *Buck*, by Chad Stuart

San Francisco, CA: RAM-10, Hamilton House Publishing, 1975, 189 pages, stock #113, $2.25, mass market paperback.

The ride was going to be a long easy one. A perfect one. No fouling at the gate. This was going to be one of those beautiful 'high pointers', one of those big-paying experiences. Out of the gate. Into the sunlight. Ride like you've never ridden before. Roll with the feel of the animal beneath you. God, it would be exhilarating.

Buck found the euphoria he was seeking. It came from somewhere inside of him, flooded out of his finger tips, uplifted him, swallowed him. Sex was the closest Buck could come to the ecstasy he felt on a good ride.

* * * * * * *

WORLD CHAMPION BULL RIDER
BUCK KNEALY

The rectangular championship buckle was gold and silver filigree, measuring five by three inches. It was affixed to a genuine alligator strap that passed through faded jean belt loops on the pair of Levi pants carefully folded and placed over the back of the chair.

The body belonging to that belt, 5'8," 145-pound Buck Knealy, was naked on the bed, his muscles glossy with a covering of sweat, bunching with the strain of pushing and pulling the eight inches of his hard cock in and out of Blake Tanners' solid, round and upturned ass. The five-inch ridge of scar tissue on Buck's back, the result of a goring in the rodeo at Big Piney, Montana, three years before, appeared white against the darker flesh.

The two men straining on the bed were surprisingly similar in physical appearance: young faces, trim and muscular bodies. Their arms and shoulders were powerful, with a thickness that was retained through the necks. There was only half an inch difference between them in height: Buck being the taller. Both wore a 15½" neck shirt with a 33" sleeve. Both wore 8D boots. They both had grey eyes, brown hair.

43. *A Presidential Affair*, by Chad Stuart

San Francisco, CA: RAM-10, Hamilton House Publishing, 1975, 186 pages, stock #119, $2.25, mass market paperback.

43A. Reprinted as: *The President's Men*, by Scott Weyburn. North Hollywood, CA: Power Force Series, Arena Publications, 1985, 186 pages, stock #PF-136, $3.95, mass market paperback.

To Our Readers,

The sexual revolution which had been taking place for a number of years in the United States has dramatically influenced many people's personal codes of sexual morality. Many sexual practices which were formerly forbidden are now either accepted or are rapidly gaining acceptance. What was once done but never openly discussed, is now widely talked about and often openly flaunted.

Today, discussion and even adoption of what were previously considered to be the darker aspects of human sexuality have permeated all levels of our society. In fact, formerly taboo practices such as homosexuality, bi-sexuality and even pan-sexuality have not only been accepted but have—if one reads the society columns of our daily newspapers—become almost fashionable.

* * * * * * *

Paul's body was made even more golden by the moonlight that filtered into the cabin through the opened porthole. His tanned chest shone with a veneering of sweat coaxed through the pores by a summer's heat which had lingered well beyond sundown. The pectoral muscles were domed mounds completely absent of hair. The hard flesh of the chest curved to a meeting with a ridged and scalloped abdomen. The first clusters of hair began at the belly button, blond strands huddled at the small pit. Pubic hairs pushed fuller on the lower belly, thriving at the roots of a cock that was, at that moment, standing hard between muscular thighs.

Paul's cock was a powerful instrument. From its thickly rooted base hung two massive and hairy balls. The sac hung low and brushed the youth's inner thighs. The skin shifted, the nuts rolling in accompaniment to the occasional nervous jerks of the hard cock. From the cock's base, which defied even the largest handspan, the penis reared upward: an arching of hard meat that was latticed with thick veins. It wasn't a perfectly round cock. It was flattened across its belly and back. It formed a gentle curving that bowed outward and upward from its base. The cockhead was a fisted mass of swollen flesh.

"God, you're handsome," Jay Tambu muttered appreciatively.

44. *B&D Boys*, by Lambert Wilhelm

San Diego, CA: Adonis Classics, Greenleaf Classics, 1976, 173 pages, stock #AC124, $2.25, mass market paperback.

A question often asked by those who deal with psychological problems is: What is normal? The answer to that seemingly simple question will probably never be answered.

For example, it is normal for some primitive inhabitants of South American jungles to perform, before the entire village, what Americans would consider depraved sexual acts.

The people within a particular society usually are well-aware of what is considered acceptable behavior for them. And therein lies the problem for the main character of this novel....

* * * * * * *

The waistband of Stan's white and tight-fitting gym shorts hugged the youth's stomach just below the belly button. The crotch of the shorts was bulged despite the fact that the concealed bulk of thick cock and balls was snugly contained by the elastic jockstrap. Muscled thighs filled the legs of the shorts, solid upper legs tapering beyond the knees to well-developed calves.

There was sweat on Stan's belly, glossing his chest, dampening his face. The young man was hardly aware of the sweat, his mind occupied on the sequence of his exercise. He was striving diligently for proper form. Exercise was an art. There was a right way and a wrong way of doing it. Stan worked hard on the right way.

Each lifting of the weight was done smoothly with no jerking, his legs firmly planted on the floor, his back straight.

45. *Leather Bound*, by Lambert Wilhelm

San Diego, CA: Adonis Classics, Greenleaf Classics, 1976, 156 pages, stock #AC127, $2.25, mass market paperback.

If is not without continual doubt that we negotiate life's daily transitions, answering questions that will shape our lives, never having the wisdom of hindsight. For many, making a sexual transition is the most difficult question life poses.

Gary Wenlock, at fourteen, had to make a change. His mother had died when he was young, and his father had turned to drinking and sleeping with a live-in whore. Gary was unimpressed with his surroundings, and even less with the girls in his neighborhood. Life had become pointless, and there was no promise of anything better. And thus, Gary began his transition to the homophile world.

LEATHER BOUND is the story of Gary's journey through question, guilt, image-chasing, and promiscuity. A story that reminds us society often fails us in one respect, but offers its rewards in another.

* * * * * * *

Gary's cock lost its virginity in the city park. That wasn't the least of things that had happened there. Not long ago, the police found two naked bodies hidden among some thick pines. Of course, they never found the murderer. But they might have found Gary getting his cock sucked. Stripped and bound to a tree, Gary wondered how he'd let himself get into such a predicament.

How? Out of a sense of adventure? Out of a sense of trust? Trust? Yes, trust. Yes, adventure. Gary had an inherent trust in the healthy butch stud who was even then prepared to sexually take him. Gary trusted the rugged blond wasn't a killer. How many victims had been fooled by the innocent air of their murderers? Wasn't that part of the adventure, too?

Still, wasn't there a line between trust and foolishness? Trusting the blond was one thing. Making no protest while he tied Gary to a tree was quite another. Wasn't it? So, why had Gary allowed it? Why had the boy made no protest, willingly complying as if he were a calf with no choice in the matter? It wasn't only because those two unidentified bodies found in the park had been girls; although, that was probably part of it. It was something much more. It was a realization that it would be now or never. That nowhere would Gary likely find a more attractive candidate to be the instrument of his deflowering.

46. *Brother in Bondage*, by Lambert Wilhelm

San Diego, CA: Adonis Classics, Greenleaf Classics, 1976, 156 pages, stock #AC128, $2.25, mass market paperback.

There are only two types of males who dare to venture into the world of bondage and degradation—those who wish to be slaves, willing to find pleasure in pain, and those who wish to be masters, willing to deal out pain to find pleasure.

BROTHER IN BONDAGE is the story of David Lamb, a four-teen-year-old boy who is mature far beyond his years. In the beginning, David is the perfect slave, a chained young Adonis willing to suffer painful passions. In the end, David becomes the master of other boys like himself, willing to degrade and debase, finding ultimate ecstasy in dealing out pain.

Yet, somewhere in the transition from slave to master, there is trauma and fear, anxiety and anguish. For no man can be master and slave for a moment or a lifetime; he can only be one or the other.

* * * * * * *

Through the gag, the grunt came out sounding like something made by a stuck pig. The first grunt was followed by a second. The fat cock continued its drive up the boy's ass. The kid's body was deluged with the pain that flooded from the passing of the cock into his butt.

He was young. He was blond. He was blue-eyed. He was getting fucked.

He'd been expecting the cock but not expecting it. He knew it would come, but he'd still been surprised by its coming. Maybe it was because they'd numbed his ass first. They'd beaten on his ass-cheeks until there was little feeling left to them. There had been only the flaming heat. And then there was the pain.

47. *Bondage Boy*, by Lambert Wilhelm

San Diego, CA: Adonis Classics, Greenleaf Classics, 1976, 158 pages, stock #AC131, $2.25, mass market paperback.

In our ever-changing and often-confusing world, a world in which it is often difficult to determine right from wrong or good from bad, things which may have shocked our grandparents, or even our parents, are often taken with a grain of salt.

Just a few short years ago it seemed that the stereotype homosexual had firmly entrenched itself in the general consciousness of our society. It would have been looked upon as absurd, for example for one to suggest that a certain professional football player was gay. After all, *everyone* knew that homosexuals were nonviolent, at best, and downright weak-kneed, at worst. It also went without saying that there were no homosexual doctors, lawyers, football players, or gymnasts. There were, however, numerous gay hairdressers, interior decorators and fashion designers. And, of course, most artists were suspect.

BONDAGE BOY is a story that "tells it like it is" in that it exposes the old gay stereotype for what it is—a lie. A compelling novel that attempts to uncover the truth in an area where the facts have been ignored too long.

* * * * * * *

Tommy hung from the still rings. He hung by his feet. His ankles were tied to the rings. His head hung suspended four feet from the floor. It would have hung closer to the floor, but Braun had raised the rings above their normal hanging height. He'd wanted access to the boy's body. He had it.

Braun's paddle whacked the already red flesh of Tommy's ass. There was a loud smacking sound. There had been many slaps of the wood against the ass flesh. The buttocks were a deep rose color. The redness overran the boy's buns and crawled along the back of his thighs.

Braun again hit the ass. The force of the blow rocked Tommy's body. Braun delivered another blow. He was sexually aroused by the wooden paddle slapping against the flesh of Tommy's ass.

48. *Strung and Hung*, by Lambert Wilhelm

San Diego, CA: Adonis Classics, Greenleaf Classics, 1976, 158 pages, stock #AC135, $2.25, mass market paperback.

A question often asked by those who deal with psychological problems is: What is normal? The answer to that seemingly simple question will probably never be answered....

* * * * * * *

Billy knelt by the side of the bed, the makeshift dildo shoved up his asshole. It wasn't a manufactured dildo. Christ, where would a thirteen-year-old kid get one of those? Oh, some young teen somewhere else might have had no difficulty. Kids at school were always bringing back tales of things they'd found while exploring in their parents' bedrooms. However, Billy's parents always seemed a bit strait-laced to Billy. The thought of either his mother or father using a rubber cock while fucking was really quite ludicrous in the extreme. Thoughts of his mother and father even fucking at all were, somehow just about equally as ludicrous.

Billy had taken a rubber and stuffed it full of cotton. His efforts had produced a quite sizable, if anemic-looking cock facsimile.

Getting his hands on a rubber was easier than getting his hands on a dildo. There was a place in the woods up above Kinnear Park where all the high-school kids drove their dates. Any enterprising youngster could find himself half a dozen disgarded [sic] rubbers on a Monday after a good weekend. There used to be more. That, though, was before even most young girls went on the pill. Pill or no pill, however, there always seemed to be a few cum-filled rubbers lying in the weeds. Doubtlessly, years of fearing unwanted pregnancy had made some guys doubly careful.

49. *Boy in Bondage*, by Lambert Wilhelm

San Diego, CA: Adonis Classics, Greenleaf Classics, 1977, 155 pages, stock #AC151, $2.95, mass market paperback.

It's been said that every person has some dark passion within his soul—some hidden desire, secret or whim that may never surface to be seen by his closest confidante, or even recognized by the person himself. Such a secret can be either a desire that is truly evil, or one that is merely frightening because it is forbidden by society.

In America, such dark passions are easily submerged and hidden by the complexities of everyday life. Yet sometimes dark passions surface—and another Richard Speck or Charles Manson emerges. Sometimes such passions are exposed—and another Watergate or Elizabeth Ray affair hits the headlines.

In this novel we see the several ways in which men hide their true passions. Some merely hide them from the outside world; other [sic] submerge their desires to the extent that they themselves do not realize them. And the representation of their true needs leads these men to acts that are unthinking and often cruel.

BOY IN BONDAGE—the story of men who find that the truth does indeed make them free. A novel of fiction for entertainment. A page of our restless society as food for serious thought.

* * * * * * *

They thought they were alone. David had certainly not expected his father to come back and find them fucking up a storm in the basement had he? Charles Ribtoff had certainly kept his suspicions well veiled. Could David have ever dreamed Charles' trip across state had been a mere ploy?

Charles hadn't gone anywhere further than across town. He'd checked into a motel. That evening he'd returned to the house. He'd found Terry's car in the driveway. Still, what did that prove? It could have been harmless. However, Charles' cautious approach would have told any witness that the father thought only the worst. What he would find in the basement would only verify his fears. Charles' fifteen-year-old son was gay.

David and Terry had wasted little time in getting together when the supposed ideal opportunity presented itself. David had called

Terry immediately. Terry had rushed right over. He hadn't made any excuses to his parents. Terry had no need to. He'd been living by himself for as long as he could remember. He'd been a *man* for years.

50. *Cop Sucker*, by Lambert Wilhelm

San Diego, CA: Adonis Classics, Greenleaf Classics, 1977, 154 pages, stock #AC155, $2.95, mass market paperback.

It's been said that every person has some dark passion within his soul—some hidden secret, desire, closest confidante, or even recognized by the person himself. Such a secret can be evil and sinister, or it may be trivial and trite....

* * * * * * *

The kid looked young enough to be Porter's son. A moment of thinking the young blond was Mat brought Porter around the block once more. Anyway, that's how Porter rationalized his return. On the second pass, Porter could well see that it wasn't Mat leaning against the side of the building there in the shadows. Oh, the age was about right, somewhere around fifteen, but the face wasn't right. The kid was attractive, but he looked tired. My God, why wouldn't he look tire out on the streets at this time of the night?

Knowing it wasn't Mat, what brought Porter back around the block yet again? Well, this time he told himself he was looking for someone else, one of the older hustlers. Of course, Porter had already told himself that the blond kid was probably the only one there. Obviously no one had told the young teenager that there'd been a raid here just the week before. The police had arrested six kids in one night. Porter knew. He'd been at the station the evening they'd brought the kids in. Porter had kept out of the limelight, though. None of the six had looked familiar, but that didn't mean one of them hadn't fucked around with Porter.

Porter was down cruising this block now because he knew there was no vice assigned here this evening. For awhile, the police chief had decided to quite harassing the gays and move on to other more important matters. Actually, Chief Harris only scheduled roundups on the gay community about once a year. If he didn't, he'd end up getting static from one faction or another of the straight establishment who thought the queers were on the move against them.

51. *Hotel Hustlers*, by Lambert Wilhelm

San Diego, CA: Adonis Classics, Greenleaf Classics, 1977, 154 pages, stock #AC162, $2.95, mass market paperback.

In our ever-changing and often-confusing world, a world in which it is often difficult to determine right from wrong or good from bad, things which may have shocked our grandparents, or even our parents, are often taken with a grain of salt.....

* * * * * * *

Hey Toby!"
Toby Dneiper turned toward the caller.
"Bran, what's up?"
"I want to borrow a few minutes of your time."
Toby, who had been heading for the volleyball game at the other end of the beach, changed his route and headed toward the stilt-supported lifeguard shack.
Bran Torber and Barry Moore watched Toby's progress through the white sand.
Toby moved slowly, aware that he was being watched by more than Bran and Barry. Toby had the attractive good looks and good physique that always drew stares form men and women alike. When he wasn't on lifeguard duty himself, like now, he was down here on the beach where he could get maximum exposure. The beach was also a good place for cruising. What else always brought Bran down here, too, but the cruising when he could have stayed in the hotel?

52. *Cockring*, by Raymond R. Lang

Santee, CA: The Blueboy Library, 1977, 184 pages, stock #80051, $2.25, mass market paperback.

Gamecock fighting, a sport banned in the U.S., is quite popular in the Latin countries to the South, popular to the extent that breeding ranches catering to just this sport abound.

It is a savage sport and one that excites the blood, and often fortunes are won and lost by the merest flicker of the cruel steel spurs attached to the birds' natural spurs. Fighting is instinctive with these fiercely territorial and possessive birds, and they have been bred for centuries for just the purpose of fighting in the ring—to the death.

And the men who adhere and participate in this sport? *Cockring* is the story of those men, their economic hopes in a poor country, of hitting the big time, their lives, their loves... Such a person is Raphael, a gamecock trainer trainee. He is also noted for his splendid good looks and is widely sought—especially by the men. Machismo is the mask that all wear in this Latin novel—but homosexuality is their motivation.

* * * * * * *

Their sex was never anything less than violent. In Juan's arms, smashed beneath Juan's body, asshole clogged with the fucking bulk of Juan's cock, Raphael could well imagine the meaning of the word rape. However, this wasn't rape in actuality. Raphael was here willingly enough, his young body prone on the bed, his fingers clawlike in the sheets, his legs splayed, his sweaty ass echoing with the pumping smacks of Juan's lower belly and swinging balls. Raphael was here, enduring this humiliation, for the money. Juan paid very well for his few minutes with Raphael, and while Raphael could always, during sex, wonder how he could sink so low as to let Juan crawl on him, he knew from past experience that you couldn't remember the pain once it was finished. It was that realization, that one piece of knowledge that kept him there pinioned on the bed, not fighting, but accepting. Eventually Juan would be finished, eventually Juan would be subdued amid a thousand guttural groanings of ejaculation and satisfaction, eventually Raphael would have his money and could sneak off to some private place to lick his wounds.

Juan was a long way from releasing his prey. His cock might well have already become lost to its balls up Raphael's behind, but the prick itself was a damned long way from completing its fuck. Despite the fact that Juan was hornier than hell, it took him a long time to cum [sic]. As sexually excited as he could become by the mere sight of Raphael's naked and available body, Juan was not one to blast his wad after only a few frantic heaves and humps. Sometimes he wished he was built differently. The passion and the pleasure that swelled inside him was [sic] often unbearable, and still he wasn't allowed a releasing until later. Sometimes he thought he would die with just the build up to an eruption, never actually be allowed to reach the supreme moment of climax; but then, somehow, just when he thought he'd never possibly get there, Juan's nuts would blow, and Juan would spasm in uncontrollable ecstasy.

During a fuck Juan looked on Raphael as nothing much more than an animal to satisfy Juan's animal lusts: a bitch to play off Juan's dog in rut. As a means of compensating for his deep-rooted guilt feelings in enjoying man-man sex, Juan always assumed dominance in his relationships, never was fucked himself or gave head, and always treated his partners violently if only because he blamed their young male bodies for arousing him to such fever pitch. Juan did feel guilty because (despite his butch good looks), he didn't like sex with anyone but boys. While he could get a hard-on at the drop of Raphael's pants (actually well before Raphael even got around to dropping them), Juan just couldn't get aroused by women. Ever since he'd been young enough to shoot his wad, Juan had been embarrassed that he couldn't make it with women. The fact that he couldn't also had made him the object of much joking by some of the women (especially those who were jealous that a young boy could do for Juan what they couldn't), and made him the object of much disgust from his father (who had liked boys, too, but had been "man" enough to marry and father children as had been expected of him). Thus Juan's psychological problems made sex for anyone subjected to Juan's incessant battering anything but a picnic.

53. *The Secret of the Phallic Stone*, by Raymond R. Lang

Santee, CA: The Blueboy Library, 1977, 184 pages, stock #80059, $2.25, mass market paperback.

Two top U.S. Scientists mysteriously drop dead while doing research on moonrocks, and immediately an investigation is underway with the shadow of fear hanging over every step. Thousands of miles away, in a top-secret Russian laboratory, changes are being made which baffle our intelligence researchers. Efforts by both sides are confused and obscured by shifting loyalties and sexual ties between those very researchers...and all clues point to a mysterious organism which may have come with the rocks—but is no longer in evidence.

Suspense and hard action mark the tortuous trail of *The Secret of the Phallic Stone,* with a surprise twist in the resolution of this spy-mystery.

The love of Man for Man is as old as Man himself. Much of the Western world's ancient history has been altered and purged of sexual references by overzealous religious and political monopolies in the name of sanctity and decency, yet there are truths and events impossible to totally expunge from the record of Mankind. From Alexander the Great through the lover-warriors of Sparta through such literary greats as Oscar Wilde to the present day, the homophilic man has been represented in history. Not always accepted by the majority of society, that man has had to fight for his place, his right to life, liberty, love, and the pursuit of happiness.

* * * * * * *

"Nothing," Peter Stort said, flopping exhausted into the chair. "It's definite that something is going on, but the Soviets are really keeping a lid on this one."

"That's unfortunate," John Wimer replied, pyramiding his fingers beneath his chin. "I was hoping you would have come up with something by now."

"This is not just any case. You don't just walk into the Soviet's top research laboratories and come out with top-secret files."

"My comment was no reflection upon your ability as an agent,"

John said easily. "In a way, it was a lamentation for my own present predicament. I was counting on you to bust this project for me, Peter. I don't know what I'm going to do without you."

"What's that supposed to mean?" Peter asked.

"You've been reassigned," John said, standing. "Get your things together as soon as you can. There will be a plane to pick you up at the airport at eleven."

54. *In the Hole*, by Raymond C. Lang

Santee, CA: The Blueboy Library, 1977, 184 pages, stock #80062, $2.25, mass market paperback.

Parents, especially concerned mothers, still whispered tales about this place: tales to scare inquisitive children away from the mouth of the mine.

There was a story of the cave-in back in '54. That was when the place was going full swing. Twenty-four men went down into the blackness and never came up again. To this day, they waited down there for some smart-ass kid to come walking by. They were mighty hungry for meat after all of these years.

Or, what about Joey Martin? He was always wandering off where he wasn't supposed to. He wouldn't listen. He disappeared. Old Lady Mackay remembered seeing him wandering around in the dilapidated mine buildings on that fateful day. A rescue party, venturing back into the catacombs beneath the mountain, spent three days looking for signs of Joey. So where do you suppose he went? Parents said he was probably still trying to find his way out. Paul Martin, Joey's brother, however, let it drop around school that Joey had merely skipped town to get away from a stepfather who was getting a little too familiar.

* * * * * * *

Mat didn't believe all of that "haunted" bullshit now that he was fifteen. Anyway, that's what he would have told you if you had asked. Sometimes, he would have told you even if you hadn't asked. All that crap was fine for prepubescent babies; but, once your balls dropped, you had to come to your senses.

Still, having been led blindfolded and gagged into the mine, walked around until he didn't know whether he was coming or going, and then left tied up for what seemed an eternity, was enough to conjure up some of those old fears even in the likes of Mat Marlow.

What if they'd left him? What if they'd forgotten where they'd put him? What if they'd gone off and weren't returning? What if... what if...what if?

55. *The Siegfried Mating*, by Chad Stuart

Santee, CA: The Blueboy Library, 1977, 184 pages, stock #80089, $2.25, mass market paperback.

Darwin theorized that man in his lowest stages was essentially an animal, and the upward progress of man is viewed as effected by natural causes, chief among which is the action of natural selection. His pronouncements were greeted by enraged outbursts by those of us who had long believed we didn't belong to the rest of nature but stood somehow apart, being a different and superior being.

However, those men who were able to cast aside the assumed insult to their human dignity sided with Darwin. They accepted this new awareness of their evolutionary origins. They accepted the fact that human behavior does obey the laws of natural causation. They were prepared to cast aside a spiritual pride which had heretofore supported man in his reluctance to accept natural laws as determinants of his own behavior.

Adolph Hitler, as but one in a long line of German leaders, kings, philosophers, and historians, saw life as Darwin saw it: a struggle for survival between the fit and the weak. Hitler, though, was prepared to go one step further. Natural selection, while Nature's valid way of eliminating the sick and the weak, was often a tedious and lengthy process, taking hundreds or even thousands of years. If man was indeed an animal, couldn't he, too, be improved by the more controlled methods of artificial selection, as other animals, specifically livestock, were?

* * * * * * *

-1945-

"They took the children away today, didn't they?" Arndt asked.

"I should have known you'd realize what was happening," Geerman said. "Others would go to their deaths in ignorance; but, you would know."

"The children will be safe, won't they?"

"All efforts will be made to protect those few who were chosen," Geerman said. "Some had to die of course."

"My son was saved, though, wasn't he?" Arndt asked, sitting up in bed, looking to his companion. "You did arrange for him him [sic] to be among he survivors?"

"Doesn't that go without saying?"

"It will be easier knowing he, at least, will go on."

"Your progeny will one day rule the world," Geerman said.

56. *Gusher Comin'*, by Chad Stuart

Santee, CA: Surree House, 1977, 185 pages, stock #HIS69203, $2.25, mass market paperback.

An offshore oil platform mysteriously abandoned, an entire drilling crew missing with no trace. Two investigators suddenly and without warning enjulfed [sic] in a fiery death when Platform number one finally blew, and now Derek, son of the oil company's magnate must make Platform number two a success—without incident—or the whole Pacific operation will fail.

As with so many other men-only wilderness operations, these men will seek relief from their pent-up drives and daily frustrations, if not by themselves, then with others. Derek, suspect for his high connections within the conglomerate was no exception, and, in fact, his preference for men soon made him a trusted "one of the boys!"

* * * * * * *

The phone began ringing while Kyle was making love. He didn't answer it. He was too far gone to even care who was on the other end. He was too far gone to even care that it was likely someone important. It was, after all, two o'clock in the morning.

Making love for Kyle was always a good feeling. Answering the phone at night usually meant other than pleasurable repercussions. A phone call usually meant he would have to get up out of bed, get dressed, go somewhere where he was immediately needed.

Fuck whoever was calling! Kyle wasn't ready yet to come back to the reality of Conglomerate Oil International. He was momentarily content with the subtler world his cock up this butt was creating for him. This world, conjured as it was within the confines of his king-sized bed, was far more enjoyable than his other world. Here, flowing on the wave of building ecstasy, Kyle was little concerned with oil boycotts, oil spills, oil cartels, oil sheiks, oil pipelines. The only oil important was the natural lubricating oils which were leaked from the pouting mouth of his cock's meatus and turning Craig's bowel into a slideway [sic] for Kyle's thick cock inches.

57. *Black Room Terror*, by Chad Stuart

Santee, CA: Hard Trade Special, Surree House, 1977, 185 pages, stock #HIS69215, $2.25, mass market paperback.

According to Robert M. Goldenson, Ph.D., in his *THE ENCY-CLOPEDIA OF HUMAN BEHAVIOR: PSYCHOLOGY, PSYCHIA-TRY, AND MENTAL HEALTH*, the correlation existing between sexual arousal and emotional experience can be a particularly close one. Certain experiences involving fear can and do become erotically stimulating for certain types of individuals.

Why is this the case? Actually, the reasons are primarily still unknown to the scientific community. The human being is a thoroughly complex mechanism, driven by motivations which are, more often than not, understood by no one—scientists or layman alike.

Whether completely explainable or not, some of us do get turned on by riding in fast cars. Some of us do get turned on by exposing our genitals or flashing our bare buttocks in public places. Some of us do get our thrills by watching people through keyholes, or by dressing up in leather.

* * * * * * *

Charles Kamulu knew what to do. Paul Gradner had given him exact instructions.

The Negro slipped into the underbrush, coming out in a small stretch of grass that bordered the top of the cliff. Below him stretched the African night, punctuated here and there with occasional lights that eventually sunburst into the illuminated port of Mambala harbor.

Charles spread out a blanket on the grass in a position that gave anyone on the blanket an uninterrupted view of the harbor. He then began to undress.

58. *Animal Man,* by Chad Stuart

Santee, CA: Hard Trade Special, Surree House, 1978, 183 pages, stock #HIS69227, $2.25, mass market paperback.

"Man," said Arnold Gehlen, "is by nature a jeopardized animal."

There exists proof that African Australopithecines first invented stone tools and then proceeded to kill his fellow man with them. There is further evidence that the first ancient man to use fire, the Peking Man, used his knowledge to roast for dinner not only game but his peers.

Indeed, Konrad Lorenz, outstanding naturalist, has even suggested that modern man has a measure of aggression bred into him for which he has no adequate outlet but violence.

* * * * * * *

They were long and thick and phallic. They coiled about one another in a mass of twisting flesh that resembled bodies writhing in orgy. They were nonpoisonous and, thus, would be transported in sacks.

The poisonous ones, like the Thai viper, were shipped out in boxes. Gregory Lai took great pleasure in every Thai viper he took from the jungle. He would like to have taken them all.

"Bastard!" Gregory spat at the blunted head that slithered amongst shifting coils. Gregory then slammed down the crate lid with a bang.

Gregory, when he was much younger, had been bitten by a Thai. They'd had to amputate Gregory's left leg just below his knee to save him. There'd been no antiseptic except whiskey. There'd been no operating equipment except for a machete and a hacksaw. Thank God for the hacksaw! Without it, they would have [sic] to go to the knee where it was possible to slice through the joint. It had been an experience Gregory would always remember as having barely survived.

59. *Incestuous Summer*, by Wilhelm Mauser

South Laguna, CA: Family Series Books, Publisher's Consultants, 1978, 159 pages, stock #FAM110, $2.50, mass market paperback.

Bondage and discipline, wife swapping, incest: three phenomenon found in our society today. Nor have these aspects of living arrived full-blown on just the present scene. They've been with us a long time, and they will probably continue on after our generation is gone.

The Marquis de Sade (1740-1814) and Leopold V. Sacher-Masoch (1836-1894) were so noted for carrying bondage and discipline to extremes that they've since lent their names to those words in our vocabulary denoting such excesses.

Vance Packard in his *THE SEXUAL WILDERNESS* quotes a marriage specialist as saying: "If we are moving into a new pattern where we are not claiming that marriage can do all things that have been assumed, we may be moving into a kind of situation where there will be more than one partner."

* * * * * * *

Both seventeen-year-old girls were excited. That excitement could easily be read in Cindy's dilated China blue yes and in Paula's large feline green ones. It could easily be seen by the tautness of their quarter-size nipples that pressed button-like bumps into the material of Paul's tight-fitting sweater and Cindy's diaphanous blouse.

The two were seated in the car and had been sitting there for the past half an hour. They were intently watching the sparse evening traffic passing by on the highway directly in front of them.

"You wouldn't be pulling my leg, would you?" Cindy Kraft asked, using long tapering fingers to nervously rearrange several stray strands of her Farrah Fawcett-Majors hair style. She was acutely aware of a wet-warm sensation that had taken root between her creamy thighs and was even then spreading upward into the pit of her firm and slightly concaved stomach.

60. *The Incestuous Stepfather*, by Ernst Webber

South Laguna, CA: Family Series Books, Publisher's Consultants, 1978, 160 pages, stock #FAM112, $2.50, mass market paperback.

"There is no question of the fact that the human male's sexual responsiveness wanes as he ages," say William H. Masters and Virginia E. Johnson in their book *HUMAN SEXUAL RESPONSE.*

That doesn't mean that every man can easily accept the fact that his sexual performances today can't necessarily match up to those of yesterday. As a matter of fact, the decline of a man's sexual activity has often been known to cause acute anxiety.

When these fears of approaching impotency, waning masculinity, and decreasing virility, take root (state Masters and Johnson), it is sometimes the case that a middle-age man will turn to a younger female partner for sexual stimulation in his subconscious need to reestablish sexual potency in his own eyes and to support his ego by proving repeatedly his sexual prowess.

* * * * * * *

Donna came into the house and tossed her school books into the nearest chair. She gave a toss of her tawny blonde hair, catching her reflection in the mirror over the couch.

At seventeen, Donna was pleased with what she saw. Her pimple days (she'd never had many), were behind her. She now had a completely flawless complexion. Her skin was clear and lightly tanned around wide, thickly-lashed sapphire-blue eyes, pert nose, and fully sensuous coral-pink lips.

In the kitchen, Donna found the note from her mother, saying that Babs had gone to a baby shower for Cynthia Powell. Donna didn't know anyone called Cynthia Powell, but that didn't mean some pregnant woman by that name didn't exist. She was probably one of the women from one of the clubs Babs was always joining.

61. *Lessons for Mother,* by Wilhelm Mauser

South Laguna, CA: Family Series Books, Publisher's Consultants, 1978, 160 pages, stock #FAM114, $2.50, mass market paperback.

It is a common fact that in societies like ours, based as they often are on rather puritanical ethics of morality, that sexual abstinence is presented as a virtue, as something which is not only ideal but somehow beneficial in the bargain. Because of this many young people often go through long periods of trying to check their powerful sex drives. If they are less than completely successful in these endeavors—which is more often than not the case—they experience feelings of guilt and shame, feelings so deeply rooted as to actually endanger their health and happiness in any future marriages.

"This permission to have sexual relations in the marital union does not in all instances resolve the problems that have been created by these feelings," states Hugo G. Beigel, Ph.D., in his chapter "Abstinence" in Dr. Albert Ellis and Dr. Albert Abarbanel's *Heterosexual Relationships.* "Many girls can comply with the moral restrictions only by convincing themselves of the lewdness and ugliness of all sexual matters. When they later marry, they cannot free themselves of the disgust they had cultivated to fortify their chastity."

The problem of Kathleen Morley then, as presented in the following novel, is not a unique one. What is, perhaps, unique is the way in which her family bands together to find a solution to Kathleen's unnatural paranoias.

* * * * * * *

"What in the hell is going on around this house?" Morinda Morley asked, entering her brother's bedroom and shutting the door behind her.

"Don't you ever knock when you enter someone else's room?" Kyle asked his pretty sister. "Or don't they teach such things as good manners in that snooty-ass girls [sic] school you now go to?"

They teach a lot of things at Briarhaven," Morinda said, coming over to the bed and sitting down next to Kyle. "Some of the things I've learned there, I'm quite sure, would even surprise you. I know it would certainly surprise dear mother and dad."

62. *Abducted Daughter*, by Wilhelm Mauser

South Laguna, CA: Captive Women Series, Publisher's Consultants, 1978, 180 pages, stock #CWS113, $2.50, mass market paperback.

There are few behavioral scientists in this day and age who will argue the point that man is prone to a violent nature, his primitive instincts held in check and balance by a set of complex rules and regulations which have been laid down *by* society for the protection *of* society.

"We all suffer to some extent from the necessity to control our natural inclinations by the exercise of moral responsibility," states Konrad Lorenz in *ON AGGRESSION.*

Man, over the years, though, has consistently found ways and means to assuage his overpowering needs.

* * * * * * *

Susie eased the flashy Lincoln Continental around the corner, knowing immediately that it had been a mistake bringing the big car. She should have rented a VW. Maybe then she could have gotten through the gate—somehow—before the mine strikers realized she was the boss' daughter. Well, it was too late now to be thinking about what she SHOULD have done.

Susie checked all of the car doors, making sure they were locked. She experienced an involuntary shiver that went all of the way up her spine and then all of the way back down again. It somehow seemed of little consolation that there were men hired by her father, waiting to act in case the strikers put up too much of a stink regarding the inward passage of "scabs" or management personnel. And since Susie had called, she knew her protectors would be on the lookout for her.

Susie honked the car horn, as much to announce her arrival to her father's men as to part the mass of rough-looking men who were purposely blocking her way.

63. *The Gang-Ravished Teacher*, by Wilhelm Mauser

South Laguna, CA: Monterey Library Press, Publisher's Consultants, 1978, 160 pages, stock #MLP 132, $2.50, mass market paperback.

"There is a really low class here that is a lulu," says Henry Dodson in August B. Hollingshead's *ELMTOWN'S YOUTH*. "It is made up of families who are not worth...a damn, and they don't give a damn. They're not immoral; they're not unmoral; they're plain amoral.... They have animal urges and respond to them. They're like a bunch of rabbits.

Some people would go so far as to argue that what Dotson said about the lower class of Elmtown could be applied today to the lower class found in many large American cities; could be applied to many people who live in decrepit slums and find their few pleasures whenever and wherever they can; could be applied to the students in the following story—the students at Westhaven High School. For the students at Westhaven, like those described by Allison Davis, University of Chicago sociologist, in Vance Packard's *THE STATUS SEEKERS*, are young kids who spend their days and nights in sexual exploration, constantly seeking out "visceral, genital, and emotional gratification."

What happens when there is thrust into just such an environment a woman, an attractive teacher, subconsciously drawn to the decidedly masculine, virile, vigorous, potent, and rugged aura exuded by some of these slum-bred boys? What's more, what happens when these students are sexually drawn to her?

* * * * * * *

At four o'clock Tuesday morning, Melinda Caine decided she would go on living after all. She knew the time exactly, because she glanced at the pale green illuminated dials of the clock on the table by her bed.

By four-ten, Melinda was throwing back the blankets and crawling free of her covers.

Melinda walked through the bedroom. She paused just inside of the bathroom door long enough to turn on the light.

Melinda went directly to the shower, turning on its water. She

avoided the mirror. She could well imagine what any reflecting surface would play back to her: tear-stained cheeks, blood-shot eyes,
uncombed hair.

64. *An Incestuous Stepmother*, by Wilhelm Mauser

South Laguna, CA: Family Series Books, Publisher's Consultants, 1978, 158 pages, stock #FAM117, $2.50, mass market paperback.

It is an often quoted fact that bad news seems to make the best news. Meaning that crime, murder, and wars are usually given more air space and newsprint than are other less destructive aspects of our society.

This phenomena has carried over into those various research projects that probe into our psyches, our family lives, and our sexual mores, in that there has been a somewhat morbid concern with those of us who fail to make the psychological adjustments, rather than with those of us who have managed quite successfully to do so.

Thus, our libraries are filled with clinical volumes devoted primarily to research having used people who have somehow drifted away from the long-accepted norms and have been adversely affected because of it.

* * * * * * *

Carol Clanton knew her husband was asleep. She could hear him breathing deeply and regularly beside her.

Carol, though, wasn't asleep. She was quite awake, acutely aware of the cold sperm which was still leaking from her cunt and down along her ass crack.

Carol shuddered slightly as she recalled the grunts and groans which had accompanied the placement of that semen up her vagina. She shuddered again as she remembered that male hardness violating the sanctity of her tender cunt.

Jesus, she could have easily borne everything else, if it just wasn't for the sex. Because, she did love Torne Clanton, didn't she? Yes, as a matter of fact, she did. Torne was a good, kind man who had showed Carol a good deal of consideration. And knowing what rights a husband had in the bedroom, Carol felt she had no valid reason for asking Torne to keep his hard maleness away from her. Carol's mother had told her just to grit her teeth and bear it.

65. *Stocks & Bonds*, by Kyle Reich

North Hollywood, CA: Golden Boy Books, Arena Publications, 1978, 160 pages, stock #GB102, $2.50, mass market paperback.

65A. Reprinted as one-half of: *Gay Collection Series, Book #5.* South Laguna, CA: Publisher's Consultant, 1978?, 160 pages, stock #GY105, $2.95, mass market paperback; bound with *New York Night School*, by Marvin Page (not written by William Maltese), which is the first book in the anthology.

65B. Reprinted as: *Daddy's Big Boy*, by Doug Mason. North Hollywood, CA: Driveshaft Library, Arena Publications, 1983, 160 pages, stock #DS123, $3.95, mass market paperback.

"I don't think the term 'sadomasochism' is appropriate for the so-called heavy sex I get into," said a gay to Bill McLoud in the latter's *BLUEBOY* article *Beyond Sexual Barrieres* [sic]...." When I bet my buddy's ass or punch him in the chest it's not pain he's experiencing, it's pleasure—*strong* sensation. I'm getting off on making him feel. And I want to *feel* it, too. 'Pain' is just misunderstood in this context."

Aspects of sadomasochism and/or bondage-discipline have long been an intricate part of hetero- as well as homosexuality. Why?

"For reasons that are largely unknown, experiences that involve fear or pain...are often erotically stimulating," says Robert M. Goldenson, M.D., in *THE ENCYCLOPEDIA OF HUMAN BEHAVIOR: PSYCHOLOGY, PSYCHIATRY, AND MEDICAL HISTORY.* "...When a person finds himself in a threatening situation, large quantities of adrenalin are secreted, quickening the heartbeat, sending blood to the brain and muscles."

* * * * * * *

Dorn Wilcox came awake with a start. It took him a good minute to realize where he was.

He'd been having his same old nightmare. He realized that finally. It had somehow been triggered by Greg's return home for the summer. The nightmare could be counted on to arrive with Dorn's young son, just like clockwork.

Dorn shut his eyes, waiting for the tightness in his throat and in his chest to subside, waiting for his heart to quit beating quite so hard.

He was sweaty. His body, pajamas, and the sheet beneath him were all drenched in his perspiration; even though, sometime during the course of the night, Dorn had managed to kick off most of his covers.

"Be calm...be calm...be calm," Dorn chanted to himself, slowly—ever so slowly—feeling himself beginning to relax.

66. *Flight into Sodomy*, by Chad Stuart

North Hollywood, CA: Golden Boy Books, Arena Publications, 1978, 158 pages, stock #GB103, $2.50, mass market paperback.

For years the "straight" society mistakenly viewed all homosexuals in the stereotype image of the effeminate individual whose every gesture and mannerism—the effusive, peening [sic] exhibitionism—supposedly labeled him a homosexual as effectively as any sign hung around his neck might have done.

However, as pointed out by Jess Stearn in his *THE SIXTH MAN*: "Effeminate features or mannerisms...do not necessarily signify homosexuality. And, paradoxically, an inveterate homosexual may be the most masculine-looking person in the world."

Of course, on the opposite end of the scale, many "gays," as pointed out by no less an authority than Sigmund Freud in his "The Sexual Life of Man" as published in A.M. Krich's *MEN*, have gone to the extreme of saying that homosexuals "are a special variety of the human race." To prove their point, they are quick to cite such homosexuals as Michelangelo, Leonardo da Vinci, Alexander the Great, Hadrian, and Julius Caesar.

* * * * * * *

Tyler Chambers entered the Hamcroft University Gymnasium and immediately took the steps to the basement level. He was quickly confronted by the black-on-white letters stenciled on the cement wall that faced him at the bottom: MEN ONLY BEYOND THIS POINT.

Tyler made a right turn, his nostrils picking up the faintly funky odors of male sweat, dirty socks, soiled jocks, damp towels, and steam.

Several students, none of whom Tyler recognized, passed him in the hallway. But not as many as would have during a class break. The two o'clock period wasn't over yet; and, most of the guys would still be out on the track, upstairs in the volleyball, handball, and squash courts, or anywhere else males enjoyed sweat-producing physical activity.

Tyler passed one of the open doors. A fencing class was in progress. A young blond German exchange student was putting a beginning class through its positions. Tyler didn't linger. He was anxious to get to the pool; although, he wasn't sure just why he was so anxious. Whenever he had the opportunity, he stopped by the pool, taking a seat in the observation area, watching the class in progress. There wasn't really anything all that unusual about that. Tyler certainly wasn't the only one who did it. Sometimes there were several people killing a few extra minutes watching the activities.

So, why did Tyler feel so guilty about heading there now?

67. *Richard's Brother*, by Lambert Wilhelm

North Hollywood, CA: Golden Boy Books, Arena Publications, 1978, 158 pages, stock #GB104, $2.50, mass market paperback.

67A. Reprinted as: *Brother to Brother*, by Stu Chadwick. North Hollywood, CA: Driveshaft Library, Arena Publications, 1983, 160 pages, stock #DS122, $3.95, mass market paperback.

Taboo: a prohibition imposed by social customs, i.e., incest and homosexuality.

Yet, Freud held that there was from infancy a strong natural instinct to incest; and, Havelock Ellis in his "The Sexual Impulse in Children," as it appeared in A.M. Krich's *MEN*, states that man has "no anti-incestuous instinct, no natural aversion...."

Freud on homosexuality in his "Sexual Life of Man" as it appeared in MEN: "We are bound, in fact, to regard the choice of an object of the same sex as a regular type of offshoot of the capacity of love, and are learning every day more and more to recognize it as especially important." And Normal Kiell in *THE UNIVERSAL EXPERIENCE OF ADOLESCENCE*: "Kinsey's data, as has been frequently pointed out, throw considerable doubt on the assumption that homosexuality is...abnormal in the United States."

* * * * * * *

Richard was naked and in the bathroom. He turned to face the full-length mirror on one wall. The reflecting surface was far from perfect: fine cracks running its length and width, large splotches of discoloration where the silver backing had worn away, flaws that at times could give the body those too fat or too thin distortions of those carnival mirrors in the fun house.

Richard, though, was used to the mirror idiosyncracies [sic]. He was, also, familiar with his own body. Therefore, he could weed out the reality from the faulty illusion.

Richard was in pretty damned good shape, considering everything. Life, after all, was no picnic in this particular neighborhood. There was more than one kid on the block who was too thin from lack of food. At least Richard had learned early how to bring in the extra dollars needed to put meat in the cooking pot. He'd even reached the point where one paying customer was just like the last: none too horribly bad, none to horribly good.

68. *Montana Bound,* by Chad Stuart

North Hollywood, CA: Golden Boy Books, Arena Publications, 1978, 160 pages, stock #GB105, $2.50, mass market paperback.

There has long been a preponderance of psychological literature that would seem to make its readers believe that there is no such thing as a lasting love relationship between one homosexual and another.

For example, take the following statement made by George F. Gilder in his book *SEXUAL SUICIDE*: "...the life of tricks and trades is in fact agonizing for most of its practitioners. Lasting relationships are few and sour. The usual circuit of gay bars, returning servicemen, forlorn personal advertisements, and street cruises affords gratifications...brief and squalid..."

A newer approach to homosexuality," says a more enlightened Dea J. LeShan in her *SEX AND YOUR TEENAGER*, "would interest itself not in the fact of homosexuality alone, but in its place in the life of a particular human being—and the range is just as wide as it would be with heterosexuals—from frightened, destructive, miserable people, who have never found themselves, to people who live creatively, constructively and in mature and responsible love relationships."

* * * * * * *

Montana (better known as Monty to his friends), was in bed, had been in bed for four hours, but he still wasn't asleep. He wished he were. His mind kept getting cluttered with all sorts of thoughts Monty would rather have put away for some later recall—or possibly, put away all together.

Right now, for some inexplicable reason, he kept recalling that incident in prep school when he'd been fifteen. Or, maybe his remembrances weren't all that inexplicable, considering many of them concerned aspects of homosexuality—and homosexuality seemed to have occupied a good portion of Monty's life.

Not that Monty was gay! Hell, no! He thought he had pretty well proved that in prep school, and several times since, hadn't he? Not only had he not succumbed to the temptations for male-male sex (had they really been tempting?), but he had successfully fucked several girls. Which certainly proved something, didn't it? Homosexuals didn't (couldn't?) screw women, did they? Where had Monty heard that? Obviously, it wasn't true. Monty's father, after all, had screwed Monty's mother, hadn't he? If he hadn't, Monty Miler wouldn't have been here, here, and now, would he? And Gerald Miller, Monty's father *was* as queer as a three-dollar bill, wasn't he?

69. *Cop Out,* by Lambert Wilhelm

North Hollywood, CA: Golden Boy Books, Arena Publications, 1978, 160 pages, stock #GB107, $2.50, mass market paperback.

For years, it was the popular misconception held by middle-Americans that all homosexuals were effeminate, limp-wristed, swish-hipped men engaged exclusively as actors, as fashion designers, or as beauticians.

However, as people become more and more cognizant of the gay subculture, they soon begin to realize that such preconceived ideas aren't really the case. There are gays so masculine in appearance that no one could possibly single them out of any crowd. And while there *are* gays involved in the world of theater, haute couture, and who work in beauty salons, they are no more relegated exclusively to the above professions than are straights to such fields as forestry, sports, fire-fighting, and police work.

Still, it isn't unusual, even in this enlightened day and age to hear some of the old fallacies bantered about.

* * * * * * *

There was the loud crack of a damp towel being snapped against some male stud's bare ass.

"Hey, you sonofabitch!..." a not-too-angry voice replied, punctuating with another loud snapping.

The guys were playing grab-ass, letting off steam, relieved that the whole fucking training course was finally being wrapped up, finished, completed.

Chris Wanalkon left the shower area, successfully bypassing the small group of cutups as they continued to snap towels against steam-dampened flesh.

"One more time, and I start moving toward those stud balls of yours!" someone (possibly Terry Craine), threatened.

Chris continued down the line of lockers, finding his own. Draping his towel around his neck, he dialed the combination of the lock and opened the metal door.

70. *Young Men of the Night,* by Raymond Lange

North Hollywood, CA: Golden Boy Books, Arena Publications, 1978, 160 pages, stock #GB108, $2.50, mass market paperback.

Male prostitution, like its female counterpart, is not something which has just suddenly arrived full-blown on the present scene.

"...the reader," says W.W. Sanger, M.D. in his *History of Prostitution*, "would form an imperfect idea of the state of morals at Rome were he left in ignorance of the fact that the number of male prostitutes was probably full as large as that of females; that, as in Greece, the...phenomenon involved very little disgrace; that all the Roman authors allude to it as a matter of course; that the leading men of the empire were known to be addicted to such habits; that the aedile abstained from interference, save when a Roman youth suffered violence..."

Nor did male prostitution disappear with the decline and fall of the Greek and Roman civilizations in which it so flourished.

* * * * * * *

"It's five bucks if you blow me, or if I fuck you. It's ten if I blow you. It's twenty if you want your cock up my rosy red ass hole."

David turned his full attention on the kid now in the car with him. He could hardly believe what he'd just heard. Nothing had really quite prepared him for it, even if he hadn't come into this entirely naïve. He did, after all, know what these young boys were doing out on the streets after dark. Why, then, was he so shocked to hear one of them put the facts into such simple and businesslike words?

Maybe it was because the kid was so young. How young? Surely just a teenager. And, David had a son somewhere, possibly on this very street, who wasn't much older than this kid. David could shudder at the thoughts of his Timmy getting into a complete stranger's car and spouting off his price list for sexual services like some waiter verbally reciting the specials of the day.

71. *The Sweat Game*, by Lambert Wilhelm

North Hollywood, CA: Golden Boy Books, Arena Publications, 1978, 159 pages, stock #GB109, $2.50, mass market paperback.

71A. Reprinted as: *Pumping Jocks*, by Doug Mason. North Hollywood, CA: Driveshaft Library, Arena Publications, 1983, 159 pages, stock #DS117, $3.95, mass market paperback.

The straight world is considerably taken back each time an exposé reveals that gays actually participate and excel in sports. *The Washington Star*'s 1975-series of articles, uncovering the presence of homosexuality in such previously sacrosanct places as the football locker room is a good case in point. As is the candid revelations of David Kopay, co-captain of the University of Washington's 1964 Rose Bowl team, in his book: *THE DAVID KOPAY STORY.*

Yet, even with verification like the above, who in the gay community can forget the response of Tom Mee, public relations director for the Minnesota Twins, when queried by *The Advocate* concerning gay athletes in sports: "The cop-out, immoral lifestyle of the tragic misfits espoused by your publication has no place in organized athletics at any level. Your colossal gall in attempting to extend your perversion to an area of total manhood is just simply unthinkable."

Surprisingly enough, there is one athletic area, though, wherein heterosexual society has been a little less reluctant to suspect the existence of homosexuality. This being the area of body-building. Possibly this is because most people have long been confused as to whether body-building is really a sport, an art, or a male beauty contest. And there has always been that narcissistic element about the activity which has raised more than a few macho eyebrows.

* * * * * * *

The music came from the recording equipment off stage: "Thus Spake Zarathustra."

The constant roar of applause came from the nine hundred body-builders and fans who packed the Seattle Exhibition Hall.

The screaming and shouting came from the crowd, too: "Pump it, Joe!" "Jesus!" "Ahhhhh!" "Do it!" "Joe! Joe! Joe!"

The performer was Joe Delugeo. Age thirty-nine. One-time IFBB Mr. Universe. Two-time Mr. America. One-time Mr. Olympia. Star of the popular film documentary on the weight game called *Spotlights on Iron.*

72. *Black Sun*, by Kyle Reich

North Hollywood, CA: Golden Boy Books, Arena Publications, 1978, 160 pages, stock #GB110, $2.50, mass market paperback.

72A. Reprinted as: *Island Meat*, by Don Baxter. North Hollywood, CA: Driveshaft Library, Arena Publications, 1982, 160 pages, stock #DS113, $3.95, mass market paperback.

Homosexuality is not exclusive to any race, creed, or color. Japan in general, Tokyo in particular, is well known for its gay bars. The Islamic religion has numerous writings bespeaking the joys of male-male sex. The Caucasian English are rife with tales of boarding school homosexuality.

The African Negro is no exception.

"The East Africa Masai do not punish sodomy," says Edward Westermarck in his chapter "Homosexual Love" in A.M. Krich's book *MEN*.

* * * * * * *

Marc van Hooten sat in the shade of a bougainvillea-draped arbor, sipping a cool rum and cola, playing *the game*.

Marc had begun playing the game shortly after he had turned twelve. At the time, he had inadvertently stumbled upon the gardener fucking one of the houseboys. Marc was twenty-one now; but, he still remembered that sight: naked black bodies drenched with sweat; loud, guttural grunts and groans accompanying the rut; huge, blood-engorged cocks—one gone frantic up an asshole, the other being whipped by a massive black fist.

Marc had been much more fascinated by that particular mating of animals than he had ever been by the fucking of the horses or the dogs on the van Hooten farm. In the same instance, what he had seen had left a decidedly distasteful feeling inside him, despite its admittedly erotic aspects. For years afterwards, Marc had dreamed repeat performances, usually waking to find his sheets soiled with his own nocturnal discharges that had made him feel embarrassed and guilty.

73. *Men in Heat,* by Chad Stuart

North Hollywood, CA: Golden Boy Books, Arena Publications, 1978, 158 pages, stock #GB111, $2.50, mass market paperback.

If, as the *ENCYCLOPEDIA OF HUMAN BEHAVIOR: PSYCHOLOGY, PSYCHIATRY, AND MENTAL HEALTH* says, "...males become involved in homosexual behavior...where they are in close contact with members of their own sex..." then is it any wonder that men brought together in those jobs which have long been considered bastions of male exclusiveness should find themselves indulging in—or at least tempted to indulge in—homosexual activity?

What, for instance, makes so many people believe that jobs like fire-fighting, where men are required by work schedules to remain in constant contact with each other on a round-the-clock, twenty-four-hour basis, do not include men who are attracted to each other? Is it really because of the misconception held by many within the straight society that homosexuals are too visible *unmasculine to make the grade in such masculine professions! Yes, possible this is* one of the major reasons, since too many people even today, assume that *all* homosexuals are the limp-wristed little fairies who invariably end up in one or more of the stereotype "gay" professions.

However, to assume this, is to be misled. For homosexuals do not, states Wayne J. Anderson, M.D., in his *HOW TO UNDERSTAND SEX,* "...confine their occupational activities to such lursuits [sic] as fashion designing, ladies' hair styling, and the field of acting...." In fact, you are just as apt to find a homosexual (albeit, probably a closet case), in the field of fire-fighting as in any other profession picked at random.

* * * * * * *

Dan Traig and Adlar Lane took out their frustrations on the small, black, rubber ball. Each time one of them gave the ball a smack with his glove-sheathed hand, his palm stung. Each time the ball hit one of the four walls of the YMCA handball court, it left a small dark smudge to remind that it had been there.

The sounds within the enclosure were loud: as ball hit hand, hit wall, hit ceiling, hit floor; as tennis shoes squeaked on hardwood; as healthy, young lungs panted to suck up badly needed air.

"Goddamn it!" Dan grunted, simultaneously stretching for the ball but knowing he was going to miss it. He bodily rammed the far wall with a bang.

The ball hit the floor, then the back wall, then the floor. "I think that makes it my game," Adlar said, going to retrieve it.

"Shit, let's hit the showers," Dan responded, coming to a squat but leaning against the wall for support. "I am one beat sonofabitch in more fucking ways than one."

"Too much beer as of late," Adlar suggested, palming the black ball and walking over to give Dan a lift to his feet. Dan's grasp was firm within Adlar's own.

The truth of the matter was, they had both probably been drinking too much beer. And if they kept on, the handball, the jogging, and the weight work wasn't going to keep the pounds off. As of yet, it didn't show, mainly because both young men had been in tip-top shape when the fire department had gone on strike for higher pay; and, the strike was only into its third week. But it didn't take too many days of sucking up the booze to add a roll to the waistline.

74. *Meat*, by Lambert Wilhelm

North Hollywood, CA: Golden Boy Books, Arena Publications, 1978, 160 pages, stock #GB113, $2.50, mass market paperback.

74A. Reprinted as: *Hard Packer*, by Mike Woodward. North Hollywood, CA: Driveshaft Library, Arena Publications, 1982, 160 pages, stock #DS105, $3.75, mass market paperback.

Kinsey estimated that fifty percent of males have engaged in overt homosexual activity at least occasionally.

Within the remaining fifty percent can be included those to whom the very idea of homosexuality is an anathema: those who have had the opportunity for homosexual encounters but have resisted them. But there is also within this percentile group certain individuals who have not experimented with gay sex primarily because they have not been exposed to it.

It is often a very difficult procedure to "come out" in gay life, not only because of the basic underlying sexual taboos which have been set up by society (as archaic as those taboos may have become), but also because joint paranoia often makes it impossible for one inexperienced male to approach another, even if there is a definite attraction existing between the two. Despite the prevailing myth, a homosexual does not make obvious advances toward each and every member of the same sex with whom he comes into daily contact.

* * * * * * *

The bar was called The Station House because the building—many, many years back—had been a police station. The tavern didn't take up the whole building but just a corner of the bottom floor. Actually, it was rather small, looking crowded even now that there were only a few people in it.

Monty Darnel, sitting at a side table, hadn't been here before. But he figured he would come again. He liked the place. He also liked the people. The latter were clean-cut collegiate types on the whole, young men who seemed to like wearing blue jeans and cowboy boots on their nights off. Mainly the crowd seemed to be drinking bottled beer or draft. Off in a corner table, there was one dude with a girl, both of whom were drinking what looked like water but what was probably white wine over ice.

Monty was drinking Budweiser from one of those phallic, long-necked bottles that one could grip firmly like you grabbed your own cock when you masturbated. Although, the bottle felt cold in the palm of Monty's hand where his cock would have been as hot as a poker.

75. *Greek Row*, by Chad Stuart

North Hollywood, CA: Golden Boy Books, Arena Publications, 1978, 160 pages, stock #GB114, $2.50, mass market paperback.

75A. Reprinted as: *Making the Team*, by Stu Chadwick. North Hollywood, CA: Driveshaft Library, Arena Publications, 1983, 160 pages, stock #DS118, $3.95, mass market paperback.

"...homoerotic activity has been widely and powerfully defined as aberrant (though, as Kinsey has suggested, about half American males have had homosexual activity, while at least a third have had experiences culminating in orgasm). Much guilt and uncertainty must plague many of the participants in these relationships," says Lionel Tiger in *MEN IN GROUPS*.

And what about this guilt if the homoerotic relationship has been tinged with incest? Wouldn't it tend to be even greater?

"You won't find it anywhere in psychiatric literature," says Paula Burnett in a *Playgirl* article entitled "Incest" by Jeremy J. Young, "but, increasingly, we are seeing cases of incest between... father and son. It really blows people away."

* * * * * * *

Rex Crandorn, III, had a hardpon [sic]. It was a big one, if for no other reason than he had a big cock. Big cocks were part of the family heritage. Rex's brother had had one; and, the older members at the club were still taking in the locker rooms about how there would never be anything on record to equal what Rex's father had had between his legs.

Rex adjusted the placement of his hard cock inches inside of his trouser crotch, glancing out of the limousine window. The city had long ago given way to the countryside. The twilight had long since given way to the sunshine.

The road was familiar. Rex had traveled it a good many times in his forty-five years. When he and his brother had been attending Krafton Preparatory School, they used to chew up these miles behind the wheel of either Rex's Mercedes or his brother's XKE. Oh, how Tom had loved the fast cars. It wasn't so surprising, then, that one of them had killed him. What was, perhaps, ironic was that the car in question had been driven by someone else. Tom had been walking at the time.

The scenery hadn't changed much through this part of the country, mainly because most of the property was privately owned by people who could afford to keep the trees instead of having them cut down for profits. From the highway, one could almost be cajoled into believing that he was in a wilderness area, little suspecting that hidden behind the façade were some of America's still-remaining sumptuous homes. In a day and age when any ostentatious display of one's wealth was looked upon as a breach of good taste (and also as an invitation to kidnappers), those people who still enjoyed the good life (and could still afford it) felt it imperative to conceal it from the public eye.

76. *Macho Brother*, by Kyle Reich

North Hollywood, CA: Golden Boy Books, Arena Publications, 1978, 160 pages, stock #GB115, $2.50, mass market paperback.

Says Eda J. LeShan in *SEX AND YOUR TEENAGER*: "Parents will endure almost anything," a family-life educator told me. "They will put up with interracial marriages, trial marriages—even promiscuity and out-of-wedlock pregnancies, if necessary, but there is one thing I can assure you—never in your lifetime or mine, will we see parents who will truly accept homosexual relationships between their children. It goes against centuries of conditioning."

Bran Wayne, one of the characters in the following novel, is caught in a homosexual act by his father. And Bran is kicked out of the family circle, while his brother Sloane (not yet certain of his own sexuality) is left to immerse himself in a façade of masculinity designed to convince himself and his father of Sloane's inarguable heterosexuality.

But Cleveland Wayne is eventually forced into a reevaluation of his attitude toward his exiled youngest son. Because, crippled from the waist down in a fall, Cleveland soon realized that what a man does in the bedroom, can't possibly have anything to do with his worth as a human being.

* * * * * * *

"I want to see Bran," Cleveland Wayne told his oldest son, tears beading in his eyes like they sometimes did in the eyes of very old men.

But Cleveland, though, wasn't *really* all that old at sixty-five—anyway he shouldn't have been. The problem, of course, was a mental as well as a physical one. The accident, aside from its physical side affects had mentally crippled the man tremendously.

The accident. How ironic had been the accident when one thought of all the possibilities that *could* have occurred to wreak havoc in Cleveland Wayne's life.

He had played polo at one time. He *could* have fallen off his horse and gotten trampled on. He had climbed mountains. He *could* have fallen off during his successful climb of K2 and cracked open his head on the ice. He had played football in high school and college. He *could* have smashed his knees or gotten a brain concussion. Oh, yes, there could have been a thousand and one things that *could* have happened. The reality, though, had been nothing at all that dramatic.

77. *The Boy of Thira*, by Raymond Lange

North Hollywood, CA: Golden Boy Books, Arena Publications, 1978, 160 pages, stock #GB116, $2.50, mass market paperback.

77A. Reprinted as: *Hot Greek Summer*, by Adam Hayes. North Hollywood, CA: Driveshaft Library, Arena Publications, 1982, 160 pages, stock #DS114, $3.79, mass market paperback.

Sculptures from the early Greek periods have long been considered museum pieces. In fact, it is to the museums of the world that one must go to find the majority of these ancient pieces of sculpture if wishing to see them outside the pages of art books.

Any more, it is a rare occurrence indeed when a new piece of ancient Greek sculpture is brought to light. Those that are discovered are greedily hoarded by the Greek government. Too often in the past, the treasures of Greece have passed out of that country into foreign private collections or into foreign museums. Greece, a country long raped of its treasures, has now become reluctant to let anything it might have left slip over its borders.

This novel concerns one such newly discovered piece of art and how it affects the lives of the men who come to know of its existence. It's the story of those motivations that make those men do what they do: whether those motivations revolve around love of country, love of fellow man, love of money; whether they are inspired by lust, greed, boredom; or, whether they are influenced by more complex psychological undercurrents.

* * * * * * *

Both George and Chris were handsome in their own right while, despite many similar physical characteristics, managing to retain a complete uniqueness, one from the other.

They each had black hair. George's locks were cut shorter, showing his ears. Chris' were longer, more mussed in general appearance. Both young men had black-colored eyes, shielded by thick lashes and brows; although, George's eyes had a decidedly oval cast about them, while Chris' were attractively large. Their lips were full and sensuous: George's pouting, Chris' bordering on cupid's-bow.

Each had a body that looked straight from statues of a museum, although of a deeply nut-brown coloring that made no mistaking real flesh from marble. George's body was almost completely hairless, except for his head, lashes, brows, armpits, and crotch. Chris, on the other hand, had a comparatively hirsute body. His chest hair grew thick and twisting, billowing through his shirt which he wore open at the collar and unbuttoned halfway down to his navel. His arms, his legs, and his belly, were likewise covered with dark strands. His back had a sparse growth of hair on each shoulder, another in its triangular small, and fainter patches in the concaving dimples of each muscular ass cheek.

78. *Two Brothers*, by Lambert Wilhelm

North Hollywood, CA: Golden Boy Books, Arena Publications, 1978, 160 pages, stock #GB117, $2.50, mass market paperback.

78A. Reprinted as: *Brothers All the Way*, by Mike Woodward. North Hollywood, CA: Driveshaft Library, Arena Publications, 1983, 160 pages, stock #DS124, $3.95, mass market paperback.

Survival of the species has long been recognized as a driving force existing within man and animals. Nowhere is this instinct more often made apparent than in those drives which compel man to bear and rear children. And while now, in this over-populated age, our species is actually more threatened by continual propagation than by any stemming of it, there are still those of us driven not only to reproduce but who try, to the best of our efforts, to mold our offspring in our own exact image.

The following novel is the story of two brothers: one forced into following in the butch, macho role assigned him by his father; another better able to discover and explore his own sexuality at a more leisurely pace. It is the story of people who sometimes come to confuse masculinity with feats of physical skill and daring which, in the final analysis, have nothing whatsoever to do with the definition of a real man.

It is a story of brothers drawn to each other in a way that goes a bit beyond the more "normally accepted" fraternal relationships: brothers who need an unfortunate family crises to let themselves realize that certain archaic taboos and out-of-date standards of living have really very little to do with the real world and the most effective ways of dealing with their living in it.

* * * * * * *

When Greighton Glaceen woke up, it took him a moment to become oriented. It was still dark; and, the sound of the wind was audible even through the muting walls of thick natural rock. And even snuggled as he was within the womb-like cocoon of his down-filled sleeping bag, Greighton was aware of the obvious coldness of the air around him—not a gently [sick] chill but an all-prevailing coldness that could freeze over-exposed skin to the bone, numb it, blister it with white sores the color of hoarfrost.

"Dad?" Greighton asked. He was aware of the movement off in the darkness to one side of him. It had been the movement which had made him come awake to begin with. He had been dreaming fitfully of riding in a dogsled through miles and miles of arctic waste, while wolves howled off in the darkness of a six-month night.

"You're awake, then?" Donald Glaceen asked his eldest son, lighting one of the Coleman lanterns that were in permanent residence. The resulting light suddenly cast a glare that left only the few shadows in the corners of the room.

79. *Night of the Animals*, by Kyle Reich

North Hollywood, CA: Golden Boy Books, Arena Publications, 1978, 160 pages, stock #GB118, $2.50, mass market paperback.

"We can see," Havelock Ellis, a respected contimporary [sic] of Freud once wrote, "How, if pain acts as a stimulant to emotion, it becomes the servant of pleasure…"

And the following story is about pain, and pleasure, and emotion. It is about a certain sexual need inside several young men that goes deeper than just their homosexuality; although, at least one of the characters you'll read about in this book is momentarily so caught up *just* with inherent fears of his possible gayness that the finer nuances of his sexual awareness are threatened with being overshadowed.

"The relation of love to pain is one of the most difficult problems, and yet one of the most fundamental, in the whole range of sexual psychology," states Ellis. "Why is it that love inflicts, and even seeks to inflict pain? Why is it that love suffers pain, and even seeks to suffer it?"

* * * * * * *

It was all a complicated game of power, wasn't it? This car. This expensive suit. This Cartier watch and cufflinks. This gold chain that hung around his neck and would be visible only when Peter Weston unfastened his tie and unbuttoned his Cardin shirt.

The *other* concerned itself with power, too, didn't it? This cruising of the streets in this particular neighborhood. Because Peter could lord it over the young men he picked up here, where he couldn't have been able to do quite such a good job of it with someone he got through the "modeling" agencies whose members were also at his disposal. The kids from the agencies were used to picking up a hundred dollars an evening, where those who stood on these street corners between Carlyle and Lansing were lucky to come away from any blow-job or ass-fuck with more than a five-dollar bill in their pocket.

Peter always paid more than a five-dollar bill. Sometimes, he even paid a hundred bills, watching how the greedy, desperate faces lit up at even the mention of so much cash. Paying more gave Peter the power he wanted over these people. It made them do whatever it was Peter wanted them to do. It always surprised Peter how much could be coaxed out of a kid for a mere hundred bucks.

80. *Up on the Floor,* by Chad Stuart

North Hollywood, CA: Golden Boy Books, Arena Publications, 1978, 160 pages, stock #GB119, $2.50, mass market paperback. (CHECK DATA)

There was a time in the not too distant past when everyone seemed to "know" what and who a homosexual was. He was an effeminate, limp-wristed, lispy-voiced male who wasn't good at athletics and would eventually choose dress designing, hair-styling, interior decorating, or maybe acting as a career.

Recently, however, amid a surge of gay awareness, these old myths are finally being exploded. Gays are not the old stereotype, nor—for that matter—have they ever been. They are people, like everyone else, who differ only in what they do in the bedroom. They certainly can't be singled out in a crowd by an [sic] distinguishing physical characteristics. They can be found on the sports field, in government, on the battlefield, like any of their heterosexual counterparts.

Says Eda J. LeShan in *Sex and Your Teenager*: "A newer approach to homosexuality would interest itself not in the fact of homosexuality alone, but in its place in the life of a particular human being—and the range is just as wide as it would be with heterosexuals—from frightened destructive, miserable people, who have never found themselves, to people who live creatively, constructively, and in mature and responsible love relationships."

* * * * * * *

It was the last sixty minutes of the film that had been shown on all the major news networks. It was, however, that last minute of film which Eton Kleig liked the least. As a matter of fact, he got slightly ill every time he saw it—Just as he got slightly ill when he had captured the decidedly tragic piece of history on celluloid. Actually his illness at the time had occurred *after* the incident was over. Before that, things had been happening so fast that Eton had been too immersed in the swift movement of events around him to have been really cognizant of them. He had seemed momentarily like someone moving in slow motion within an environment which had sped up around him.

Eton's mind was once again brought back to a focus on the movie screen in front of him, drawn there by the beauty of what his eyes were registering.

Beauty. God, yes, beauty on this first part of the reel! And where in the hell was that beauty (once so thoroughly recorded) now?

There was a boy trapped within those whirling feet of film: a boy preserved there—as he was on countless paper pages—who was destined to, after time, relive on that film those past moments leading up to and including the bullet that ripped his chest and splattered his white T-shirt with a sunburst of scarlet.

81. *Love's Courage*, by Anna Lambert

North Hollywood, CA: Carousel Romances, American Art Enterprises, 1979, 160 pages, ISBN 0-89784-036-4, $1.50, mass market paperback.

"I've been wondering why we had separate bedrooms," Marie said, smoothing a stray lock of black hair from her husband's forehead. "Maybe we could do some rearranging, do you suppose...?"

"I'd like that," he replied....

Marie Carmaux exclaimed her pleasure in response to what Pierre Yonne's pointing finger had apparently conjured from the seascape just for her: the domed head of Mont D'Esnembuc.

82. *Brothers in the End*, by Lambert Wilhelm

North Hollywood, CA: Golden Boy Books, Arena Publications, 1979, 154 pages, stock #GB121, $2.50, mass market paperback.

"First loves are rarely forgotten," states Norman Kiell in *THE UNIVERSAL EXPERIENCE OF ADOLESCENCE*, perhaps not so much for the pleasure derived as from the pain experienced."

And, what additional pain exists when this first love is of a boy for a boy? Or, of a brother for a brother?

"By and large," Kiell tells us, "homosexual activities at adolescence represent normal behavior in experimentation or in developmental tendencies, and usually leave little or no trace of psychic trauma."

* * * * * * *

Kyle Storm was dead.

The crowd moved, shifted, flowed, appearing more like a swarm of insects than people. A girl had died in this crowd: two days, ten hours, and forty minutes after the news had been leaked about Kyle Storm. Her name was Kathy Condulum from Butte, Montana. She was fifteen. When the cordon of police had pushed the crowd back to allow the entrance of another of the big limousines through the mansion gates, Kathy had fallen. She had died before anyone would let her come up for air. The authorities feared Kathy wouldn't be the only fatality. Daily, hundreds more of the curious flocked to the mansion, hoping, by some stroke of fate, to get through the main gate to view Kyle Storm's coffin. And if they couldn't do that, then just being near him seemed to be good enough. Kyle Storm, after all, had been around for as long as most of these young kids could remember. A world without him was suddenly hard to take.

Kyle Storm was dead.

And Talbot Powers was hauling in the dough. He was selling black T-shirts with a picture of Kyle Storm in white on the front. Kyle was posed in one of his classic sexual posturings, guitar lowered to his crotch so that the long fretted guitar neck looked very much like a large erection sprouting from between Kyle's legs. Talbot had sold out his first batch of T-shirts. He now had his wife working on new T-shirts back in their basement apartment while he hawked the finished goods to the fans. He wasn't the only businessman on hand. There was John Danner who was selling Kyle Storm mourning bands. There was Casey Dukes who was getting up to ten dollars for the largest of his Kyle Storm posters (Kyle in a stance similar to the sexy pose on Porter's T-shirts). There was Kitty Miles who had made tapes of all her Kyle Storm oldie-but-goodies and was uncaring that her transactions in selling them was in direct violation of several copyright laws.

83. *Hung Father,* by Lambert Wilhelm

**San Diego, CA: Adonis Classics, Greenleaf Classics, 1979, 148
pages, stock #AC211, $2.95, mass market paperback.**

Many Americans have treated homosexuality like an ostrich
with its head in the sand—they simply refuse to believe that man
could actually physically love another man. For those open-minded
individuals who have realized that homosexuality is another facet of
the human condition, their problem is that they believe homosexuals
are vastly different from themselves.

HUNG FATHER is a story which shows homosexuals have all
the human elements found in everyone else—they suffer from the
same frailties and short-comings as anyone else, yet they can also
enjoy the same intense happiness of any person. Domination, vengeance, ecstasy, sorry, love, hate—all these emotions are found in the
characters in this novel.

HUNG FATHER—undoubtedly a shocking story for some, but
a story which does not ignore the fact that homosexuals exist, a story
which shows that the members of the gay society are truly human.

* * * * * * *

He was an ass! Oh, he was a priest, too: Father Daryl Mason.
But at the moment, he was more of an ass than a priest, wasn't he?

Did an alcoholic go out of his way to put himself into a position
wherein liquor bottles were piled around him? Did a reformed dope
addict purposely seek out every pusher in the neighborhood just to
prove to himself he was cured? Well, while Daryl was neither an
alcoholic nor a reformed dope addict, those similes were still apropos in that Daryl did have a monkey on his back. And being here—
now—certainly wasn't the smartest way to throw it off.

Daryl opened the car door and stepped out onto the garbage-
strewn street. He knew he was in worse shape than he thought, for
he was comparing his temptations to the temptations of Christ. Because Daryl Mason—Father Daryl Mason—wasn't without sin. Oh,
no! He had slipped over the brink more than once. And equating his
inner turmoil with that once experienced by Christ in His confrontation with Satan bordered on blasphemy. Daryl was destined to spend
many hours on his knees, begging forgiveness, because of his

thoughts this evening—let alone for anything that might come about as a result of his stepping through that door across the way.

84. *Oil Rig Boys*, by Lambert Wilhelm

San Diego, CA: Adonis Classics, Greenleaf Classics, 1979, 149 pages, stock #AC212, $2.95, mass market paperback.

There has recently been a surge in the number of homosexuals coming out of their closets—publicly proclaiming "Gay is Good!" and smashing age-old stereotypes. Homosexuality is finally taking definite steps toward making itself an acceptable life-style in our increasingly complex world.

Yet this is not to assume that each and every gay is able to successfully come out into the open. Bryan Balon suffers through guilt and insecurity as he struggles to come to grips with his sexuality. Eventually, sexual violence becomes the catalyst which provides Bryan with a deeper awareness of his true identity.

OIL RIG BOYS concerns itself with men who are having definite problems being gay in a basically straight society. As these men attempt to solve their problems, they provide a definite message for our times.

* * * * * * *

Bryan Balon didn't want to fuck her. Hell, he didn't even like her.

But then, he hadn't loved, liked, or enjoyed any of them, had he? Not really. Not Melissa. Not Joanne. Not Carolyne. Ad infinitum. And there had certainly been enough of them, hadn't there? All of them grunting and groaning, smelling of sweat and perfume. All of them screaming out how they loved his big, fat cock churning up their juicy cunts. All of them begging for more and more. All of them squealing through a whole series of orgasmic shudders before Bryan could finally manage to get his own rocks off—if he ever did manage to climax.

Bryan sat on the edge of the bed, his bag open beside him and almost filled with everything he thought he was going to need. He wasn't even worried about Celine and his child inside her. Actually, Bryan figured this kid, too, had probably already been aborted. And Celine was probably off somewhere counting her newly swollen bank account. Oh, she would have cried up a storm, screaming bloody murder that she wanted the baby. But Bryan knew better.

Nobody did anything that his father John Balon didn't want them to do. And John Balon did not want any child rooted in Celine Jackson's lower-class womb!

85. *Raped Stud*, by Lambert Wilhelm

San Diego, CA: Adonis Classics, Greenleaf Classics, 1979, 151 pages, stock #AC213, $2.95, mass market paperback.

Many Americans have treated homosexuality like an ostrich with its head in the sand—they simply refuse to believe that a man could actually physically love another man. Perhaps that is why so many parents cannot confront the fact that their son may have homosexual tendencies—because they can't believe the condition exists.

For those open-mined Americans who have realized that homosexuality is another facet of the human condition, their problem is that they believe that homosexuals are vastly different from themselves.

RAPED STUD is a story that attempts to show that homosexuals have all the human elements that everyone else has—they suffer from the same frailties and short-comings as anyone else yet they can also enjoy the same intense happiness as any person. Domination, vengeance, ecstasy, sorry, love, hate—all these emotions are seen with the characters of this novel.

* * * * * * *

Roger Craine dropped to his knees in front of Jeremy Morris, his knees resting against the hard asphalt that paved the small alleyway.

Roger's fingers deftly unfastened the snaps that held the young man's fly closed The resulting parting of the denim material revealed a bush of curly brown hair—Jeremy wasn't wearing any underpants.

The last snap unfastened, Roger could see the lower inch of Jeremy's cock. The rest of the boy's prick was swollen downward into the ramped space afforded between Jeremy's muscled thigh and his pantleg [sic].

86. *Son Loving Father*, by Lambert Wilhelm

San Diego, CA: Adonis Classics, Greenleaf Classics, 1979, 148 pages, stock #AC218, $2.95, mass market paperback.

In our ever-changing and often-confusing world, a world in which it is often difficult to determine right from wrong or good from bad, things which may have shocked our grandparents, or even our parents, are often taken with a grain of salt....

* * * * * * *

Tyler Balor's young body hung from the chain-supported manacles that wrapped his wrists.

The teenager's muscles were stretched into erotic lines, veeing downward along his hairless chest and belly, focusing attention on the jutting hardness of his cock thrust upward from his blond-haired crotch.

Below Tyler's sizable cock shaft, suspended in a large sac covered with stiff blond hair, were two bull-like balls chock full of teenage cum.

His ass was twin mounds of hard athletic flesh and skin, white compared to the tan that bronzed the majority of his youthful physique.

87. *K-YMCA*, by Chad Stuart

North Hollywood, CA: Golden Boy Books, Arena Publications, 1979, 154 pages, stock #GB124, $2.50, mass market paperback.

87A. Reprinted as: *"YM" Weekend*, by Norm Peters. North Hollywood, CA: Power Force Series, Arena Publications, 1985, 154 pages, stock #PF-151, $3.95, mass market paperback.

"With the new tolerance, there has bloomed in most major cities in America the 'gay' (homosexual) world," says Tristram Coffin in *THE SEX KICK*. "It has its own communities, its own 'marriages,' its own grand balls in costume, its special hangouts or bars, its own communications, its own prostitutes."

The process of a young gay *coming out*, then, certainly isn't as difficult as it once was, especially in the larger cities where media exposure often informs interested men where they can go to make contact with those in the homosexual community. Where a gay or an older generation was often forced into suspecting he was alone in his sexual leanings, the modern youth in the city has only to scan a whole gamut of magazines found on the newsstands to find hints, clues, and even direct references made to places where gays gather.

Unfortunately, there is still an uninformed segment of America that continues to exist beyond the new enlightenment found in the cities. There are small towns that have no visible gay life: places where a young homosexual can still feel isolated and completely alone. Many gay men, born and raised in these locales, stay there, suppressing inner needs and desires for which they have no visible outlets. Others are somehow able—through luck or chance—to discover that they are not alone, that there are literally hundreds of young men out there in the world who are of equal sexual persuasion.

* * * * * * *

Bobby Powell, age eighteen, scrunched down in the seat of the Greyhound bus and, turning toward the darkness outside, caught sight of his reflection on the glass of the window. Bobby scrutinized his features, wishing—as he often did—that he looked a little less boyish. His shock of white-blond hair, his large blue eyes, his pouting mouth, all combined to give him an appearance of boy-next-door youthfulness that Bobby—now moving out into the big world—would just as soon have outgrown. There was just something about looking young that made people take you a hell of a lot less seriously than they did if you—say—looked twenty-five when you were only eighteen.

Still, Bobby was somewhat consoled by the knowledge that he wasn't ugly. Bobby wouldn't want to have been ugly like some guys he'd seen. What Bobby wanted was the handsome good looks of Tyler Bailey. Now, there was someone—at least as far as Bobby was concerned—who had it all: good looks, good body, and a big cock

Bobby found himself blushing at his thoughts regarding the dimensions of Tyle's [sic] cock. There were a few things about Tyler that were forever making Bobby blush whenever he allowed himself to think about them.

88. *Enlisted Man*, by Cort Forbes

North Hollywood, CA: Golden Boy Books, Arena Publications, 1979, 152 pages, stock #GB126, $2.95, mass market paperback.

88A. Reprinted as: *G.I. Jock*, by Mark Richards. North Hollywood, CA: Driveshaft Library, Arena Publications, 1982, 152 pages, stock #DS115, $3.95, mass market paperback.

"While there are many people who accept the romantic propaganda about male homosexual existence, the life of tricks and trades is in fact agonizing for most of its practitioners," states George F. Gilder in *SEXUAL SUICIDE*. "Lasting relationships are few and sour. The usual circuit of gay bars, returning servicemen, forlorn personal advertisements, and street cruises affords gratifications... brief and squalid..."

Obviously though, there are those more than ready to disagree with Mr. Gilder's resounding statement, among them Arthur Bell who, with Martin S. Weinberg, recently wrote *HOMOSEXUALITIES*. Said Bell in a recent "*People Weekly*": "Don't leap to the conclusion that the kinds and numbers of partners homosexuals have indicated an unhappy state. Among the cruisers were found no psychological misfits."

There is no doubting, however, that even with the growing acceptance of homosexuality as a valid life-style, there are some gays who adapt less easily than do others. After all it is often exceedingly difficult to shake off old taboos and prejudices which have been built up by years of repression by church and state without first undergoing a certain amount of soul-searching and wondering if life wouldn't, in fact, be somehow better if one could adjust—somehow—to the more acceptable sexual norm.

* * * * * * *

Tad Gilbert kept his steady stroll down the street. The car followed behind him, gained on him, passed him and disappeared. That had been the third time. It was so familiar!

He turned into the little doorway with the lights blaring out the kind of beer being sold inside. He moved in and found a seat. Sam Murray was sitting at the bar. Sam was putting on weight. Sam was with a sailor. The latter was the young, innocent type who looked as if he was out for his first weekend. He had probably moved up to LA when the going got crowded in Dego. God, but he looked like a kid.

"Sam is going to get tried for statutory rape," Mark Herald said while enroute [sic] to the can. Tad barely caught what Mark said.

It was a good thing Sam hadn't heard. Sam had a tendency to get nasty if given the least provocation.

89. *Big Foot*, by Alex Mann

North Hollywood, CA: Golden Boy Books, Arena Publications, 1979, 154 pages, stock #GB125, $2.95, mass market paperback.

89A. Reprinted as: *12 Inches*, by John Anderson. North Hollywood, CA: Driveshaft Library, Arena Publications, 1982, 154 pages, stock #DS112, $3.75, mass market paperback.

"Long before Oscar Wilde went to jail for 'the love that dared not speak its name,'" says Jess Stearn in *THE SIXTH MAN*, "the Anglo-Saxon world was embarrassed by even the mention of homosexuality.... Two generations have passed since the names of Wilde and Lord Alfred Douglas were linked together. Homosexuality is now much more open in many social areas, and it certainly has more acceptance...."

And that begrudging acceptance by society has actually allowed some gays to grow to relative maturity without being so much concerned with what they do in the bedroom as they are concerned simply with the sometimes difficult day-to-day chore of living.

Thus, the characters in the following novel, though they are gay, could just as easily be straight. For their primary concerns—beyond the sexual—do not arise so much because these people are homosexuals as they do because these young men have the same "other" basic drives of their heterosexual counterparts. Such needs as to be liked, to be accepted, to belong. All of which, according to Norman Kiell in *THE UNIVERSAL EXPERIENCE OF ADOLESCENCE*, "are universal feelings."

* * * * * * *

Craig Masterson came awake to the darkness. His ears strained to again hear the sounds or series of sounds which had brought him so abruptly from his slumber. He had been dreaming. He had been naked in a blissful forest meadow, complete with wild flowers. He hadn't been alone. There had been this well-muscled, good-looking, well-hung stud who looked surprisingly like Roger Powell. Craig and his lover had been into some pretty hot petting. Craig still had a hard-on. It had been all too pleasant a fantasy to be pulled back to the reality.

The night wasn't silent; but, then, it never really was, was it, especially out here in the woods? However, the noises now playing on Craig's ears weren't eatraordinary [sic]: wind in the pines, wind-slapped waves from the nearby lake, more water splashing to the rocks from the small waterfall just through the trees, crickets calling to one another and being answered. There was nothing more. So, what had he expected? Obviously his dream had been getting too good, and his subconscious had merely seen fit to interrupt it before Craig creamed a mess into his sleeping bag.

"Craig, are you awake?" Roger whispered from beside Craig. Craig should have guessed Roger was awake. One of the familiar sounds which had been missing had been Roger's open-mouth snoring.

90. *Shaft*, by Bryant Tyler

North Hollywood, CA: Golden Boy Books, Arena Publications, 1979, 152 pages, stock #GB127, $2.95, mass market paperback.

90A. Reprinted as: *Deep Load*, by Rick Taylor. North Hollywood, CA: Driveshaft Library, Arena Publications, 1983, 152 pages, stock #DS120, $3.95, mass market paperback.

The white population of South Africa occupies a position of supremacy over all other races in residence in that country. They base their dominance on history and custom. They buttress their position with stringent laws. Not only are African trade unions not recognized in industrial bargaining, but only whites may legally possess firearms or be weapon-carrying members of the military and police forces.

Apartheid, an Afrikaner word meaning "apartness," denotes officially polices which can find their roots as far back as the first white settlement in 1652. Such segregation is based on sociological and theological assumptions that races are a basic division of the human species, and that each race had its own particular culture and destiny which cannot come to pass if subjected to races mingling within a common society.

Apartheid is a taboo in South African law as well as in custom. Every resident is, thus officially classified by his race. And sexual relations of any kind between different races are severely punishable crimes.

* * * * * * *

Christopher de Vorden was beginning to suspect that they weren't coming. He adjusted his position in the hay, taking another look through the two slats he had pried apart to give him a view of the area below. No sign of anything down there; nothing but livery equipment hung on the walls and a collage of shadows.

Christopher brought his wristwatch up to a convenient position and checked out the luminescent dials. If they were coming, they should have been here by now. Christopher wasn't planning on waiting around forever. Staying up here in these cramped little confines was one thing if he could expect to see something or hear something. However, Christopher had no intentions of substituting a night in the stable for a night in his own comfortable bed.

Actually, Christopher wasn't in a stable. He was in one of the buildings used for storage that was set off to one side of the stable. Oh, there was still hay in the small loft, but it wasn't fresh hay. There was still the smell of horses, but that came only when the wind blew in the right direction.

Most of the equipage hung on nails around the walls and was propped in the corners. It hadn't been used in a long time. Although, there was a surprising smell of freshly oiled leather about the place which Christopher couldn't adequately account for.

Damn it, where were they? Christopher had done enough spying over the past couple of days to pinpoint this place as where Korden headed every time he left the house late at night. And Korden was joined here by M'daba. And the two of them stayed behind these closed doors for hours at a time. Christopher had more than once been tempted to sneak up and peek in. He had decided, though, that doing that risked discovery. What he would do was conceal himself inside and watch from a viewpoint that neither his brother nor M'daba would expect him to occupy.

91. *Teacher in Chains*, by Kyle Reich

North Hollywood, CA: Golden Boy Books, Arena Publications, 1979, 155 pages, stock #GB128, $2.95, mass market paperback.

"The Senate subcommittee to investigate juvenile delinquency reported last year that school violence had become so common that the only difference between 'tough' city schools and those in the suburbs was one of degree," stated Marguerite Michaels in her 26 February 1978 *PARADE* article *Our Nation's Teachers Are Taking a Beating*. "In a three-year period attacks on teachers were up nearly 80 percent, assaults on students up 85 percent."

Dr. Alfred Bloch, a Los Angeles psychiatrist, reported in the same article that teachers "suffer from the same wartime psychological symptoms: emotional tension, anxiety, insecurity, nightmares, blurred vision, dizziness, fatigue and irritability."

But what happens when a man, an ex-GI, a decorated veteran of the Vietnam Conflict, a man trained in actual combat conditions, arrives to teach in one of these "tough" city schools? What happens when the school roughnecks suddenly find themselves confronted with a man well-trained for survival in a war zone? What happens when this new teacher begins a determined compaign [sic] to tame the worst of the lot in his classrooms, utilizing techniques that, while unauthorized in their aspects of sexual humiliation, seem to do the job?

* * * * * * *

Ernst Klammer knew he had their attention. He could feel their dark eyes staring at him, boring holes into him. Did they think they scared him? Hell, after all Ernst had been through in Nam, these kids were nothing. *Nothing!* Ernst could only hope that they would partially fill the void that had somehow appeared when the war had finally ended and Ernst had found himself suddenly a civilian once again. Frankly, these bastards didn't look all that much of a challenge, did they? But then, Ernst would wait and see. After all, some of those gooks in Nam hadn't looked all that tough, either, had they? Looks could sometimes be deceptive.

Ernst had everyone's attention for two main reasons at that point of his arrival at the doorsteps of Garfield High (this being before the school grapevine got around the word that the new teacher was a decorated Nam veteran). First, Ernst was blond: and, blondness in that neighborhood was indeed a rarity. These were slum children, after all, and tended to all derive from ethnic backgrounds that contributed to dark (often black) skin, black (or brown eyes), black (or brown) hair. Second, Ernst was physical [sic] impressive in that he stood well over six-feet tall, had broad shoulders, narrow waist, well-deleloped [sic] chest, and flat belly. And, he didn't look in the least bit afraid. Quite to the contrary. He strolled through the curious onlookers as if he were out on a Sunday stroll in the middle of an average American suburbia. And only a fool, or a special brand of man (even a well-built one) could enter these premises without being a little afraid.

A black kid stepped to stand in front of the door to block Ernst's entrance. The kid: Mexican-Puerto-Rican, leader of The Spanish Toreros. He had knifed a classmate and had almost killed him. He had a knife scar on the left side of his face that had puckered to give him a kind of hair-lip appearance. If anyone could strike fear into the heart of an interloper, Juan Catalina was it.

92. *Love's Emerald Flame*, by Willa Lambert

Toronto, Canada: Harlequin Books, Harlequin SuperRomance #2, 1980, 380 pages, ISBN 0-373-70002-4, $2.25, mass market paperback.

92A. Reprinted as: *Love's Emerald Flame*, by William Maltese Writing as Willa Lambert. Rockville, MD: The Borgo Press, an Imprint of Wildside Press, 2007, 380 pages, ISBN 1-4344-8152-2, $19.99, trade paperback.

"SHALL I CARRY YOU ACROSS IN MY ARMS?"

Sloane led Diana toward the bridge, laughing when she gasped in alarm. It was nothing but a collection of swaying vines and rotting pieces of wood. The walls of the gorge were so steep that Diana's head spun when she looked down at the distant ribbon of water at the bottom.

"I'll carry my own weight," she said with a shaky voice. Sloane moved up close, his body behind her guiding her across.

93. *Vanessa in White Marble*, by Anna Lambert

North Hollywood, CA: Carousel Romances, American Art Enterprises, 1980, 160 pages, ISBN 0-89784-044-5, $1.75, mass market paperback.

Why couldn't she believe it would last?

Oh, how wonderful it would be if there could be a forever...with Roberto...with the feel of him...the touch of him...the wonder of him....

Why weren't dreams possible?

94. *House of the Brave Bulls*, by Anna Lambert

North Hollywood, CA: Carousel Romances, American Art Enterprises, 1980, 160 pages, ISBN 0-89784-059-3, $1.75, mass market paperback.

Mary Ann Weiss ran delicately tapered fingers through her tumbled mane of lion-gold hair and watched the dusty Spanish countryside go by beyond the window of the speeding car.

They were driving fast (Mary Ann thought too fast) along a narrow road heading east out of Trujillo. The flatlands and low hills, punctuated here and there by olive groves, were burned, merging shades of ochre and tan in the hot Iberian sunshine. The temperature was somewhere in the hundreds.

This was the region called Extremadura. Empty country. Rocky. Southwest from Madrid and hugging a shared border with Portugal.

95. *The Last Galaxy Game*, by Karl Klyne

North Hollywood, CA: A Carousel Science Fantasy, American Art Enterprises, 1980, 158 pages, ISBN 0-89784-079-8, $1.75, mass market paperback.

> The sky was as blue as a robin's egg.
> The wheat was as yellow as a sea of gold.
> Sky and wheat field met in a straight line on the horizon.

96. *The Crystal of Power*, by Adriana deBolt

North Hollywood, CA: A Carousel Science Fiction, American Art Enterprises, 1980, 159 pages, ISBN 0-89784-086-0, $1.75, mass market paperback.

A prequel to *The Galactic Arena*, by Christopher Dane (#109).

> *And, on the Fourth Day of Klindoria, Kyrie did ride the Weirles to Tonkeri and did stop in the Wen of Zantinum for a period of forty latrums.*
> *And he did neither eat nor drink, for, as he had told his multitude of followers:*
> *"Behold, I will make fast in order that I might be strong in faith during my confrontation with Dyrynum.*

97. *The Alien Within*, by Adriana deBolt

North Hollywood, CA: A Carousel Science Fiction, American Art Enterprises, 1980, 160 pages, ISBN 0-89784-090-9, $1.75, mass market paperback.

A prequel to *Michael: The Master*, by W. Lambert III (#114).

The Battle of Tyrog-D had been raging for days without letup, although Commander Dillon, with the assist of data flashed incessantly on the readout screen of Computa-104, counted his side in the advantage—despite the fact that three of his five forceshields were down; that he was out of communication (audio and visual) with Captain Traine in the rear section of the AsterShip.

Tyrog-D was a two-sun, twenty-planet system on the edge of the Plethegra Galaxy. The cleanup operations of the system had been going on ever since the Tyrogs had decided to make their move against defenseless ZnX-II

The Tyrogs of the Tyrog-D system (only one of the twenty planets, Tyrog, being habitable), were warlike in the extreme. Their devotion to war had supplied them with an arsenal which had made their planet supreme in the system named after it.

98. *Homecoming Buddies*, by Lambert Wilhelm

San Diego, CA: Adonis Classics, Greenleaf Classics, 1980, 150 pages, stock #AC220, $2.95, mass market paperback.

Many Americans have treated homosexuality like an ostrich with its head in the sand—they simply refuse to believe that a man could actually physically love another man. For those open-minded individuals who have realized that homosexuality is another facet of the human condition, their problem is that they believe homosexuals are vastly different from themselves....

* * * * * * *

Ernst Hoffman nuzzled his large cockhead against the asshole. Although it was dark in the room, Ernst knew the asshole belonged to Peter. Ernst was used to running the dark gauntlets and singling out his specific prey from among the myriad forms and shadows. But, then, he had had a lot of practice. He came here, usually, at least three times a week.

Ernst was lucky to have gotten to Peter's ass first. Peter, after all, was stud material by anyone's standards. He had a nicely muscled body, attractively butch features, blond hair, big cock, and a tight asshole. He reminded Ernst of Lief.

Peter stood facing a wall. His hands were pressed against the graffiti-covered wood. His towel was dropped to a white puddle around his feet. His ass was jutting back slightly.

99. *Cruising Cops*, by Lambert Wilhelm

San Diego, CA: Adonis Classics, Greenleaf Classics, 1980, 149 pages, stock #AC221, $3.95, mass market paperback.

Many Americans have treated homosexuality like an ostrich with its head in the sand—they simply refuse to believe that a man could actually physically love another man. For those open-minded individuals who have realized that homosexuality is another facet of the human condition, their problem is that they believe homosexuals are vastly different from themselves....

* * * * * * *

Patrolman Kevin Kane was jacking off his cock while watching the two guys getting it off together on the other side of the air vent that separated the storage room from the restroom.

There was a broken mirror in the storage room, one once used in a Christmas display in the main window of Kleindale's Department Store. That mirror was now reflecting the erotic picture Kevin presented with his huge cock jutting from the open fly of his police-uniform trousers. The eroticism wasn't lost on Kevin, either, who was voyeur enough to appreciate viewing his own cock, his hand working up and down along its stiff length.

Kevin was handsome, and he very well knew it, without ever coming across as being stuck-up. There was something about his muscled young body poured into his policeman blues, set off by his short-cropped blonde [sic] hair that was a sexual turn-on. His boots helped, too, polished as they were to a sheen that reflected almost as well as the mirror was doing.

100. *College Buddies*, by Lambert Wilhelm

San Diego, CA: Adonis Classics, Greenleaf Classics, 1980, 149 pages, stock #AC223, $3.95, mass market paperback.

Many Americans have treated homosexuality like an ostrich with its head in the sand—they simply refuse to believe that a man could actually physically love another man. Perhaps that is why so many parents cannot confront the fact that their son may have homosexual tendencies—because they can't believe the condition exists....

* * * * * * *

Rock Harrison scrunched down in his theater seat while two hunky studs fucked in larger-than-life Technicolor on the silver screen before him.

Rock assumed the blond doing the fucking was the star, somebody billed on the marquee as Dick Goliath. The kid was probably called that because he had a cock as big as that legendary giant. Dick was fucking another kid called Dan. Then again, maybe it was Ted or Jim he was fucking Rock couldn't keep track, since the movie had been merely a series of fucks that had involved the hero in one sense or another.

The present victim was hung from the ceiling while Dick Goliath fucked away.

101. *Snowbound Studs*, by Lambert Wilhelm

San Diego, CA: Adonis Classics, Greenleaf Classics, 1980, 153 pages, stock #AC224, $3.95, mass market paperback.

In our ever-changing and often-confusing world, a world in which it is often difficult to determine right from wrong or good from bad, things which may have shocked our grandparents, or even our parents, are often taken with a grain of salt.

* * * * * * *

Talbot Winnet heard the wind even above the slurpy, sexual sounds Eddie Hampton was making over stiff cock. The sound of the cold wind, seeping in through the tightly fitted logs of the small cabin two-thirds up Bear Creek Mountain, made Talbot even more appreciative of the warmth from the fire and the warmth spawned by the up and down movements of hot mouth and throat over his hard prick.

Neither young man was aware of the snow that was beginning to fall. Even if they had been aware of it, they wouldn't have been too concerned. At 10,000-foot elevation, the area was often sprinkled with the white stuff even in midsummer.

The wood in the fireplace shifted as the lapping flame ate away more of the supporting fiber. The resulting rise of sparks cast an attractive glow over both Talbot, who was standing naked, and Eddie, who was naked and on his knees.

102. *Fun House Buddies*, by Lambert Wilhelm

San Diego, CA: Adonis Classics, Greenleaf Classics, 1980, 149 pages, stock #AC227, $3.95, mass market paperback.

In our ever-changing and often-confusing world, a world in which it is often difficult to determine right from wrong or good from bad, things which may have shocked our grandparents, or even our parents, are often taken with a grain of salt....

* * * * * * *

Tim Jacobs grunted lowly as Michael Windfield's large cock sped inward along the slick lubricant greasing his gripping asshole.

"Fuck me!" Tim moaned in follow-up, feeling Michael's muscled belly come to a grinding stop against his firm buttocks. "Oh, Jesus, yes, stud, fuck me raw!"

Michael had all intentions of doing just that. Tim was one hell of a sexy young stud. Michael always got a charge out of fucking someone so evidently turned on by gay sex.

103. *Tied Up Ranch Hands*, by Lambert Wilhelm

San Diego, CA: Adonis Classics, Greenleaf Classics, 1980, 149 pages, stock #AC228, $3.95, mass market paperback.

In our ever-changing and often-confusing world, a world in which it is often difficult to determine right from wrong or good from bad, things which may have shocked our grandparents, or even our parents, are often taken with a grain of salt....

* * * * * * *

"You want it, don't you?" Rolland Drake asked.

"Yes," Grahm said. His voice sounded slightly breathless.

The two were in the back room of the OK Corral bar. The room was made to look like a barn. There was hay on the floor. There was more hay in the loft. There were stalls. There were ropes on the wall for use in tying. There were wagon wheels and sawhorses to which one could be tied.

104. *White Water Buddies*, by Lambert Wilhelm

San Diego, CA: Adonis Classics, Greenleaf Classics, 1980, 150 pages, stock #AC230, $3.95, mass market paperback.

It's been said that every person has some dark passion within his soul—some hidden secret, desire, closest confidante, or even recognized by the person himself. Such a secret can be evil and sinister, or it may be trivial and trite....

* * * * * * *

Tyson Riley rolled on his back. Myler Baker rolled to cover him.

Myler's cock battled for space with Tyson's cock between their muscled bellies. Finally, the two cocks aligned, one beside the other. Their cocks were hard.

Tyson's hands ran the length of Myler's back. His fingers came to rest finally on Myler's firm asscheeks. Moving his fingertips inward, he glided them into the faintly damp crease of his ass. His middle finger fond the pucker and stroked it.

105. *Call Boy Brothers*, by Lambert Wilhelm

San Diego, CA: Adonis Classics, Greenleaf Classics, 1980, 149 pages, stock #AC234, $3.95, mass market paperback.

In our ever-changing and often-confusing world, a world in which it is often difficult to determine right from wrong or good from bad, things which may have shocked our grandparents, or even our parents, are often taken with a grain of salt....

* * * * * * *

Chris Oates opened his thighs, letting his older brother's lower body fit in between them.

Larry laid his belly on Chris' belly. He laid his chest on Chris' chest.

Chris, raising his legs to lock his ankles in the small of his brother's back, was simultaneously positioning Larry's cock to his asshole.

106. *B&D Buddies*, by Lambert Wilhelm

San Diego, CA: Adonis Classics, Greenleaf Classics, 1980, 149 pages, stock #AC235, $3.95, mass market paperback.

A question often asked by those who deal with psychological problems is: What is normal? The answer to that seemingly simple question will probably never be answered....

* * * * * * *

"Get your ass over here, you cock-hungry bastard!" Steve Mellon said. His command was part of the game, just as his uniform was part of the game, just as his uniform was part of the game. The latter belonged to his father, Sergeant Timothy Mellon, New Mexico Highway Patrol. Nevertheless, it fit. Steve, at eighteen, had a body just as studly and well built as that of his father. In fact, the shirt was actually a little tight over Steven's muscled chest.

Antony Wells, the other game player, crawled on his knees, his hands handcuffed behind him. His hard cock weaved in front of his belly. His arms hurt where they were pulled back at the shoulders. The floor, though, was covered with rug, so there was little discomfort for his knees.

Where Steve was decked out in his father's uniform, Antony was stark naked. Like Steve, he had a well-delineated physique honed to a perfect edge by participation in high-school athletics. Track and swimming had kept the boy slim, while gymnastics had molded each and every muscle to the perfection it now was. His stomach was scalloped, punctuated by a slightly indented navel. His biceps and triceps were round and powerful. His waist was small, giving a decided veeing to his upper torso. His ass was compact, solid as a rock. His cock was ten good inches of stiffness in its present erection, his balls as big as hen's eggs, held in a tan scrotum that was covered with brown hair more wiry and curly than the tousled brown hair on the boy's head.

107. *Balling Brothers*, by Lambert Wilhelm

San Diego, CA: Adonis Classics, Greenleaf Classics, 1980, 154 pages, stock #AC238, $3.95, mass market paperback.

"Fuck me!" Tom Linery said, bucking his hips back from his dog-style position on the floor. He was attempting to get his asshole, skewered more quickly by Casey Carlyle's enormous cock. The cock, however, was slightly out of alignment, sliding down and under Tom's asshole to jab the young man's big balls.

"Come on, sexy bastard! Jesus, come on! Ram that cock of yours so far up my tight asshole that I can feel it jabbing through my belly and into the base of my throat!" Tom continued.

Casey's cock was certainly hard enough for fucking. It was slick enough, too. Tom had, moments before, taken the cock deep inside his mouth and throat to cover it with sticky spit. Wherever the cock now touched, it left a tracing of Tom's spit and Casey's leaking cum.

108. *Voyage of the Trigon*, by Adriana deBolt

North Hollywood, CA: A Carousel Science Fiction, American Art Enterprises, 1981, 160 pages, ISBN 0-89784-097-6, $1.75, mass market paperback.

The presentation was over.

The Vasery of Kahilur, Jarun Faralum, the insignia of his nobility strung around his neck on a chain of golden asterisks, talked with His High Commander of Krale, Emperor of Kam, Filar, and Ming, Faceen of Warlo-IV and Kinto-VI, King of the Xxl Solar Worlds.

"I would have thought, Jarun, after your long absence from us that you would have been desirous of staying put for a while to enjoy your recent accolades," The High Commander said, sipping amber-tyine from a vee-shaped crystal. But, what should I see upon my desk this morning but a request for permission to go rocketing off on this latest venture."

109. *The Galactic Arena*, by Christopher Dane

North Hollywood, CA: A Carousel Science Fiction, American Art Enterprises, 1981, 159 pages, ISBN 0-89784-103-4, $1.75, mass market paperback.

A sequel to *The Crystal of Power*, by Adriana deBolt (#96).

Then, suddenly, he knew that The Beast knew everything. He didn't think, suspect, even fear that it knew. He *knew* it knew.

It knew about the experiments Mannix had done in his lab, locating the family on Thear whose selective breeding would finally deliver up a woman, Warla Tyler, whose gene makeup was as near as possible to the original contributor, David Misstol.

It knew Warla Tyler had been purposely mated with The Beast (in The Beast's male form of Dielum of Thear),in order to further reach for a duplicate of that original Altan species—all of whom had died except Myra Morgana.

110. *Bohack: Symbiotic Worlds*, by L. Linehan

North Hollywood, CA: Carousel Science Fiction, American Art Enterprises, 1981, 160 pages, ISBN 0-89784-127-1, $1.75, mass market paperback.

Kalyle Microna was worried. Not that that was anything unusual for The Keeper of The Machines. He had been worried ever since he had ascended to his august position and had been informed by the dying Karoon Jakila that no Keeper had really known how to operate The Machines for the past two-thousand tireum. The Machines operated them-selves. The Keeper was merely there to offer an illusion that such weighty matters as the ejection of waxo-lictic gas into the atmosphere was actually under human control.

"We have lost the knowledge of The Old Ones," Karoon had told Kalyle, sequestered as they had been at the time during those ceremonies which had singled Kalyle out from all the other proselytes. "The Ticol Plague in the Ramas Years went through the scientific community and left us only with the books and diagrams that no one could read, one cannot now read. One day, The Machines will break down of malfunction, and pity the poor Keeper who officiates at the religious functions at that time, unless he has the forcefulness to transfer the blame to the multitudes, blaming everything on their sins."

The Old Ones: they had built The Machines. Kalyle didn't remember them. Karoon Jakila didn't remember them. But, the legend of them persisted, as well as the results of their labors. They had come riding through space on the planet Bomial, turned loose from that planet's orbit when the gaseous globe Fira-B began its final heat mold toward disintegration. They had scoured the universe in search of waxo-lictic gas, that basic ingredient of which they had been deprived when their source, the gaseous glob Fira-B, had dissolved. They had found it on Hacksolm-II, a planet orbited about the Red Dwarf Star Mylosol-Beta. Rather, they found it not *on* Hacksolm—but *in* it.

111. *Riders of the Dragon*, by Christopher Dane

North Hollywood, CA: Carousel Science Fantasy, American Art Enterprises, 1981, 160 pages, ISBN 0-89370-137-9, $1.75, mass market paperback.

> *"There is no one here!"*
> —Last words of Banic Zoph, Dragon Rider, Go-rillean Nights 19, before dying.

It was easy for Mam Moog to find babies of both sexes in those lean years of The Fonfonal Plague and The Parolic Famine. The presence of male children, laid out on the slopes of The Barren Weld, was more indication than any of the dire condition of the times. No man, unless bordering on the very edge of existence, would have ever consented to laying out his male child. But, these were not normal times. Nor had the aristocrats been spared, as had sometimes happened in the past. Famine, Plague, and Pestilence, were no honorers of the caste system. And, in those years, many an aristocratic family was lowered to the level of commoner, if not by official ranking then by the circumstances.

All of the wealth of the great Kinoil family perished when The Plague affected cownals as well as people. For the Kinoil family's claim to wealth had always been their monopoly on the meat source afforded by the butchering of their cownal herds. All of the wealth of the great Bowly family was wiped out when The Plague swept through the slave corrals at Winset, Pyrone, and Kleg, leaving one alive out of every two hundred workers. Even more than that perished when The Famine made it impossible for the Bowly family to feed itself, let alone its dwindling herds of people.

112. *Encores in Fade*, by W. Lambert III

North Hollywood, CA: Carousel Science Fantasy, American Art Enterprises, 1981, 160 pages, ISBN 0-89784-145-X, $1.75, mass market paperback.

> *And his father asked him what it was he wanted for his Yomsul Celebrations.*
> —Excerpt from The Beginning.

Deja-vu!

Gamil Forner had been here before. He had stepped into this arena many times, just as he would step into it now. How many times, he really couldn't remember. Which was strange. Why, after all, could he remember some but not all? How could he remember times that hadn't yet been?

113. *Jason and the Astronauts*, by Karl Klyne

North Hollywood, CA: Carousel Science Fiction, American Art Enterprises, 1981, 160 pages, ISBN 0-89784-153-0, $1.75, mass market paperback.

At eighteen years of age, Kyphol Mandran was a Priest. At nineteen, a matter of a mere couple more hours, he would be something more. For, he had been chosen by the Poponal Dinkar to succeed him, even though it had been thought by many that the Poponal Dinkar would find no one suitable. The ascension from Priest to Poponal was a complicated procedure, necessitating favorable omens from many different quarters. For years, those favorable omens had not come, and the Poponal Dinkar had grown older and older. Until, at 99, he wavered continually on the brink of death.

It was whispered as ill augury that a replacement had been found so late in the Poponal Dinkar's life. There were more whispers that the Keenlae had a part in it, though few could venture just how that had been accomplished. The fact being, the Poponal Dinkar dying without substitution in the Deified Priesthood, the Keenlae would have been at the advantage in the roll calls of the Control Board. Not that there hadn't been imbalance there before. In Zila-240, the Poponal Minar had died without replacement, and in Zila-614, the Poponal Ryen had likewise died. But, both of those deaths had seen the advent of wars which had endangered Planet 1046-B and had seen the Keenlae chip away bits more of the civilized worlds. Bits which, even until this age, were lost to unabashed barbarism.

However, neither Minar nor Ryen had been of Planet 1046-B. While the Poponal Dinkar was. As a death of a Poponal without successor allowed for a period of grace for the involved planet left representationless, some thought the deeper danger to their safety was now in the presence of a mere boy being the dying Poponal Dinkar's successor. No ascension, after all, was possible for anyone *under* the age of nineteen; so, nineteen to many—especially in the present day and age—seemed too young. There were, after all, dark sides to the Deified Priesthood that were capable of infinite shades of persuasion as regarded neophytes to their number. A Poponal, after all, might enter the Priesthood on one side, but that did not mean that he couldn't shift if he was so inclined to do so.

114. *Michael: The Master*, by W. Lambert III

North Hollywood, CA: Carousel Science Fiction, American Art Enterprises, 1981, 160 pages, ISBN 0-89784-155-7, $1.75, mass market paperback.

A sequel to *The Alien Within*, by Adriana deBolt (#97).

"So, why didn't you stay in that world?"
"I came back for my son."
"Your son? I'm the son of Michael Mylo before he mutated into something else."

115. *Assignment: Grey Area*, by W. Lambert III

North Hollywood, CA: A Carousel Adventure, American Art Enterprises, 1981, 160 pages, ISBN 0-89784-156-5, $1.75, mass market paperback.

Betty Mae Jenks would never forget the Tomb of the Noble 35A carved into the sandstone of the West bank of the Nile at Aswan. Oh, she would certainly forget the name of the noble himself. By that time, she had been subject to a whole gamut of those funny Egyptian names (Thutmosis III, Mentuhotop I, Amenemhat), during her vacation, and one more had about as much chance of sinking in as had all the others. Betty Mae actually wasn't all that "in" to Egyptology and wouldn't have even contemplated making the trip on her own; but, it had always been a dream of Clarence's. And, never in a million years would Betty Mae have dreamed that one of Clarence's distant uncles would up and die (one Betty Mae had never met and Clarence had almost forgotten), to leave her husband enough cash to pack the both of them off on a whirlwind jaunt to the land of the Pharaohs. Betty Mae could have certainly found a better use for the cash, but....

Anyway, the tomb was 35A. That much was sunk in her memory about as far as it could possibly go. And, at the time of her stroll through the dim-lit passageways of that tomb, Betty Mae was beginning to wish there were a few less tombs in Egypt to which her husband could get them access.

Tomb 35A (Tomb 34, 35, 36, and 37, too, for that matter), had seen Betty Mae and Clarence riding a camel for an hour before being dropped on top of the escarpment. The damned camel ride had cost ten times more than their tour agent had told them to pay (ten Egyptian pounds came out roughly as fifteen American dollars). The constant lope of the ship of the desert had been continually opposed to the natural movements of Betty Mae's body atop it. The jolting had given her a backache and a headache (the latter, she figured, coming in exceptionally handy that evening, since desert nights seemed to have been aphrodisiacal as far as Clarence was concerned). Not only that but her kidneys weren't what they should have been. Which might have accounted for the rather embarrassing accident which occurred when the light of the flashlight finally illuminated what was down in the bottom of that gloomy hole.

116. *Abort Project K!*, by Lambert Wilhelm

North Hollywood, CA: A Carousel Adventure, American Art Enterprises, 1981, 159 pages, ISBN 0-89784-181-6, $1.75, mass market paperback.

Jesus, the blood! It was all over him, all over the corpse, all over the room. He'd done a messy job of it. Damn, but he had done a messy job!

The blood stunk: a rich, rotting stench. Not only that, but it was coagulating on his underpants, turning them stiff like semen. It was coagulating on his fingers, making them stick together as if he'd dipped them in glue.

He moved his fingers, feeling the pain.

117. *Bodybuilding Buddies*, by Lambert Wilhelm

San Diego, CA: Adonis Classics, Greenleaf Classics, 1981, 149 pages, stock #AC239, $3.95, mass market paperback.

"Oh, sweet Jesus, fucking God!" Brad Pilar said, following with several loud grunts that signaled the inch-by-inch insertions of John Perry's large cock up his ass.

John's cock was a big one, too, weighing in at a heavy ten inches when stiff. It had a way of plowing up Brad's asshole that made it seem as if it were shoving his guts to one side in the process. It was so big around, it felt as if it were a fist.

"I'm in all the way!" John said, giving a grunt of pure animal satisfaction. He had an asshole wrapped around his hard cock from his cocktip to its bottom. His balls were squashed along the crack of Brad's muscled ass. His washboarded belly was mashed against Brad's butt, his well-developed chest mashed against Brad's back.

118. *Into Leather, into Bondage*, by Lambert Wilhelm

San Diego, CA: Adonis Classics, Greenleaf Classics, 1981, 149 pages, stock #AC244, $3.95, mass market paperback.

It's been said that every person has some dark passion within his soul—some hidden desire, secret or whim that may never surface to be seen by his closest confidante, or even recognized by the person himself. Such a secret can be either a desire that is truly evil, or one that is merely frightening because it is forbidden by society....

* * * * * * *

"Oh, Jesus, yes, fuck me with that big cock of yours!" Tyner Baxter said, his voice low and guttural.

"Yeah, I'll fuck you all right," Jed Dawner said, pulling his cock out until only its pulpy tip was being gripped by Tyner's tight pucker. "I'll screw you so hard and so deep that you're going to think my cock has pierced your guts all of the way into the base of your throat."

When he pushed his cock back into the snug asshole, he was true to his word. As far as Tyner was concerned, it did feel as if Jed's big cock had shoved his guts to one side. Jed's sizable balls whacked Tyner's asscheeks, the blond hair on he sac mingling with the sweaty black hair that lined the crack.

119. *Well-Hung Hustlers*, by Lambert Wilhelm

San Diego, CA: Adonis Classics, Greenleaf Classics, 1981, 150 pages, stock #AC246, $3.95, mass market paperback.

Many Americans have treated homosexuality like an ostrich with its head in the sand—they simply refuse to believe that a man could actually physically love another man. Perhaps that is why so many parents cannot confront the fact that their son may have homosexual tendencies—because they can't believe the condition exists....

* * * * * * *

Logan Riley felt a sudden wet warmth engulfing his cock, and he thought it had to be a dream. Halfway between sleep and consciousness, he knew that he and Dan were on the bus. It therefore hardly seemed possible that someone could be going down on his stiff cock, unless it were a wet dream. On the other hand, the sensations were more real than any Logan had ever dreamed before. As he felt himself quickly progressing toward an orgasm, he struggled to come completely awake. He hardly wanted the sudden spray of cum which would undoubtedly be difficult to clean up, considering the present circumstances.

He awoke completely, and the waves of pleasure didn't stop. If anything, they became even more intense. In automatic reflex, his right hand dropped to his groin to pinch off his explosion. His fingers made contact with the head that was burrowed there.

Logan suddenly knew full well what was happening. Dan Westcastle had somehow unfastened Logan's fly while Logan was asleep. Dan had also managed to pry free Logan's cock. Leaning sideways, he had then opened his mouth and begun sucking.

120. *Midnight Hustler*, by Lambert Wilhelm

San Diego, CA: Adonis Classics, Greenleaf Classics, 1981, 149 pages, stock #AC247, $3.95, mass market paperback.

Many Americans have treated homosexuality like an ostrich with its head in the sand—they simply refuse to believe that a man could actually physically love another man. For those openminded [sic] individuals who have realized that homosexuality is another facet of the human condition, their problem is that they believe homosexuals are vastly different from themselves....

* * * * * * *

The cock was big. Jesus it was a giant! It was long and it was thick, and each time it jammed deep inside Gerald Raspin's asshole it made his mouth open in a low groan.

"Oh, God that feels good," he said as Kyle Winter's cock pulled out to its rubbery tip and then rammed back inside to collide with Gerald's prostate.

The kid had said his name was Kyle, but you could never tell what a kid's real name was, especially out on the street. Most of them were runaways who changed their names as often as they dropped their pants.

121. *Hazards of Hustling*, by Lambert Wilhelm

San Diego, CA: Adonis Classics, Greenleaf Classics, 1981, 149 pages, stock #AC249, $3.95, mass market paperback.

Many Americans have treated homosexuality like an ostrich with its head in the sand—they simply refuse to believe that a man could actually physically love another man. For those open-minded [sic] individuals who have realized that homosexuality is another facet of the human condition, their problem is that they believe homosexuals are vastly different from themselves....

* * * * * * *

Jack Mason, Jr., was sucking cock like crazy! When he swallowed, he took Dan's nine-inch erection all the way down to the point where his lips were flattening the black pubic hair clustered on the young hustler's muscled lower belly. When he released those inches of stiff prick, he traveled all the way back up the cock until his lips had fallen into the groove beneath the flare of the circumcised cockhead.

His mouth was full of soupy saliva. His cheeks were compressed to hug the priming erection like a rubber glove molding a hand. His tongue worked. Jesus, did it work! It whipped the cock like a cat-o'-nine-tails beating on a muscled slave.

His left hand was clamped hard on the hustler's studly ass, feeling the muscled asscheek dimpling beneath a pair of faded jeans. His other hand was working the stud's hairy nuts, rolling them between his fingers, pinching and squeezing them, pulling on flesh that had a tendency to want to lift out of reach.

122. *B&D Hustlers*, by Lambert Wilhelm

San Diego, CA: Adonis Classics, Greenleaf Classics, 1981, 153 pages, stock #AC254, $3.95, mass market paperback.

A question often asked by those who deal with psychological problems is: What is normal? The answer to that seemingly simple question will probably never be answered.

* * * * * * *

"Ball me! Jesus, ball me!" Michael Dysic screamed, his ass getting fucked royally by the frantic pumping of Jeff Heathrow's big stiff cock.

"Damn right I'm going to ball you, stud!" Jeff said, his hips on a forward swing to ram his eight inches of cock in so far that his blond pubic hair was suddenly meshed with the equally blond hair lining the crease of Michael's firm ass. "Ball you! Fuck you! Screw your tight asshole until I cream my soupy white cum up your as!"

"Aaaaggghrrruughh!" Michael groaned, his voice low and guttural. Another withdrawal of Jeff's stiff prick to its pulpy, uncircumcised head had sent Michael's pleasure soaring to yet higher plateaus of enjoyment.

123. *Stud on the Rings*, by Lambert Wilhelm

San Diego, CA: Adonis Classics, Greenleaf Classics, 1981, 149 pages, stock #AC256, $3.95, mass market paperback.

Many Americans have treated homosexuality like an ostrich with its head in the sand—they simply refuse to believe that a man could actually physically love another man. Perhaps that is why so many parents cannot confront the fact that their son may have homosexual tendencies—because they can't believe the condition exists.

* * * * * * *

"Fuck me raw, stud!" Tony Maxton said and moaned, keeping his voice low. Even though the Westbrook Coliseum was pretty much deserted, there were a few circus people and die-hard fans left who might have heard the sounds and been drawn to them.

Tony was beneath the bleachers. They rose on four sides of the room to give a full view of the three rings which had been set up on the auditorium floor. He was there with Michael Draegar of the Flying Draegar Family.

Tony's faded jeans had been peeled down his young body and were now dropped in a pool around his Justin cowboy boots. His tight asshole was plugged with good, long, thick Draegar cock—just as good, long, and thick as Tony had always known his cock would be.

124. *Hunter Stud*, by Lambert Wilhelm

San Diego, CA: Adonis Classics, Greenleaf Classics, 1981, 150 pages, stock #AC260, $3.95, mass market paperback.

Many Americans have treated homosexuality like an ostrich with its head in the sand—they simply refuse to believe that a man could actually physically love another man. For those open-minded [sic] individuals who have realized that homosexuality is another facet of the human condition, their problem is that they believe homosexuals are vastly different from themselves....

* * * * * * *

"Fuck my tight asshole, stud!" Jim Pasteur said, down on his knees, leaning forward over the bale, feeling the compact hay scratch his naked and muscled chest and belly. "Screw it like only you know how!"

Hunter Fanbert didn't have to be asked twice. He was hot, horny, and ready for a good time. His cock was ready, too. It was a massive hunk of stiff erection that jutted upward from the black hair that covered his balls. Hunter never really realized just how much he missed having sex with another warm body until he renewed his experience. And, since he lived alone in his mountain cabin, this was only possible when he came down for supplies, such as he had done today.

He used his calloused right hand to fist his cock, stroking up and back along his big prick, milking it for more sticky juices. He caught the resulting drool on the flat of his thumb and veneered the sex juice along the domed top of his cockhead. With a torquing movement, he smeared the wetness along the whole length of his massive erection.

125. *From This Beloved Hour,* by Willa Lambert

Toronto, Canada: Harlequin Books, Harlequin SuperRomance #23, 1982, 383 pages, ISBN 0-737-70023-7, $2.50, mass market paperback.

125A. Reprinted as: *From This Beloved Hour,* by William Maltese Writing as Willa Lambert. Rockville, MD: The Borgo Press, an Imprint of Wildside Press, 2007, 383 pages, ISBN 1-4344-8153-0, $19.99, trade paperback.

"ABDUL HAS OFFERED TO GIVE UP THE CHASE."

Sharp sarcasm edged Peter's words. "Damned good of him to give you up, don't you think? Not every man would make such a sacrifice out of gratitude."

Jenny was stunned. "Do you mean that because you saved Sheikh Abdul's life, he's agreed to stop seeing me?"

126. *Heavy Cruisers*, by Lambert Wilhelm

San Diego, CA: Adonis Classics, Greenleaf Classics, 1982, 150 pages, stock #AC263, $3.95, mass market paperback.

Many Americans have treated homosexuality like an ostrich with its head in the sand—they simply refuse to believe that a man could actually physically love another man. Perhaps that is why so many parents cannot confront the fact that their son may have homosexual tendencies—because they can't believe the condition exists....

* * * * * * *

"Tell me you like my hard cock fucked far and deep inside of you!" Barry Gayner commanded in a low, guttural voice, fucking all of his thick prick up the asshole of his sister's studly husband.

"No, goddamn it, no!" Darryl Dwayne said in protest to any such insinuation. Darryl's ass had been virgin up to this moment of his life. He felt as if Barry's big cock had penetrated his ass, his belly, and his chest cavity, into the base of his throat.

"Fucking-A, it's what you've been wanting," Barry said in contradiction, drawing out his cock until only its tip was being squeezed by Darryl's asshole. "It's what you've been wanting ever since you set your pervert eyes on me, isn't it?"

127. *Country Studs*, by Lambert Wilhelm

San Diego, CA: Adonis Classics, Greenleaf Classics, 1982, 154 pages, stock #AC265, $3.95, mass market paperback.

It has been noted by psychologists that man is a gregarious creature whose need for affection and acceptability is as strong a motivation as his need for food and shelter. Approval is a social need that is reflected many times over in our everyday lives.

Frequently, however, one's need for approval and acceptance undergoes a serious challenge, especially in those instances where behavior reflects a departure from what sociologists would consider the norm.

COUNTRY STUDS chronicles just such a challenge. Two brothers, Ken and Peter Cleaver, have developed a physical attract to one another, yet it is only through a series of encounters with mutual buddies in their rural community that they will finally be able to understand the true meaning of their attraction.

* * * * * * *

"Yeah, you studly bastard, fuck my tight asshole!" Henry Wilcox said, his voice a low grunt as he felt the big cock fuck all of the way up his ass, the giant balls banging against his sweaty asscrack.

Those giant balls, plus the accompanying big cock, belonged to Gil Sampson. Gil was a stud from the word go, and Henry had known that from the moment he had spotted the kid hitchhiking along that dusty country road. There was no way Henry could have driven right on by without stopping. He'd played his cards right, too. If the kid hadn't fucked male ass before—which Gil had said was the case—he had certainly taken to the male-male fucking like a duck took to water. In fact, Gil fucked ass so well, Henry wasn't at all sure the kid had been telling the truth when he had said it was his first time. Henry certainly hadn't gone at ass-fucking with quite as much gusto, his first time around. But, then, the kids in this day and age were a hell of a lot less paranoid regarding gay sex, or any kind of sex, than the kids had been in Henry's teenage years.

"Like that?" Gil asked, pulling his big prick outward until only the large head of his cock was held entrapped within the gripping sphincter of Henry's asshole. The sphincter was a tight one, giving the definite impression of being a rubber band wrapped around the top of the prick. But the gripping pressure was pleasurable, the pleasure becoming even more intense each time Gil pushed to fuck all of his cock deep into the snug tightness of Henry's asshole.

128. *In Stocks and Bondage*, by Lambert Wilhelm

San Diego, CA: Adonis Classics, Greenleaf Classics, 1982, 153 pages, stock #AC267, $3.95, mass market paperback.

Many Americans have treated homosexuality like an ostrich with its head in the sand—they simply refuse to believe that a man could actually physically love another man. Perhaps that is why so many parents cannot confront the fact that their son may have homosexual tendencies—because they can't believe the condition exists....

* * * * * * *

"Oh, God, easy! Easy! Eeeeeeeeasy!"

But Stock Bradley didn't fuck anyone easy. He was known for his rough fucks. This fucker he was screwing knew Stock was known for rough fucks, and that was why the bastard had approached Stock in the first place.

"Easy my ass!" Stock said, pulling his long and powerful cock out of Harold Wiley's asshole and fucking his prick back in again to the black hair on Stock's big balls. The handsome stud's muscled and hairy belly smacked Harold's sweaty and hairless asscheeks. Bang went the goddamned collision of flesh against flesh. Bang, bang, bang, it went again and again and again as Stock really got down to the nitty-gritty of fucking.

129. *Masters and Slaves*, by Lambert Wilhelm

San Diego, CA: Adonis Classics, Greenleaf Classics, 1982, 152 pages, stock #AC269, $3.95, mass market paperback.

A question often asked by those who deal with psychological problems is: What is normal? The answer to that seemingly simple question will probably never be answered.

It is normal for some primitive inhabitants of South American jungles to perform, before the entire village, what Americans would consider depraved sexual acts. Such behavior would probably result in arrests ands convictions, if not a full-fledged riot, in the U.S.A.

The people within a particular society usually are well aware of what is considered acceptable behavior for them. And therein lies the problem for the main characters of this novel.

For the men who become slaves in this novel, they have already accepted and adjusted to their world of homosexuality. Yet, they are given an insight into another side of gay sex—into the dark world where souls mix pleasure with pain, agony with ecstasy, delight with domination.

MASTERS AND SLAVES deals with a sexual dilemma that confronts all of us in one form or another. We cannot pass judgment on how individuals seek and find pleasure—we can only look at them with an open mind, seeing how some members of our society face the problem.

* * * * * * *

"Goddamned, fucking good!" Dennis Larriet said, thrusting his ass upward in order to assure his asshole took all of the hard inches of cock that Post Welaney was hot to feed it. "Jesus, Jesus, good!"

It was good, too. Fucking with Post was always good. The only thing was, at least lately, Dennis had begun to suspect there was fucking that went beyond good. And, as much as he would have preferred exploring those new avenues with Post, he somehow doubted that was going to be the case. He had already sent out feelers, indicating the way he thought their sex should go. Post, though, hadn't taken the bait. In fact, as if in a direct attempt to thwart what Dennis had in mind, Post had proceeded to make their fucking even less rough and tumble than usual.

The two were fucking in the bedroom of Dennis' apartment, which explained the presence of all the mirrors to reflect a never-ending playback of the two attractive studs at rut. Dennis always had been the more experimental of the two. He had early seen the erotic possibilities to be had from mirrors. Post, although he had likewise seen the potential, had been conservative enough not to rush out and buy mirrors with which to experiment. Dennis could understand Post's reluctance, up to a point. After all, why should Post go to the bother of checking out the turn-on of mirrors when it had been obvious from the start that Dennis would take the lead? What Dennis didn't understand was how Post had kept from buying mirrors for his bedroom once the guy had seen, thanks to Dennis, just how much of a turn-on they could be. Post just remained too much the conservative farm boy, while Dennis saw himself leaving Post behind as far as adapting to the big-city ways.

130. *Golden Shower Slave*, by Lambert Wilhelm

San Diego, CA: Adonis Classics, Greenleaf Classics, 1982, 151 pages, stock #AC272, $3.95, mass market paperback.

A question often asked by those who deal with psychological problems is: What is normal? The answer to that seemingly simple question will probably never be answered....

* * * * * * *

"Yeah, kid, whip it, whip it, fucking whip it!" Baylor Niles screamed, his voice muffled by the plastic visor of his motorcycle helmet and by the wind buffeting around him.

Tim Jaxon couldn't really feel the warm flesh of Baylor's cock, which he held gripped so firmly in his hand, because he was wearing leather gloves. But he could detect the hardness of that stiff prick that jutted so powerful from Baylor's leather pants as the two men rode together on the big Harley.

It was late and the surrounding traffic was scant. It was doubtful anyone but the two cycle riders knew just what Tim was doing to Baylor's cock as they rode along. Seeing a guy getting his meat beaten while he was cruising along at sixty miles an hour wasn't really what anyone expected to see on any freeway.

131. *Black Room Buddies*, by Lambert Wilhelm

San Diego, CA: Adonis Classics, Greenleaf Classics, 1982, 150 pages, stock #AC273, $3.95, mass market paperback.

A question often asked by those who deal with psychological problems is: What is normal? The answer to that seemingly simple question will probably never be answered....

* * * * * * *

"Oh, Christ, what a tight ass!" Kyle said, pumping his thick prick into place and corkscrewing his cock against Gerald's prostate.

Actually, Gerald Claynesbourg's asshole wasn't the tightest Kyle Stevens had ever fucked, but it wasn't the loosest, either. It fit snugly enough around his fucking prick, so there was plenty of friction to tease the cock toward orgasm and get Gerald to climbing the walls. Of course, Gerald's pleasure was supplemented by Kyle's hand fisting his cock. There was nothing Gerald enjoyed more than fucking a gripping hand while getting fucked in the ass by a very big cock. Gerald was getting fucked dog style in the middle of the bedroom floor.

"Stud, oh, Jesus, stud!" Gerald said, his voice a low and guttural grunt as his prostate received another battering from the fucking cock. "That is good, good, good. It's just the way I fucking like it."

132. *Love's Golden Spell*, by Willa Lambert

Toronto, Canada: Harlequin Books, Harlequin SuperRomance #59, 1983, 380 pages, ISBN 0-373-70059-8, $2.95, mass market paperback.

132A. Reprinted as: *Love's Golden Spell*, by William Maltese Writing as Willa Lambert. Rockville, MD: The Borgo Press, an Imprint of Wildside Press, 2007, 380 pages, ISBN 1-4344-8154-9, $19.99, trade paperback.

"TELL ME YOU'RE NOT GLAD TO SEE ME...."

Such a sexy voice he had—all ripe peaches and heavy cream.
"I'm not," Janet said. She should struggle—scream, shout. She didn't.

133. *Emerald-Silk Intrigue*, by Willa Lambert

Murray, UT: Heritage Romances, Wordspinner Press, 1987, 212 pages, ISBN 0-939043-06-8, $3.95, mass market paperback.

133A. Reprinted as: *Emerald-Silk Intrigue*, by William Maltese Writing as Willa Lambert. Rockville, MD: The Borgo Press, an Imprint of Wildside Press, 2007, 212 pages, ISBN 1-4344-8149-2, $14.99, trade paperback.

Slowly he folded her against him until she could feel her heart beating in time with his. His mouth lowered to hers until their lips met. Tentatively at first, then more firmly. Thought of the future left her mind, leaving only sensations of Jeff, his scent, his texture, the strength of his good arm around her.

"Just in case you're not speaking to me tomorrow at this time," he murmured, breaking the contact of their lips. "I've wanted to kiss you since I first saw you, and the thought that something might happen to keep me from it in the future makes me quite brazen."

FROM THE AUTHOR: After three successful SuperRomances published in fourteen countries by Harlequin, I'd like to thank Beverly King and Heritage Romances for launching my long-contemplated "Seven-Continent" series of LDS-oriented romantic mysteries, consisting of seven separate and individual novels, one set on each of the seven continents, beginning with *Emerald-Silk Intrigue* which takes place in Asia. It is followed by South America in November 1987 and North America in February 1988. We will also cover Africa, Europe, Australia, and Antarctica. Each book contains its own cast of characters who mirror high standards, while proving a lie to the misconception that life for such people need be unexciting, unimaginative, unglamorous, and unfulfilling.

* * * * * * *

Jessica Miller cringed as she heard Jeff Billings shout, "What skeletons are you so intent upon keeping in the family closets?"

Roman Whyte ignored the words as he slammed the limousine door and signaled his driver to leave. The Church members seemed mesmerized by the proceedings.

She'd never dreamed when she offered to show Jeff the way to the Bangkok chapel this morning that he was coming solely to interrogate Roman. He'd mentioned that he wrote unauthorized biographies, but she had no idea that Roman was his quarry. She'd think twice and quell her missionary spirit before she ever again helped a stranger find the church.

134. *Jungle Quest Intrigue*, by Willa Lambert

Murray, UT: Heritage Books, Wordspinner Press, 1987, 223 pages, ISBN 0-939043-09-2, $3.95, mass market paperback.

134A. Reprinted as: *Jungle Quest Intrigue*, by William Maltese Writing as Willa Lambert. Rockville, MD: The Borgo Press, an Imprint of Wildside Press, 2007, 223 pages, ISBN 1-4344-8150-6, $14.99, trade paperback.

"LAURA."

LIKE HAIL, PIECES OF ROCK RAINED FROM THE UNSEEN CEILING. Painfully pelted by falling stone, Laura crawled quickly toward Kurt's voice and collided with him. They pulled each other together and melded against the solid stone of the iceberg-like chunk they hoped would protect them from its smaller cousins. Rocks, once they hit the ground, emitted soft plopping sounds as if they erupted fine dust from deep, dry puddles.

The earth groaned and a gigantic reverberation, then another and another, rocked the entire area.

* * * * * * *

Fear dilated Laura Lexly's blue eyes as she glimpsed snag-like treetops perilously close. Absentmindedly, she twisted an unruly strand of her short-cropped, sweat-saturated blonde hair that had lost all of its attractive beauty-parlor curl. She swallowed hard, and her mind flashed visions of horrendous disaster; no matter Jim Kenner's already proven worth at the controls of this small singe-engine plane. Her stomach churned, giving rise to the nausea she'd barely controlled throughout most of her wild roller-coaster-like ride through the turbulence percolating upward from horizon-to-horizon jungle and from upthrusts of ragged stone.

"Jim's landings here are always a bit hairy," Kurt Reiger confessed, nervously chewing on his lower lip. His violet eyes, purple against the mahogany tan of his face, were dark with concern, and the deep dimple in his right cheek wasn't punched there by amusement. Anxiously, he ran his large and well-formed fingers through his thatch of cut-short curly black hair and, doing so, contributed to the tousle of interlocking stands.

Laura could see much of the boy-she-remembered in the man-Kurt-had-become. Although, calling Kurt a boy at fifteen, when Laura had last seen him twenty-four years before, was probably a misnomer. More to the point, Laura, eleven at the time, had been a girl: a slow bloomer who hadn't exploded into official womanhood until a whole year after the tragedy and after Kurt had been spirited away.

135. *Moon-Stone Intrigue*, by Willa Lambert

Murray, UT: Heritage House Books, Wordspinner Press, 1988, 212 pages, ISBN 0-939043-10-6, $3.95, mass market paperback.

135A. Reprinted as: *Moon-Stone Intrigue*, by William Maltese Writing as Willa Lambert. Rockville, MD: The Borgo Press, an Imprint of Wildside Press, 2007, 212 pages, ISBN 1-4344-8151-4, $14.99, trade paperback.

MELISSA REFUSED TO SUCCUMB TO FEAR.

She'd dumped a madman over her head and down a flight of stairs; survived a crash landing, a waterfall, bears, a machine gun, a kidnapping. She could survive this, too

She walked faster and heard footsteps behind her. She hurried to escape them, down the sidewalk, though the shrubs and to the closed glass door that separated her from the private elevator in the private lobby.

* * * * * * *

Melissa Jordan's black hair danced in the down draft.

"Tell me, Melissa, does your associate see me as some kind of monster?" Christian shouted above the noise of the rotors as he assisted Melissa across the storage bay of the large helicopter. "Miss Howard seemed reluctant to let me hitch this ride."

He was certainly perceptive. Elizabeth hadn't trusted Christian from the start. She felt that meteorites should be used for research not frivolously wasted on knife handles.

136. *Diary of a Hustler*, by Joey

London, England: Just Eighteen Series, Prowler Books, 1997, 140 pages, ISBN 0-9524647-6-4, £5.99, mass market paperback.

136A. Reprinted as: *Diary of a Hustler*, by William Maltese (Told by Joey). Albion, NY: MLR Press, 2007, 156 pages, ISBN 978-0-9793110-7-9, $14.99, trade paperback.

"I want you to bend your legs at the knees," Thane says. "Kind of like you're inviting me to climb on up and slip my big weenie between your sexy buns, missionary position."

I oblige, because I want this over and done. All of my expendable hair not yet removed, I already feel far more naked and far more vulnerable than seems commensurate with the mere removal of so few totally useless pubic hairs.

"That's the way," he says. His fingers and the razor are far down beneath my balls, searching out and toppling the very last strands that survive between my scrotum and my asscrack.

* * * * * * *

I'm about to get my asshole fucked royally by Thane Calendar. I can think of worse fates, because Thane is one helluva nice looking not-all-that-old man.

Thane's hair is black, cut short at the sides and in back, left fairly long on top and in front. He doesn't use hair spray, so his hair in front is always falling into his startlingly green eyes, and Thane is always either running his hand through his hair to unlock his vision, or he has this attractive way of giving his head a little flick that does the job, but not usually all that well.

His eyebrows are thick and the kind you feel sure would meet across the bridge of his nose if he didn't keep the space plucked, or shaved, or whatever. Maybe the space never does grow hair but merely gives that impression. His eyelashes are sexily long and lush.

137. *Young Cruisers: An Anthology*, by Cort Forbes

London, England: Just Eighteen Series, Prowler Books, 1997, 142 pages, ISBN 0-9524647-7-2, £5.99, mass market paperback.

137A. Reprinted as: *Young Cruisers: An Anthology*, by William Maltese. Rockville, MD: The Borgo Press, an Imprint of Wildside Press, 2007, 142 pages, ISBN 1-4344-1846-8, $13.99, trade paperback.

A short story collection. Contents: "Been There, Done That," "Black and Blue," "Performing Arts," "Play It Again, Sam," "Poet-Voyeur," and "When Opportunity Knocks."

"You like getting fucked in your ass," the man panted in Sam's ear, and it wasn't a question. "You like getting it from a real man. He-man prick pushed in and pulled out of that rear end of yours? Big male cock stuffed so far and so deep up your guts that you feel it in the bottom of your throat. My blasted wad going to blow right on out the other end of your mouth, like great wads of white water geysered from Old Faithful."

On cue, the man's cock swelled even bigger. Its additional size caused additional friction from each and every pump within hugging asshole walls. The more the friction, the more the exquisite pleasure/pain that sunburst from Sam's molested asshole to the rest of the youth's body.

Sam pressed his face into the hard ground. Mashed and moist leaves clung to his cheek. He moaned and felt bits of dirt on his wet lips and tongue. He smelled the pungency of damp earth.

* * * * * * *

BEEN THERE, DONE THAT

Sloppy sounds could be sexy sounds. That these weren't, Ty Jackson's rubberized dick doggie-fucking a customer's ass, was a bit disconcerting to Ty who hoped he wasn't bored. A bored hustler was right up there with warm ice cream by way of desirability.

Ty couldn't blame Carr (with two r's) Milder...or Milner...or Maxner. Who the hell cared what his name was, since it was probably as play-baloney as they came? Ty always used his real name, but that was only because everyone assumed "Ty" had to be as phony as the next name.

Anyway, Carr wasn't all that bad to look at, especially considering he'd paid for the screw. He was probably in his early forties. He still had a full head of hair, gone only slightly salt-and-pepper… more likely, salt and cinnamon, since the natural color seemed more brown than black. He had dark-colored eyes. Black, brown, maybe even dark blue. It had been just dark enough when he'd approached Ty that it had been impossible for Ty to tell. He had a regular nose. He had an attractively full-lipped mouth, probably really nice for sucking cock; Ty wasn't into mouths for kissing.

138. *Slaves*, by Alex von Mann

London, England: Prowler Books, 1997, 137 pages, ISBN 0-9524647-9-9, £5.99, mass market paperback.

138A. Reprinted as: *Slaves*, by William Maltese. Rockville, MD: The Borgo Press, an Imprint of Wildside Press, 2007, 137 pages, ISBN 1-4344-8145-X, $13.99, trade paperback.

He turned his well-formed butt to the mirror. His was a firm ass. His was a studly ass. So what that it was a white and not a black ass? This was fantasy time!

"Maybe, this time, I'll grab that big black prick of yours and whip it for white cream, even while I fuck the shit out of your cat-o'-nine-tails whipped black ass with my lily-white dick," Jack said. "Would you like that?"

No pillory in the hotel room, but Jack imagined Konoco secured in one. If Jack laid on the hotel bed, the mildew on the bedspread clammy beneath his butt and back, he was, in his mind, standing behind Konoco, his cock ready for the hot plunge up restrained Negro's funky ass.

* * * * * * *

The space in the first-class restroom, on the flight from Johannesburg to Dar Es Salaam, was cramped. It helped that the young flight attendant had fucked there before. Timothy knew right where to stand to advantage what little space he had. His pants (he wore no undershorts), were dropped around his ankles. His large dock and large accompanying balls, the latter within their containing sac of blond-haired skin, were propped upon the leading lip of the cool porcelain sink.

He handed a condom packet to the young man positioned directly behind him.

"By the look of that long-lasting boner in your trousers, I decided 'Large' was your size," Timothy said. "Lubricated, because it's been a long time since my butt ate such a hefty meal."

139. *California Creamin' & Other Stories: An Erotic Anthology*, by William Maltese

London, England: Prowler Books, 1998, 260 pages, ISBN 1-902644-04-2, £7.95, trade paperback.

139A. Reprinted as: *California Creamin' and Other Stories: An Erotic Anthology*, by William Maltese: London, England: Prowler Books, 2001, 318 pages, ISBN 1-902644-43-3, £7.95, trade paperback; excludes "Poetic Defense of One-Hand Readers."

139B. Reprinted as: *California Creamin' and Other Stories*, by William Maltese. Albion, NY: MLR Press, 2007, 288 pages, ISBN 978-1-934531-35-8, $16.99, trade paperback; cover title: *California Creamin' & Other Stories*.

A short story collection. Contents: "What If...?," "Poetic Defense of One-Hand Readers," "Cowboy Boots," "Pumping Gas," "Mensur," "Fucking Drunk," "Variations on a Tale of Two Cities," "Food Chain," "Robinson Hole, Wyoming," "Counterfeit Cowboys," "California Creamin'," "Users," "Football," "Open Fly-Fishing Season," and "Uniform Sex."

Rob pumps his dick harder and faster. His pleasure swells with each rise and fall of his fist over his stiff meat. He raises his knees higher and higher. His knees, thighs, and feet tightly entrench the boot's sole more and more firmly against Rob's nuts. Finally, Rob's left ankle, still crossed by his right ankle, almost touches Rob's ass, and the boot between his legs really mashes his testicles which are prominently kept elevated by the way the front of his jocksock is still latched beneath his cum-bulged testsicles [sic].

"Oh, yes," Rob congratulates. No way does he stop the onslaught of orgasm this time. Doing so would require more know-how than he's mastered during all of his admittedly extensive sexual experimentation.

He pumps his dick harder, and each downward pass of his hand over his cock jams the heel of his fist against his balls and additionally squashes his gonads between Rob's fist and the strategically laced jocksock-hammock accordianed [sic] more and more by the pressure of boot leather.

* * * * * * *

WHAT IF?

I'm wearing a white shirt, grey shorts, sneakers. Six other guys wear the same, although the colors differ. It's the costume geared to make us all look younger, and it basically does the trick. When I see my reflection, I look about twelve. It's hard to believe I, and the other six, are legal and then some. One of the guys, Brent, looks so young even I have trouble believing his balls have dropped or his cock is capable of achieving boner-status.

The way I have it figured, Rodrigo Maurez liking his one special boy-toy to look young, Brent is the one of us about to collect $200, do not pass Go.

The party we're attending isn't being thrown by Rodrigo but by a Mr. Sanchez who Rodrigo knows from their early days in Cuba. Mr. Sanchez, from what I can tell, just by following the way he works his own party, prefers his tricks a little older-looking than Rodrigo does, although he's well aware of how we young-looking stuff liven up things, if just by providing something seemingly-chicken to look at.

140. *Summer Sweat: An Erotic Anthology*, by William Maltese

London, England: Prowler Books, 1999, 210 pages, ISBN 1-902644-10-7, £7.95, trade paperback.

140A. Reprinted as: *Summer Sweat: An Erotic Anthology*, by William Maltese. Rockville, MD: The Borgo Press, an Imprint of Wildside Press, 2007, 210 pages, ISBN 1-4344-8147-6, $14.99, trade paperback.

A short story collection. Contents: "Fetish?," "The Music, Man," "Guess Who?," "Cop Out," "Doubting Thomas," "Eating Crow," "Comes a Naked Stranger," "Changing of the Guard," "Crapshoots," "One...Two...Three...Out," "Abracadacus," and "Summer Sweat."

FETISH?

"For what are we looking?" always asks the sidekick of just about every television or big-screen detective there ever was, his boss and he having just entered the apartment of a murder victim or the residence of some prime suspect.

"I'm not sure," always comes the reply, "but we'll know it when we see it."

Bullshit!

Some people haven't a clue. Not even when it jumps up and bites them on the ass, not once but time after time. I know from personal experience, albeit not as a detective, nor as the sidekick of some gumshoe investigating a crime. More of the "what" later.

For the moment, let's take a closer look at Marky and see how close he stands to an epiphany. My guess is about as far away as the North Pole stands from the North Star.

In short, Marky doesn't have even a hint. Actually, he's likely all the more confused, because he's such a little cutie and probably can't begin to fathom that none of this has anything whatsoever to do with looks. Because in the world in which Marky exists—hustling—looks play too much a part, too much of the time, for a kid like him to remove them entirely from any equation.

141. *A Slip to Die For: A Stud Draqual Mystery*, by William Maltese

London, England: Lambert III Library for Prowler Books, 1999, 211 pages, ISBN 0-9672420-0-2, £7.95, trade paperback.

141A. Reprinted as: *A Slip to Die For: A Stud Draqual Mystery*, by William Maltese. Rockville, MD: The Borgo Press, an Imprint of Wildside Press, 2007, 211 pages, ISBN 1-4344-8148-4, $14.99, trade paperback.

A prequel to *Thai Died* (#146).

HE HAD ME SECURELY LOCKED AGAINST HIM

There was no give to his body. His left arm, like a strong metal vise, was slung around in front of me; it and its accompanying hand pinioned my arms against my sides. His belly ground my butt. His chin wedged over my left shoulder, against my neck; his whisker-stubbled right cheek exerted pressure that kept my head from shaking off his other slab-like hand that anchored over my face.

"Don't fight me, damn it!" a whispered command in my ear.

I had no choice but to struggle. My brain, deprived of oxygen, sent instructions for survival that didn't include passive resistance. I was suffocating in the airless vacuum between his hand and my face.

* * * * * * *

The bullet punched black silk slip was a sensuous lake beached across the shore of the corpse's muscled thighs; the exposed length of flaccid penis placid and calm on its raft of coarse dark hair.

The silk was Draqualian, the end product of a sophisticated and very exclusive manufacturing operation in upstate New York where ravenous silkworms gobble mulberry leaves treated with a secret formula and then excrete gossamer strands of protein in every color of the rainbow.

Draqualian silk is exorbitantly expensive, but Don deZinn could afford the exorbitantly expensive. As that cross-dresser, model, underground movie star, and high-class call-boy confessed to me on more than one occasion: "Stud, I've come a long way since I walked the streets and peddled my cock and ass to the highest bidder."

142. *When Summer Comes*, by William Maltese

London, England: Prowler Books, 2001, 289 pages, ISBN 1-902644-33-6, £7.95, trade paperback.

142A. Reprinted as: *When Summer Comes*, by William Maltese. Rockville, MD: The Borgo Press, an Imprint of Wildside Press, 2007, 289 pages, ISBN 978-1-4344-8165-8, $15.99, trade paperback.

Summer comes. Maybe just around the next corner. Talbot Crane, Marky Matthews, and Jeffrey Layins can tell, even this far south where even winters are mostly sunshine and warm breezes. This sunshine is more intense, this breeze is more noticeably warm than when the trio weekended here just a couple of months ago. This summer-on-its-way late-spring surf has an entirely different intensity than winter-in-full-swing. These sea-to-shore cascades aren't nearly as stirred to wildness and fury by mid-Pacific storms.

Their cock-in-ass, cock-up-ass, cock-wrapped-by-hand daisy-chain fuck, complete with their collective heaves for breath, is audible, even above the distant sounds of water crashing on isolated Baja California coastline. Oak leaves tremble, within the large canopy of limbs that overhangs them, seemingly disturbed by the guttural sounds of these three rutting prime specimens in heat.

"Oh, Jesus, yes!" Talbot says. His hand is on a down-stroke along the powerfully uplifted length of his massive erection. By luck (or un-luck) of the draw, his boner is the only one of the three not occupied by tightly squeezing asshole. The heel of his descending hand mashes his red-haired testicles. His scrotum pleasure-compacts to the shape and size of a regulation basketball.

143. *The Brentridge Gold: The Pleiades Portals Series*, by W. Lambert III

Lincoln, NE: Writers Club Press, 2002, 119 pages, ISBN 0-595-65325-1 and ISBN 0-595-25775-5, $20.95 and $10.95, hardcover and trade paperback.

NO LONGER A MYSTERY

Once he had expected the Brentridge gold to be panned from some river lost to anyone but Indians and Brentridges, within Deadmen Hills. Maybe even a river, hidden underground, like the water of the rumored Payne Reservoir. By the first time he'd reached this exact location, he'd changed his opinion to imagine a large vein of gold. But Brentridge gold didn't start out as nuggets, or as shimmering glitter implanted amid black lava stone, the latter bound to have confused and amazed geologists who'd always predicted against it.

Brentridge gold was something far more eye popping. Something that drooped mouths in awe, even as David's mouth had dropped, that first time, and every time since. Just as David's jaw went slack this time as he turned the mist enshrouded corner …

* * * * * * *

The poison bloated its victims, and this poor sucker had been so desperate he'd plunged right in. He'd figured to bathe and drink at the same time, or maybe he'd toppled in afterwards, the result of gut pains and disorientation.

Water-filled boots dragged on the bottom of the pool, and the corpse floated, bent from its waist. With the pool's depth at less than three feet, it made the body about five-nine. Not short, at least by the thinking of the man, who stood poolside, taking in the grisly scene, because David Brentridge was only an inch taller.

David squinted his turquoise eyes against the blinding New Mexico Territory sun, his head automatically bobbing in tempo with the corpse's head that bounced slightly in currents formed by deadly artesian seepage.

144. *SS Mann Hunt,* by William Maltese

Lincoln, NE: Writers Club Press, 2002, 171 pages, ISBN 0-595-26188-4, $12.95, trade paperback.

"YEAH, I'LL SETTLE FOR THAT," HE ADMITS

"I'll even settle for killed and cannibalized by natives, or eaten by wildlife. I'll settle for any fate except the one that paints my father as a Nazi monster out to cover his tracks. Because I remember him, you know? I wasn't so young at the time he disappeared that I didn't know with certainty who and what he was. And I tell you, he was a good, kind, caring human being, man and father. He had his faults, but they weren't of the magnitude, or of the grotesque nature, insinuated by muckraking journalists who took advantage of a real tragedy to run down the character and reputation of a man unable to defend himself."

* * * * * * *

Concern dilates my blue eyes as I glimpse snag-like treetops perilously close. Absentmindedly, I run my fingers through the unruly stands of my short-cropped, sweat saturated blond hair. I swallow hard, and my mind flashes visions of horrendous disaster; no matter Jim Kenner has already proven his worth at the controls of this small single-engine plane. My stomach churns, giving rise to the nausea I've barely controlled throughout most of this wild roller-coaster-like ride through the turbulence percolating upward from the horizon-to-horizon South American jungle, and from the up-thrusts of ragged stone amongst all the greenery below us.

"Jim's landings here are always a bit hairy," Kurt Mann confesses, nervously chewing his lower lip. His violet eyes, purple against the mahogany tan of his face, are dark with concern, and the deep dimple in his right cheek isn't punched there by amusement. Anxiously, he runs his large and well-formed fingers through his thatch-short curly black hair and, in doing so, contributes to the tousle of interlocking strands.

Within the suffocating cramped and super-heated confinement of the small plane, I can still see much of the boy I remember within the man Kurt has become.

145. *Dog on a Surfboard (and the Rest of the Adventure)*, by Billy Lambert

Lincoln, NE: Writers Club Press, 2003, 163 pages, ISBN 0-595-65572-6, $22.95 and $, hardcover and paperback.

A young adult novel.

JEFF HELPED HIS DOG ON THE SURFBOARD

Kamehameha didn't have to struggle to keep from being washed off the board. The sea obligingly pulled them and their board closer and closer to the horizon.

Somewhere behind them, although it was night, a flock of birds took flight, circled once, circled twice, and amid the sounds of their furiously flapping wings veered inland.

* * * * * * *

It was a summer's last gasp, unfamiliar to most northern climes in that it didn't tinge trees heavily with reds, oranges, yellows, and browns. Nor did leaves droop wearily to flutter free on any blasts of icy breeze. For this was a tropical isle. Where the sun shone upon a continuing lush greenness. Wherein birds busily fluttered and never surrendered their nests to fly south.

It wasn't any one cloud appeared on the horizon and lazily drifted across the sun, nor any one flower suddenly wilted on its vine, nor any one bird call to the night, nor any distant mountain suddenly turned purple within sweeping misty haze…

It *was* the change of the ocean waves that told Jeffrey Hyves and his Irish terrier Kamehameha that it was time to leave. The pale-blue seawater simply humped too imperfectly on the shore. The wet curls might be bigger than they had been throughout the course of the summer, but each collapsed its total length at once now, with a loud splash rather than merely folded first on edge to roll shut like a zipper in one gradual, continual, final…

…Whooooooooosh!

146. *Thai Died: A Stud Draqual Mystery*, by William Maltese

San Francisco, CA: Green Candy Press, 2003, 172 pages, ISBN 1-931160-13-9, $14.95, trade paperback.

A sequel to *A Slip to Die For* (#141).

THE WHOLE WORLD BURNED AROUND ME!

What little breathing I managed became even more of a chore as billowing smoke grew thicker. I leaned exhausted against hot stone, part of a large seated Buddha that was mostly lost to the murk and the gloom. I turned head-on into a smoky breeze that reached me over a limestone Hari-Hari whose two left arms, one hand holding a seashell, laid broken at the figure's feet. I stumbled forward, past a terra-cotta deer whose folded legs gave it the collapsed appearance of a poor animal already succumbed to asphyxia.

Escape for me, if it existed, remained hidden within a river of smoke that grew thicker by the second. I surrendered to whatever my remaining survival instincts, held my breath, and plunged forward. Desperately, I tried to see through the smoke, through the soot, through the ash, and through the heat-distorted air. I hadn't a clue how long I could hold my breath, or how long I could keep going. My legs had about carried me to the limits of their and my endurance.

* * * * * * *

Whoever slit Rhee Dulouk's throat should never have let the victim, second mouth still bubbling blood, reach Jeff Billing. Billing would have been gone in another day … or two … or three. As he'd left the Philippines, Borneo, Bali. As he'd left Australia, Cambodia, Burma. As he'd left Spain, France, Germany.

For Billing, Thailand was just another stopover on the way to… he never knew where…just somewhere.

Rhee Dulouk wasn't a particularly great lay. He wasn't even Billing's type. He was just another wham-bam-thank-you-man someone. One of many. A diversion. An exotic. Another notch on Billing's belt. One more fuck in Billing's ongoing fuck of the world.

A keeper, beyond the first fuck, only because of a bit of pillow-talk that interested Billing, who knew a little something about Far-East antiquities. But not likely to keep Billing's interests for long.

Therefore, Rhee Dulouk dead on someone else's doorstep would have been one thing. After all, there had been plenty of other bodies in Billing's life...in the deserts of the Gulf, in the mountains of Iraq, in the back alleys of Afghanistan. Bodies left behind. Throwaways. Job-product.

Rhee Dulouk dead on Billing's doorstep, though...somehow... made the death personal. Not only to Billing but to me.

Thought I sure as hell didn't know it at the time.

147. *A Conspiracy of Ravens: A One-Hand Read®*, by William Maltese

Lincoln, NE: iUniverse, Inc., 2003, 79 pages, ISBN 0-595-29162-7, $9.95, trade paperback.

THE FOG SWIRLED AROUND HIS FEET

He stopped, his ears pricking like those of an animal. He listened. God only knew for what he listened. He thought he heard distant footsteps, water dripping, the hoot of an owl. Part of it, all of it, merely imagined? He tried to shake his growing dread. It was ridiculous to let his imagination get the best of him. He had to get a grip on himself.

He started walking again. His footsteps echoed on the flagstone. The fog parted for a second in the distance. Brian saw the section of fortress wall were Tad lived. It was dark.

* * * * * * *

Patrick Mulligan's hand, with red-hair knuckles, pulled a handful of loose outer flesh down around the more solid inner core of Ian Riley's cock. He couldn't help wondering what they would say back in the States if they could see him naked and playing with another man's healthy dick. His mother would have cried, his father would have been boiling mad, and his closest friends would have suddenly begun seeing him as something less than a man. Even his grandmother, whose savings had been responsible for sending him to school in Ireland, wouldn't have understood. She had expected, indeed hoped sincerely, that exposing her *green-eyed, red-hair, little darling* to his roots would make him a different man, but her definition of *different* did not go so far as to encompass homosexuality.

Homosexual sex was the last thing that Patrick expected to encounter in Londonderry. Even when he began to learn that his new mates looked upon male sex with a good deal more acceptance than did Patrick's family and friends back home in Middle America, he never dreamed that within a few months of his arrival in Ireland he would be rooming with an openly gay Irishman he could admit to loving.

Ian stirred in his sleep, his leg and chest muscles elongating in a stretch that didn't disturb his erotic dreaming. Had he known what Patrick was thinking, he would have been amused. Ian had been aware of his own personal sexual preference for men since shortly after exploding into puberty. Not only had he recognized his particular passions, but also he had straight away set out to satiate them. He'd quickly found more than his share of those willing to assist him. Even at an early age, he hadn't looked young. He'd always had the butch, dark-complexion, square-jaw, cleft-chin good looks and stocky build that made anyone who picked him up confident he was someone above the age of consent, even when he had been significantly underage.

148. *circuSex: A One-Hand Read*®, by William Maltese

Lincoln, NE: iUniverse, Inc., 2004, 97 pages, ISBN 0-595-31761-8, $10.95, trade paperback.

148A. Reprinted: Albion, NY: MLR Press, 2010, __ pages, ISBN, $, trade paperback.

I STILL HAD TROUBLE
BELIEVING THAT I SAW WHAT I SAW

The one wall of the shower stall that faced me, from across the room and slightly down the hall, was opaque. Once Darrel was latched inside, washed down with water, he continually pressed segments of his wet body against the inside glass. Each time he did so, whatever tattoos were inked on those segments of his wet skin miraculously appeared, only vaguely distorted, through the glass on my side. It was as if I viewed a heavily misted jungle, gusts of wind constantly blowing away bits of the mist to unveil an exotic flower here, a succulent plant there, a monkey, a peccary, a parrot, a large-winged butterfly. When Darrel pressed his ass hard against the glass, and provided for my viewing pleasure the head of the jaguar that was tattooed, whiskers and all, on the canvas provided by both of Darrel's firm buttcheeks, my cock leaked a genuine flood of pre-seminal goo in appreciation.

His anaconda of green-and-black indelible inks was a genuine sight to behold. It anchored its tail over the instep of his right foot, curled its thickly sensuous body counterclockwise around his right leg, up and over his right hip, onto his stomach and into a narrow oxbow up and over his knotted navel, before it flowed straight down to his shaved crotch, and narrowed only slightly as it blossomed three-dimensional along the thick neck of his cock (snakehead and cockhead one and the same).

* * * * * * *

MR. NOT-SO-SMALL

"MY NAME IS MR. SMALL," Jeremy said.

There were chuckles from those of us who had been there be-fore and knew what was coming. There were a few downright laughs from the newcomers who thought his name a gimmick, come after the fact.

In actuality, the dwarf's name was Mr. Small. Mr. Jeremy Small.

And this is Mr. No-So-Small," Jeremy said and opened wide the front of his robe to flash his gasp-producing erection which had to be seen to be believed. Even seeing it didn't truly convince, because it was not only unimaginable in size but precariously sprouted from the few red hairs at the crotch of someone who stood only a mere three-feet on tiptoes.

"Every time I see his cock, and I've seen it plenty of times, I don't believe it," Robert Six (my boss, Jeremy's boss, and owner of Circus Six), whispered to no one in particular; I knew *just* what he meant.

149. *Slovakian Boy*, by William Maltese

San Francisco, CA: Green Candy Press, 2004, 177 pages, ISBN 1-931160-30-9, $14.95, trade paperback.

WILLIE

Brat. Slovak for brother.

Although the word I want is the one that best describes my one-hundred-percent Slovak *brat*'s one-hundred percent Slovak cock.

Big-dick big *brat*? Nah! Not that Pavel's prick is small. It's just right. *Just right* two words.

You want big dick, there's mine. My pecker you can't believe. It's long. It's fat. I'm hardly able to get my hand around it. My cockhead would choke a horse before the rest of my prick slid inside.

Nice would work to describe Pavel's dick. *Tasty* would work, too.

Uncut for sure. When his dick is soft, his foreskin is an attractive snout that reminds me of one of the *Demänovská* caves. Not one of those linked by underground lakes and waterfalls; one of the smaller caves, with its almost invisible entrance. Once squeezed into, it gets a bit wider but not much. Suddenly, there's this boulder completely blocking the way. That boulder reminds me of Pavel's cockhead locked within its cave-like foreskin. Pavel could describe the cave better. Pavel could even tell you how it was formed. Pavel's a spelunker. He genuinely likes that sort of thing. Caves, especially the *Demänovská* caves, make *me* feel closed in.

150. *Bond-Shattering*, by William Maltese

Kingman, AZ: Nightwares Books LLC, 2005, 243 pages, ISBN 1-931160-13-9, $16.99, trade paperback.

150A. Reprinted: Albion, NY: MLR Press, 2007, 176 pages, ISBN 978-1-934531-34-1, $15.99, trade paperback

ON PLANET JIRAT, DEATH IS ON THE PROWL...

Roynoldo tried to recall the first part of the nightmare, the part that brought him to this point. He couldn't remember anything but that it had been especially nasty. The taste of that nastiness refused to leave him, even as the darkness refused to go.

He was in a room with no windows, and everything that surrounded the bed was lost in deep shadow. The shadow completely concealed whomever or whatever was in the room with him.

* * * * * * *

AND MEDEEK LOOKED DOWN upon all He had created. And, lo, He observed that Adar was lonely and yearned for the companionship of his own kind. And Medeek took pity upon Adar and provided him Biolab-1, saying: "Scientif and multiply!"

—excerpted, page 2, Chapter One ("Life from the Void"), THE GREAT BOOK; loca date banks Clan Julius Archives, WARXII.

SYCRAIAN MELAT-ADVISER BANEUS THO had witnessed nature's equivalent to this man-made disaster. He'd been on the slopes of High-Mountainclimb, at the time; when across the valley, one small crystal of fall from the sky ice touched down, mingled with dormant of its kind, and began to move the lot. Soon a small, moving ball, to gather more mass. Then, an all consuming roar that sucked up, pasted on, and devoured all, including one small village. Nothing recognizable in its wake, as if ice had become permanent eraser.

Here, *now,* on this scene, if presently off center-stage, was Thuam Moore, of deposed planet Hylan royalty, emigrant to planet Sycra, become catalytic ice crystal of his own. The product not only of the unchecked passions of Sycraian Melat Gaylan West for Thuam, but the duo's involvement in the disastrous plan to capture planet Hylan's City Hideo Max and put Thuam back on the Hylanian throne. Resulting in the kidnapping by the Hylanian ruler, Quin Xu, of Gaylan's Warrior Clan bond-mate Dovio Lix; too, threats made the latter having become a burr to anger the Warrior Universe with whom Baneus had so diligently sought to open a viable channel.

So far culminating with this: an incoming message. The message's unknown content every reason to make Sycraian Melat Gaylan West and Sycraian Melat Adviser Baneus Tho anxious. For, if it bore good news for Gaylan, something might yet be salvaged from the input of the power hungry bastard Thuam Moore. For, if it bore bad news, more disaster was risked than the mere erasure of some small village in a High-Mountainclimb valley.

151. *Beyond Machu,* by William Maltese

Binghamton, NY: Southern Tier Editions, Harrington Park Press, 2006, 206 pages, ISBN 978-0-73946-825-8 and ISBN 978-1-56023-568-2, $17.95? and $14.99, hardcover and trade paperback.

151A. Reprinted: Albion, NY: MLR Press, 2008, 221 pages, ISBN 978-1-934531-68-6, $14.99, trade paperback

DAN GREEN didn't know the man who sat down to join him at the restaurant table. In case his expression didn't sufficiently denote that fact, he quickly reinforced it verbally. "I beg your pardon?" His forkful of *cebiche de corvina* was interrupted halfway to his attractively pouted mouth.

"I'm sorry I'm late." As if this guy, with an accent Dan couldn't place, had known Dan for all of Dan's twenty-five years.

Dan felt suddenly as if he were a character in a low-budget film. The locale was certainly exotic enough.

"I see you've gone ahead and ordered the fish." The stranger flashed a wide smile. His lips were sensuously full and revealed a wide expanse of large white teeth. Not only did the locale suggest some B-grade movie, but the man seemed to fit the bill, too. He had the rugged good looks that one would attribute to an actor still quite handsome but past the allure of youth.

Dan looked curiously around the room, wondering if he was unknowingly appear on that popular old television rerun *Candid Camera* but doubting that its crew would be sent all of the way to Lima, Peru.

152. *The Gomorrha Conjurations*, by William Maltese

Rockville, MD: The Borgo Press, an Imprint of Wildside Press, 2007, 164 pages, ISBN 0-8095-0126-0, $14.95, trade paperback.

II PETER 2:6
And turning the cities of Sodom and Gomorrha into ashes condemned them with an overthrow, making them an example...

INTERLUDE 1

THE WIRE LOOP PENETRATED like a knife through warm butter. There was a whoosh of air prematurely released from human windpipe. Short fingernails clawed briefly but frantically at the slicked sliced throat and left bloody smear marks.

It was the second time Dr. Tye Winslow had killed that evening. Along with his first body, he had left chunks of his own partially digested vomit. This time had been easier. Still, he didn't look at his second victim's blood-drooling nose and mouth, death-bulged eyes, or bloody neck. He hurried into the darkness, followed by the nauseating stench of the dead man's uncontrolled release of bladder and bowel.

153. *Ardennian Boy*, by William Maltese and Wayne Gunn

Albion, NY: MLR Press, 2007, 224 pages, ISBN 978-0-9793110-3-1, $14.99, hardcover and trade paperback.

PAUL
Paris: 15 March 1887

THIS ASS I FUCK dog-style on this filthy bed of this seedy Paris hotel room is tight and will coax my sticking dick to ejaculation, but it isn't Arthur's tight asshole. This kid may have a thick and unruly head of auburn hair, a slender body streaked and multi-layered with days of dirt and grime, but the thickness of his hair isn't the right thickness, its color isn't the right shade of chestnut; his dirtiness isn't layered and grimy enough.

His breath doesn't smell of absinthe. His eyes aren't the hauntingly strange blue of Arthur's eyes. This young male whore resembles Arthur Rimbaud about as much as does the Caravaggio-like boy-whore depicted in Fantin-Latour's *Corner of the Table*; neither painted canvas *nor fucked-by-me-in-real-life* hustler is anything but a caricature of the real thing.

154. *Heart on Fire: A Romance*, **by William Maltese writing as "Willa Lambert"**

Rockville, MD: The Borgo Press, an Imprint of Wildside Press, 2007, 148 pages, ISBN 1-4344-0027-1, $14.95, trade paperback.

"I DO WISH YOU'D RECONSIDER this Mt. St. Helens business," Grace Woof said to her daughter. "Who knows when it'll explode again? You? The scientists who didn't have a clue the first time?"

"They're monitoring the mountain more closely, these days," Janine argued, for not the first time. "I'll be fine. Besides, I need something to keep me occupied until Marine World gets refurbished after the fire. You want me hanging around here, all of the time, and making a nuisance of myself?"

Grace shook her head at the ridiculous suggestion that her daughter would ever be a nuisance. "You know we'd love to see more of you."

155. *SS & M: Being Excerpts from the Nazi Death-Head Files*, by William Maltese

Rockville, MD: The Borgo Press, an Imprint of Wildside Press, 2007, 148 pages, ISBN 1-4344-0024-7, $14.99, trade paperback.

"YOU ARE NOTHING MORE THAN a piece of meat," Colonel Saber said, pacing in front of what was once a pretty young woman. "Actually, you are less even than meat. Meat can at least be eaten; not even a Jew would eat fellow pig, would he?"

His words barely penetrated to Marta's brain. There'd been so much pain, so very much, that the shrieking hum of it still remained to the distraction of everything else. It played loudly against her one punctured eardrum. It pulsed throughout her body like a second heartbeat.

Colonel Saber moved Marta's head with the tip of his highly polished black boot. In a way, it was a shame that she'd been so difficult. She had, after all, been a very attractive member of her sub-human species. She could have had a few more months left to live in one of the special prostitution establishments staffed by non-Aryans. And, not even Saber had anything against a German fucking a Jew. That was certainly no different than fucking a dog: something done by at least one member of Hitler's High Command.

156. *Anal Cousins: Case Studies in Variant Sexual Practices*, by William Maltese

Rockville, MD: The Borgo Press, an Imprint of Wildside Press, 2007, 167 pages, ISBN 1-4344-0039-5, $15.99, trade paperback.

A book of supposedly nonfiction case studies.

"I JUST ABOUT HAD my cock on target at the opening of her snatch when she slapped my pecker away; damn, did that sting.

"'Wait a minute, boy,' she said. She was calling *me* boy. That made me so goddamned mad. She was younger than I was and was treating me like a fucking child. Truth of the matter, as regards sex, she probably *was* a lot more knowledgeable about it than I, even now, am.'

"'What do you mean, *wait*?'"

157. *The Fag Is Not for Burning: A Mystery Novel*, by William Maltese

Rockville, MD: The Borgo Press, an Imprint of Wildside Press, 2007, 250 pages, ISBN 978-1-4344-0074-1, $14.95, trade paperback.

MORGAN

"WAS I SURPRISED?" Morgan G. Kent asked, rephrasing Detective Cord Maxwell's question and pouring himself the drink the policeman declined. The *Chevas Regal* formed an immediate stripe of pale amber that glistened through the refracting lead crystal of the tumbler. Morgan drank the booze English-warm while Lake Union dock lights and attending flotilla offered him and his Seattle penthouse a dazzling backdrop through two-story-high picture windows. "As early as two years ago, an acquaintance of mine commented that Horton Lendland would undoubtedly die violently. I was possibly surprised by the suggestion, but probably not."

"This acquaintance?" Cord asked, looking up from his notebook and its seemingly illegible scrawl. He wrote only to look official in the presence of someone he found unacceptably disconcerting. It was more than Morgan being gay. If Morgan *were* gay. Cord was unable to find anyone to verify that on a first-hand basis, although the handsome and successful writer was always mentioned in any *who's-who-within–the-gay–community* conversations.

"I'm reluctant to give you a name," Morgan said with a wide smile that dimpled his cheeks; those attractive concaves perfectly offset the small cleft couched in his chin, "because his comment was one anyone might have deduced from the evidence. By now, even you must have enough of an overview of Horton Lendland's lifestyle to be less than shocked by his manner of dying."

158. *Gerun, the Heretic: Being Excerpts from the Clan-Missionary Chronicles: A Science Fiction Novel,* by William Maltese

Rockville, MD: The Borgo Press, an Imprint of Wildside Press, 2007, 171 pages, ISBN 978-1-4344-0058-1, $13.95, trade paperback.

Panrun-ru: Incinerate the book! For it contains heresy.

Maxlima II: Should not we first run it though complete analysis?

Panrun-Ru: We have run it through all the analysis that need be. I repeat, the contents are heretical.

159. *Goldsands*, by William Maltese

Albion, NY: MLR Press, 2007, 298 pages, ISBN 978-1-934531-04-4, $16.99, trade paperback.

They were as different as sun and moon...Gil Goldsands believed he could handle any complications that might arise on his archaeological assignment in Egypt. But he hadn't anticipated the two dynamic men who would pursue him from the moment he arrived. Powerful Sheikh Abdul Jerada—darkly handsome, openly passionate—clearly wanting Sand's [sic]. Peter Donas—elusive and as seductive as the desert; his kisses and touch as fiery and consuming as the hot Saharan sun—wanting? Goldsands wasn't quite sure.

* * * * * * *

"THE BENNU," the man said, referring to the hieroglyph of a heron with two long feathers growing from the back of its head. He'd quietly joined Gil Goldsands in the small alcove on the first floor of the Egyptian Museum in Cairo. Gil was facing forward, at the time, toward a sandstone relief that had been saved from the area around Abu Simbel when the Nile had been backed up behind the multimillion-dollar *Saad al-Ali*—the Aswân High Dam.

Gil was surprised by his sudden company. The museum was kitty-corner from the Nile Hilton and, therefore, quite accessible to tourists, but most visitors usually kept to the more impressive Tutankhamen exhibit located on the second floor. Gil was saving that until last, rather like saving a fine dessert to be savored after a thoroughly enjoyable and deliciously filling meal.

At first, Gil assumed he'd been joined by a tourist—the man spoke perfect English, albeit with a thoroughly enchanting accent that was more British than American. Gil should have been forewarned by the way the guy was able to identify a key figure in hieroglyphic script. Gil knew very few people, besides his colleagues in the archaeological profession, who were so thoroughly versed. "Yes," Gil said, turning, quite prepared to further define the heron character and prove Gil's own more-than-just-a-modicum knowledge of Egyptology. Despite being handicapped by the long-complained-about-like dimness, for which the Egyptian Museum was notorious, Gil realized immediately that it was Peter Donas beside him.

160. *Blood-Red Resolution: Being Excerpts from the Crypto-Coded Files of the United Courier Service: A Novel of Adventure*, **by William Maltese**

Rockville, MD: The Borgo Press, an Imprint of Wildside Press, 2007, 179 pages, ISBN 978-1-4344-0098-7, $14.99, trade paperback.

PROLOGUE

IT WAS TWELVE-TEN A.M., and Dayklan Incorporated's newly-launched *Spaceborn Imagining Satellite (SIS)* rose over the eastern horizon. What its electronic payload was programmed to see, record, and relay, it saw, recorded, and relayed, despite the fog at ground level.

Unluckily, for those scientists monitoring on the planet's surface, the competition's SIS had made this very same pass sixteen months before, which meant The Mentlic Group had already mapped, and acted upon, whatever the mineral resources as detected, color-coded, and spewed out on read-outs from the banks of computer link-ups below.

* * * * * * *

DANE WILCOX SET HIS TRAVEL CLOCK for a one-thirty A.M. alarm, and he dozed until seconds before the buzzer went off.

At the Machu Picchu hotel sink, he splashed his face with water that he wouldn't drink on a bet. He paid little notice to his mirror-reflected black hair, black eyes, dimpled cheeks, and cleft chin, which all came together in a rugged boyishness that belied his thirty-two years. He was no more immune than the next guy to the good-looks of other people, but he'd always considered his own physical attractiveness a superficiality.

161. *Love Hurts*, by William Maltese

Albion, NY: MLR Press, 2007, 232 pages, ISBN 978-1-934531-12-9, $16.99, trade paperback. The front cover illustration features a photograph of the author.

A short story collection. Contents: "Doppelmörder," "Hand-Picked," "Closet Case," "Lars of the Ring," "His Lord and Master," "Thou Shalt Not Covet Thy Neighbor's Torqring," "Trinity National Forest," "Anasazi Medicine Bag," "Universal City," "Lake Tahoe," "Los Angeles," "Catalyst," "Phantom Beach," "Zanzibar," "Mt. Shasta," and "Pæan to Pain."

DOPPELMÖRDER

i.

I DON'T KILL QUEERS because they're queer. I don't kill them out of any misconceived notion that in killing their gayness I eliminate my own. I kill them, because it's my calling to send to another plane certain human beings whose time has simply come. Their being queer and my being queer merely make it easier for them to be found and for me to find them.

I mean, look. I enjoy being a queer. Take this butt-fucking I'm receiving, right here and now, in the backroom of San Francisco's latest "in" gay night spot, Danny-Dean's Cowboy Bar. I'm having more than a good time. I'm having a really great rootin'-tootin' good time.

The cock up my ass has a marvelously bulbous head. It has this turn-on way of bumping into and over my prostate to get me really hot. If I'm not as excited as I would be on the receiving end of a special someone's cock—no matter its size or shape—this will do until one of those comes along. There's enough pleasure found among these run-of-the-mill dicks to hold me over. In a way, it's good the unique ones are so few and far between, because the intensity of ecstasy I feel when poked by one of them is...well...I'm not sure it's something even I (good with words as I so obviously am), can adequately express. If you're interested, though, in a more mundane but still enjoyable butt-fuck in progress, I can certainly give you a good enough account of this one.

162. *The Moonstone Murders: The Movie Script*, by **William Maltese**

Rockville, MD: The Borgo Press, an Imprint of Wildside Press, 2007, 139 pages, ISBN 978-0-941028-93-6, $13.95, trade paperback.

INTRODUCTION

This book comes to you for several reasons.

Firstly, my agent requested that I do an m/m movie script so that he could "shop" it around; more specifically, the runaway success of *Brokeback Mountain* had suddenly put "gay" movies in vogue. He had also received feelers from a producer of mainly gay porn who was looking to upgrade his company and his products' image by possibly putting into production something a little more mainstream and less in-your-face (pun intended) than his usual fare.

Shortly after I'd completed the script and passed it onto my agent, and my agent had sent it to the production company, my agent passed away. By the time the producer got back to me with his request to "possibly work with him" in getting the script "just right," I'd lost interest, having already moved on to other things.

Secondly, I recently came across the script in a drawer and, reading it over after having not seen it for awhile, I realized how the format made it far easier and faster to read than a standard novel. I had this confirmed by handing it over to a friend of mine who exhibits all of the typical tendencies of the "today" generation: he has a rather short attention span, he would rather play a computer game than read a book, and if and when he does read anything, besides game instructions, it tends to be comic books....

* * * * * * *

FADE IN:

PARIS, FRANCE
INT TOWN HOUSE
LANDON JORDAN AT 14 reads a letter from his father as

CLARK MOIRE, 14, joins him.

CLARK
Something from your father? More scrimshaw?

Clark looks at the two small stones from Landon's father that Landon shows him.

CLARK
Oh. Not more scrimshaw.

LANDON AT 14
Impressed?

CLARK
Rocks. Two.

Landon holds one small stone to his ear.

LANDON AT 14
Earring?

Landon moves the stone to the middle of his chest.

LANDON AT 14
Necklace?

CLARK
Your father must know you have all the rocks you need—in your head.

163. *Catalytic Quotes: (Some Heard Through a Time Warp): One Music- History- Literary- and Trivia-Buff's Pure Conjecture on the Seemingly Sometimes Idiosyncratic Transmigration of the Creative Muse,* **by William Maltese**

Rockville, MD: The Borgo Press, an Imprint of Wildside Press, 2008, 181 pages, ISBN 978-1-4344-7395-0, $12.99, trade paperback.

HANK AARON to WILLIAM GOLDING:
"Yep. Me. The Lord of the Flies."

HANK AARON to ELVIS PRESLEY:
"You've got to learn to *swing* from the hip."

LEON ABBOT to ETHEL MERMAN:
"We're looking for a few good people to work on the stage."

THE ABDOMINABLE SNOWMAN to DOCTOR PHIBES:
"I'm abominable?! You're the one who's abominable!"

ACE to JOHN HOLMES:
"How long?"

ADAM to FOUR TOPS:
"I was always telling Eve— 'Ain't no woman like the one I've got.'"

164. *Sucks!: Book #1 of the Draqual Vampyre Chronicles*, by William Maltese

Albion, NY: MLR Press, 2008, 200 pages, ISBN 978-1-934531-32-7, $15.99, trade paperback.

URUK
2400 B.C.

AND NIMROK DRAQUAL of Bal-Derah, until recently a farmer of cotton, does—finally!—fuck his handsome cousin Kalil Draqual of Uruk, who is a weaver; Nimrok having wanted incestuously to fuck this particular tight-ass relative (and, by An, The god of Heaven, Kalil's rectum *is* vise-like), for the whole of the preceding evening and night.

That it has taken Nimrok this long to get his thank-An still-hard cock up Kalil's asshole—only after the feasting on innocents, all that blood sucked dry, has turned into the feeding frenzy of vampire feeding upon vampire, Draqual feeding upon Draqual, each and every six participating family Draqual members turned blood-glut languid and listless by excess—is because Kalil, so stunningly handsome with his abundance of curly dark-black hair, hairy muscled body, horse-like cock, and bull-like balls, and firm cock-hardening ass, has been in much demand, as top man and bottom; Nimrok, so recently recruited from the less-civilized countryside, is exceedingly low as regards the family hierarchy, and has not dared make his move until now, having not previously been paid much mind by Kalil who has obviously preferred encounters with the more sexually experienced members of the family sextet than with his country-bumpkin cousin.

"Yes…yes…yes," Nimrok complements himself on having endured the wait, managed the crawl across the floor, achieved the lifting of Kalil's legs, put cockhead to the small hair-parenthesized mouth of Kalil's hairy asshole, plunged cock deeply into funky corridor made surprisingly none the less tight by the cocks and the cum that have preceded.

165. *Tusks*, by William Maltese

Albion, NY: MLR Press, 2008, 276 pages, ISBN 978-0-9793110-8-6, $14.99, trade paperback.

RICHARD HAD BEEN PREPARED to hate this handsome man whose touch sent uncontrollable sensations racing along his spine, whose low and melodious voice brought back memories of his childhood before it went sour.

"Welcome to Lionspride," Christopher said, and smiled. He didn't recognize Richard. Richard didn't expect he would. They weren't children now, and Richard's professional by-line was Richard *Westover*, not Richard Kelley.

Christopher's teeth were brilliantly white in contrast to a tan burnished deeply bronze by the South African sun. His golden eyes were black-flecked. He didn't look like his father, Vincent. He never had. He took after his mother's side of the family. Richard didn't remember Gretchen Van Hoon, but he remembered Christopher's father very well. There was no forgetting or forgiving him.

166. *Snakes*, by William Maltese

Albion, NY: MLR Press, 2008, 203 pages, ISBN 978-1-934531-19-8, $14.99, trade paperback.

IAN MYLOR PLACED the last inch of his very impressive dick into the slot provided by Leith Talbot's asshole and grunted appreciation for the well-remembered tightness found there. If anything could convince him that his sex, the previous evening, with Gerald Sims wasn't quite as extraordinary as he'd come to imagine it had been, it was re-familiarization with Leith's experienced and talented man-pussy.

"Oh, sweet Jesus, so good!" Ian congratulated on having found this way to steer himself clear of his helpless-to-counteract initial inclination to head on off to sample even more of the sweet sex Gerald might offer. The last thing Ian needed, at this moment in his life, was involvement with Gerald, whom Ian suspected was trouble, pure and simple.

More often than not, Ian had come to look upon Gerald as competition in their mutually shared field of expertise. Ian had commented upon it more than once—a couple of times to Gerald's face. Not only was Gerald often mysteriously on the scene wherever and whenever Ian set up shop, but he had the infuriating habit of being forever involved in research projects suspiciously parallel to Ian's: seaweed palytoxins on Maui, stone-fish palytoxins on Jamaica, tiger-snake proteins in Australia. If Gerald had, likewise, been competition for the few available research grants in those areas, Ian would have *really* resented Gerald focusing in on *Ian's territory*. As it was, while on the subject, Ian couldn't help but be a little jealous that Gerald's seemingly inexhaustible funds, from three trusts funds, left him immune from the money-grubbing and back-stabbing politicking required of most of his peers, Ian included. As much as Ian had always tried to stay out of the rat race that attended most scientific research, it was hard for him to do since he, unlike Gerald, wasn't independently wealthy.

167. *Wet Skin: Wild & Wet First-Time Stories*, by Laura Baumbach and William Maltese

Albion, NY: MLR Press, 2009, 200 pages, ISBN 978-1-9793110-9-3, $13.99, trade paperback.

Contents: "The Cataracts, Part One" and "The Cataracts, Part Two," by William Maltese; "Slippery When Wet," "The Drive Home," "Wet Sheets," "Wet Dreams," and "South of the Border," by Laura Baumbach.

THE CATARACTS
by William Maltese

This isn't the first time I've run.

At age fourteen, when my mother died of cancer, I ran. Oh, I didn't get far. I didn't have the money at my disposal, then, like now, to hop a plane to South America. Instead, I filled a paper bag with food from the kitchen and fled into the woods behind the house. My father found me, of course.

"Running never solves anything," he said.

He was always able to cope. Coping is something with which I sometimes have a problem. Maybe it was because my father or those people he hired—my father seldom around—were so good at coping for me.

Well, suddenly my father is dead, and there's no one to help me adequately cope with that.

"Oh, Harold tries, but my being courted by an older man who is also the head of the modeling agency with which I'm signed, isn't what I'm looking for. Even if I have, for years, been contemplating sex with "some" man—thinking there has to be more than what I experience with my dick ejaculating up seemingly always available pussy; being assured by more than one of my fellow models, gay, in the fashion business that that *is* the case. Harold certainly isn't all that bad to look at and has never made any bones (although he has made plenty boners) about his wanting to be my first.

I am, in a way, then, suddenly running from Harold, too. He seemed genuinely hurt when I told him I was going off alone and didn't want him along for the ride.

"I'm a big boy," I said, feeling anything but my twenty-one years. "I can certainly take care of myself for a couple of weeks. Besides, it isn't as if it's all pleasure."

"But South America?" Harold moaned. "Couldn't you go somewhere a bit closer?"

168. *Ride the Man Down: #1 in the New World Shaman Series*, by William Maltese

Albion, NY: MLR Press, 2009, 193 pages, ISBN 978-1-60820-030-6, $14.99, trade paperback.

BRENDON AND EDUARDO

"Damn, but I love your funky young cowboy ass," Brendon Ridgemont said to Eduardo Rivera.

The two teenagers were stark naked. Eduardo's head rested on his forearms that rested atop a fence railing. Brendon squatted behind; his tongue provided another long and leisurely lap from the rear hang of Eduardo's hairy scrotum to the small of the young Latino's back.

Nearby, just to one side of a large boulder, two horses, reins dragging the ground, munched what none-too-succulent scrub was immediately available.

"And I love your big cowboy cock, too." Brendon's right hand reached around and took hold of Eduardo's impressively stiff dick to provide a couple of quick but firm up-and-down strokes. "Or, are you tired of hearing how much your body turns me on?"

"Since I so love your studly body, it's always nice to hear that mine is loved in return," Eduardo said. His ass provided a small circular movement that rubbed its firm cheeks against Brendon's face. All the while, Brendon's tongue flicked, like a frog catching flies, and left dabs of accumulated shiny spit at the puckered entrance of Eduardo's tight-tight little asshole.

169. *Murder by Meteorite: A Play in Three Acts*, **by William Maltese**

Rockville, MD: The Borgo Press, an Imprint of Wildside Press, 2009, 142 pages, ISBN 978-1-4344-5703-5, $13.99, trade paperback.

MELISSA JORDAN: After five days unconscious, I continue to sleep at the drop of a hat. John says, "There's sleep, then there's sleep." Of course, Christian was discharged two days ago.

(to Kevin) Kevin, I'll understand if you want to cut your visit short.

KEVIN SILNER: (not sounding fine) I'm fine.

MELISSA: John says when the body is subjected to too much stress, the brain overloads and shuts down. Self-repair can take hours, days, sometimes even…. (she shrugs)

170. *Total Meltdown: A Tripler and Clarke Adventure*, by Raymond Gaynor and William Maltese

Rockville, MD: The Borgo Press, an Imprint of Wildside Press, 2009, 162 pages, ISBN 978-1-4344-0355-1, $14.99, trade paperback.

Anne Elizabeth Jackson, wife of President-Elect Alexander Mathias Jackson, stood only five-foot four-inches in her bare feet. She had waist-length jet black hair, slightly slanted eyes, button-nose, soft thin lips, and a fashionably slim figure; she had been deemed by the media as "a classic oriental beauty." The single child of Kokoro Narumi and Hawaii-based Pacific shipping magnate Samuel Bryant Johnston, she was born on Hawaii but was mainland-educated at The Masters in Dobbs Ferry, New York and, then, at Harvard where she'd met Alexander and they'd fallen in love. Presently she was on the faculty of the Radcliffe Institute, her recent celebrity status having projected her onto the world stage at exactly the time she was ready to make her debut. Quietly, incisively, supportively standing beside her husband and soon-to-be sworn-in President of the United States of America, it was Anne's vision that her husband and she would, together, reshape the world and make it a better place. Except that, as she stepped out of the hotel room's bathroom shower and reached for the Turkish towel her husband was extending toward her, she still had a recently realized sneaking suspicion that something was seriously amiss.

Six-foot-six, 185 pounds, well-built—muscular even under the tapered cut of his conservative grey suit—and with black hair, Jackson presented a powerful presence. His eyes, though naturally hazel, habitually reflected the color of whatever he was wearing—one of the many traits his media team had used to advantage. Right now, his eyes looked deep grey and worried. Rather than being elated by the recent incoming phone call of concession by his defeated opponent, President Harold Gallen Brown, he had hung up looking decidedly somber and frustratingly reluctant to confide the reason why. Whatever it was that was bothering him, however, he would need Anne's support and she was ready and willing to give it, in whatever manner she could, even before he gave her the specifics that would eventually be hers if she only waited patiently.

Finished with the towel, she let it slip to the floor between them, leaving her completely naked. Since her husband, to her chagrin, was too momentarily lost in thought to take her in his arms, she opened his arms for him and stepped in between, pushing her small breasts up so tightly against him that he had to feel her hard nipples even through the shirt he was wearing.

171. *The Gluten-Free Way: My Way*, by Adrienne Z. Milligan and William Maltese

Rockville, MD: The Borgo Press, an Imprint of Wildside Press, 2009, 167 pages, ISBN 978-1-4344-5719-6, $14.99, trade paperback.

This book is primarily written from the first-person perspective of my niece, Adrienne Z. Milligan, because it's mainly the ongoing story of her concentrated efforts to find the cause of, and instigate the elimination of, the initially mysterious source of health problems that were visited upon her family.

For many years, I existed on the sidelines, merely watching and being impressed by her efforts to cope, discover the culprit (gluten), and convert her family into living a completely Gluten-Free Way. In the end, of course, as a long-time published author, I couldn't help but recognize the obvious value her experiences might have for others who face similar health problems and seemingly insurmountable dietary roadblocks, sometimes without even a clue. With that incentive in mind, I approached my niece about the possibility for this collaborative effort.

Along the way, I have, of course, added my constant input, by way of hopefully stimulating, improving, and supplementing my co-author's narrative. Quite by way of marvelous side effect, I've seen my own health benefit tremendously from my participation and experimentation in the formulation, collection, and tasting of GF-Way information and recipes for this book.

172. *Dare to Love in Oz*, by William Maltese

Honolulu, HI: Savant Books, 2009, 399 pages, ISBN 978-0-9841175-4-3, $16.95, trade paperback.

"*Kenk-lum-ra!*" Gerald Simms pointed. His low voice promised the worst was over; his optimistic smile, that crinkled the edges of his velvety black eyes and deepened his already deep dimple, bolstered that promise.

Kenk-lum-ra was an actor-player in aborigine Dream Time. To Jane Mylor, disinclined to believe in mythical battles waged by half-men-half-monsters against half-men-half animals, *Kenk-lum-ra* was only a long-standing, very dead tree. If pressured, Jane might have conceded it simply a misnomer in an otherwise flat landscape without another tree, dead or alive, visible for miles. That the desiccated gum tree, bleached skeletal white by the never-kind elements of the Australian outback, hadn't been carted away, piecemeal, to fuel fire in a locale where firewood was rarer than gold, was supposedly proof-positive of its Dream-Time origins. Jane, on the other hand, suspected the tree's stick-figure existence, supported atop bone-dry earth by a root system as dead as the deadweight it supported, was more a case of no one, in his right mind, wanting to stop in such an inhospitable spot to roast marshmallows, or to camp-fire broil wieners.

Home base should be close enough to walk," Gerald offered; the Australian-blown dust had frosted his black hair with dull reddish highlights.

173. *I, Debauchee: Book #1 of the William Maltese "I" Series*, by William Maltese

Albion, NY: MLR Press, 2010, 208 pages, ISBN 978-0-60820-092-4, $14.99, trade paperback.

> Debauch:
>   … to seduce from chastity…to lead away from virtue…to corrupt by intemperance or sensuality… orgy…
> Debauchee
>   …one given to debauchery…
> Debauchery
>   …extreme indulgence in sensuality…orgies… seduction from virtue…

I fucked Mallory von Burel on the large four-poster bed…as I'd fucked him in the basement dark room where I'd chained him to a wall, shackled to a rack, where I'd manacled his arms, head, and legs to a stake…as I'd fucked him in the Main Room of the Lodge with its galleries of stuffed animal heads, so many of them with record-breaking horns, but none as horny as Mallory and I…as I'd fucked him in the manicured parkland, his back and ass cushioned by emerald-green sylvan moss….

He was on his knees, kow-towed so his ass was elevated, his arms wrapping a pillow, his right cheek against the bright orange of a Draqualian-silk sheet. The exquisite overall tan of his body, with the exception of where a small European-style bikini swim suit was worn during more than one sunning session, looked even more impressive against the colorful backdrop. The rest of our covers were thrown back so that I had full view of the exquisite handsomeness of the young man I butt-fucked. The line from his asscrack to the nape of his neck was parenthesized by an intricate interplay of muscle in movement as I pressed my cock deep inside of him, and, then, pulled free until only my cock's corona remained implanted inside the rubber-band moue that was his gumming sphincter.

I firmly gripped his hips, not only to steady him but to exert those slight pulls and pushes that first securely anchored his asshole over my dick, then, slid him almost free of it. Occasionally, my cock fully buried, I let go just long enough to put my handprints to his asscheeks in coordinated slaps that had a way of echoing loudly in the large bedroom.

174. *Africa: Spice Island Love: Book #1 of the Seven Continent Series*, by Willa Lambert

Albion, NY: Passion in Print Press, 2010, 192 pages, ISBN 978-0-60820-197-6, $14.99, trade paperback.

"Carolyne...I may call you Carolyne? And you must call me Field."

He was tall and distinguished; with a full head of frost-white hair combed straight back above his high forehead. His eyes were steely gray, his nose slightly off-center; his mouth had a full lower lip contrasted with an upper lip that seemed nonexistent. He was tanned a healthy brown that looked the result of real sunshine, not banks of tanning lights. He wore a white button-down collar shirt made whiter by his tawny complexion. His pencil-thin body was encased in a double-breasted, gray pinstripe suit of impeccable style and cut that proclaimed "bespoke," rather than "off-the-rack."

He was an impressive example of the male animal but would have seemed more so without the obvious comparison invited by the younger man's presence in the same room.

"Dirk Johnson, may I present Dr. Carolyne Mider who has agreed to join us on our little adventure."

"Actually, I've only agreed to listen to a more comprehensive proposal," Carolyne qualified.

"I stand corrected," Field diplomatically conceded. He looked noticeably pleased by the way Carolyne and Dirk shook hands. Could he possible read the electricity Carolyne immediately felt when her hand became lost, albeit for only seconds, within the grasp of Dirk's large fingers?

Dirk was someone Carolyne had never expected to see off the jackets of his popular books, or on [sic] TV screens (where he was a regular guest); he made potentially dull history palatable to the common reader. Such insinuated intelligence, along with his thick dark-brown hair, violet eyes, and rugged good looks, seemed way too good "a package" to be true.

175. *Back of the Boat Gourmet Cooking: Afloat—Poolside—Backyard*, by Bonnie Clark and William Maltese

Rockville, MD: The Borgo Press, an Imprint of Wildside Press, 2010, 186 pages, ISBN 978-1-4344-1154-9, $14.99, trade paperback.

WILLIAM—

As someone who was born and raised in the Pacific Northwest, a locale known for its preponderance of lakes and rivers...someone who's from an extended family that took its fishing damned seriously...and someone who has had the great pleasure, over the years, of having been on board ocean-going yachts and ships that boast extensive galleys and, even, extensive kitchen staffs...I've had a very long and very enjoyable exposure to the pleasures inherent in boating and the food available on board.

Early on in my life, fine dining on the water wasn't of first consideration—if, in fact, of any consideration at all—in that food consumption consisted mainly of chowing-down on whatever was conveniently packed (in paper-bag, lunchbox, or cooler) for an excursion. While this could mean any number of selections from the available menu of cold-cuts, cold fried chicken, cheese, potato salad, milk, even an apple, the closest any of this ever genuinely came to gourmet dining was on our return to the evening's campfire, or to the convenient cabin's kitchen, where the fresh catch of the day was converted into mouth-watering fried or grilled fish for much-enjoyed end-of-day feasting.

My university days saw me chumming with a crowd of young recreational boaters that could boast several watercraft, none larger than thirty feet, all with skippers and "crews" who had discovered pre-packaged meals were no longer nearly as "in" and/or as fashionable as the newly discovered wonders of freshly barbecued hot dogs and hamburgers, supplemented by crisp chips and ice-cold beer, all of which fit to a tee all of our college-boys' admittedly indiscernible palates.

176. *William Maltese's Flicker: #1 Book of Answers: First Book of the Flicker Series*, by **William Maltese**

Honolulu, HI: Savant Books, 2010, 320 pages, ISBN 978-0-9845552-4-6, $16.95, trade paperback.

AUTHOR'S NOTE

There is a long-held history in our family from a time, many years before I was born, when certain of us possessed the power of candle-reading divination, all of which faded at one and the same time Major Magic made its inexplicable exit from the world. Ever since, those of us, like me, have been relegated by friends and society to divining the future from the way steaming entrails of sacrificed animals are spilled upon slabs of cold stone, or the future from the patterns of migrating birds, and more recently, parlor tricks like mind-reading, picking correct cards from a deck, trying to decipher meaning from within crystal balls, the deal of the Tarot, a throw of dice, the lines on the palm of a hand; and, finally, twice a year, to the lighting of a ritual candle *in memoriam* of those long-gone, long-lost, mostly forgotten candle-readers.

Except...at the last biyearly lighting of a ritual candle, I truly experienced a vision, and since then, with each candle-lighting subsequent visions. All of which leads me to believe that I have been chosen, by whomever or whatever powers may be, to chronicle not only the reason behind the initial fading of Major Magic but also its recent return.

So, join me, if you will, as I light yet another candle, one made specifically for this purpose by the candle-artisan, Jfay, and begin recording for posterity, and relating to you, personally, what is even now occurring, at this very moment, in an area around a small town called Flicker in central Washington State, where there is, even as I write, fierce competition in progress between young and old, male and female, candle-readers, vampires, werewolves, shape-shifters, demons, dragons, shadow-people, chimera, tree-spirits, and all manner of other long forgotten beasts and races, some once known, some never known, but all vying for the ultimate power in Major Magic—sitting on the Master Magician's throne.

I light my candle within this dim-lit room. I relax and let myself merge with the flame, dance within its flickering glow. I gaze into its fiery center to read what is my family's heritage and my own present and future to see.

And, this is what I see...

177. *William Maltese's Wine Taster's Diary: Spokane and Pullman, Washington*, by William Maltese

Rockville, MD: The Borgo Press, an Imprint of Wildside Press, 2010, 147 pages, ISBN 978-1-4344-1160-0, $14.99, trade paperback.

I WAS BORN AND RAISED in Spokane, Washington. I went to Pratt Elementary School, Libby Junior High School, Lewis and Clark High School. I attended Washington State University in Pullman, Washington. After my graduation from the latter, I jettisoned the Spokane/Pullman area, like just about everyone else who has ever been born and raised there, to head off to places a little less quiet, a little less conservative…a lot more exotic, erotic, more culturally sophisticated, and a lot more "with it." Literally, I circled the globe a couple of times, often finding myself sipping the local wines in the vineyards of France, Germany, Italy, Spain, Chile, South Africa, and Australia….

Actually, my interest in wine occurred before I left the Pacific Northwest. My final university paper in Marketing/Advertising was based upon "The U.S. Pacific Coast. Wine Industry." However, at the time, there was no wine production in Washington State. There was none in Oregon State. Its emerging presence in California, on which I based my treatise, wasn't yet so far along that any of that state's wines were yet recognized as serious competition to its European counterparts.

My earliest ongoing long-term relationship with wine, therefore, was with those bottled by the long-established French châteaux; not so expensive, at the time that they couldn't be far more easily, monetarily, accessed and enjoyed than they are today. Imbibing Château Lafite-Rothschild, Château Margaux, Château Latour, Château Haut-Brion, Château Mouton-Rothschild, and Château D'Yquem, on the very ancient sites from which their grapes are still grown and harvested, spoiled me for years into thinking that the only really great wines were French wines. That early and long-lasting impression remained with me even as I and my nose and palate ventured farther afield with on-site sampling of German Spätburgunder, Muskattrollinger; Italian Valpolicella, Lambrusco, even Frascati whose history goes back 2,000 years to ancient Rome;

Spanish Divus, Muruve Crianza; Chilean Cabernet Sauvignon; South African Pinotage and Bordeaux Blend Stellenbosch....

178. *The "Happy" Hustler*, by William Maltese

Rockville, MD: The Borgo Press, an Imprint of Wildside Press, 2010, 167 pages, ISBN 978-1-4344-1163-1, $14.99, trade paperback.

PAUL...ET AL.

While, in retrospect, I can easily see that I was receiving money for sexual favors even during pre-pubescence, when I really didn't have a clue...and while I shall mention those incidents, herein, in passing, only since to leave them out would be to truncate my story of becoming, for the most part, a happy hustler...I have no intentions of going into the same explicit detail, in their regard, that I will do, in later chapters, when recounting my sexual encounters after I reached the age of consent. I have no desire to be accused of writing anything with even the slightest hint of seeming to pander to the prurient interests of pederasts.

So, just know that there was Donnie, the older boy, who lived next door, who enticed me with the offer of candy (yes, there is something behind that old ploy), to join him in the overly large doghouse (literally) usually occupied by his family's Great Dane, Pantegruel, when we weren't using it. While there was never any actual penile penetration, oral or anal, we did do a lot of petting and cuddling, Donnie physically spooning and stroking me from behind; which I've only now come to realize, has a sexual term that describes it—frottage—that always has me confusing it with *fromage*, French for cheese. By way of additional payment for my services, and silence, Donnie acted for years as my protector on the schoolyard.

There was Father Kinstock, the Catholic priest, who sucked my cock (which obliged him by going hard in his mouth but couldn't yet provide him even one drop of nonexistent cream; he never seemed to mind), and who rewarded me with extra sacramental wine (Moganberry, I do believe).

179. *Grit,* by William Maltese and Jardonn Smith

Albion, NY: MLR Press, 2010, [200] pages, ISBN 978-0-60820-021-1, $14.99, trade paperback.

Grit permeates each crevice of the Depression and the men living through it. This sex-saturated tale from William Maltese and Jardonn Smith is of have's and have-not's who run trains across the Dust Bowl…who hitch trains to escape poverty and despair.

* * * * * * *

THE CRO-MAGNON CROATION-AMERICAN

Wilton Zukel was a good boy. His mother said so. His aunt said so. Even his staunch and stoic father, who rarely spoke words of encouragement or praise of any sort to anybody, said so. One of the three final statements the elder Zukel left for his son, words spoken from a hospital bed where Wilton's papa lay suffering with second and third degree burns upon seventy percent of his flesh.

"Wilton," he said. "Come closer." With only the right side of his face intact and unencumbered by bandages, Mr. Zukel's Croatian-accented English was nearly unintelligible. A tent of sheer linen sealed him off from the rest of the room, as his son stood with nose touching the outside, listening while watching his father's lips. An eyewitness to the dangers of railroading in the age of steam, the younger Zukel winced at the sight of his papa, a fireman ravaged by fire.

The fireman shovels coal into the firebox. Fire boils the water that produces steam to power the drive train that turns the locomotive's wheels, but when the rear axle breaks and wheels ride on wooden ties instead of steel rails, red-hot coals are bounced from the opened-door firebox. The fireman shoveling fresh coal into the box is peppered with fired coals shooting out. They pelt his exposed skin. They find their way inside the bib of his overalls and set his clothing afire, and with continued forward motion of the locomotive, wind from its open cab fans the flames to an extent that no amount of rolling or smothering can suffocate them.

180. *Draqualian Silk: A Collector's & Bibliographical Guide to the Books of William Maltese, 1969-2010*, by William Maltese

Rockville, MD: The Borgo Press, an Imprint of Wildside Press, 2010, 303 pages, ISBN 978-1-4344-1172-3, $16.99, trade paperback.

Let me confess to being fully aware that my being who I am, today—where I am, today—with the backlog of literary work I have to my credit, today—is, in large part, attributable to some pretty damned good luck. There is simply no denying that anyone being the right person, at the right time, in the right place, can turn keys in a helluva lot of locks, to open wide a helluva lot of doors, otherwise usually kept tightly shut and secured.

Certainly, I, personally, had nothing whatsoever to do with my having been born such a mighty fine-looking baby, Baby! Seriously, I'm not saying that just because I'm narcissistic (although, I am), or because the nurse, who may well have been blind at the time, announced to the world at my birthing…, "Miss Scarlett, I don't know nuthin' about birthin' no baby!" Oops, I seem to have become a bit confused (literally? literarily?), which does happen to me, more and more often, at this junction of my long life, hopefully to get longer (since another wished-for elongation—of a certain anatomical part—never did take place). Rather, I say so, because, that delivery-room nurse wasn't the first or only person to say I was "too pretty to be a boy," quite aside from my parents and relatives, or anyone else, who might have possibly felt obligated to say it, true or not. Nor did my attractiveness wane as I proceeded into adolescence and early manhood, unlike most of those "other" very few beautiful male babies who usually turn into ogres before their testicles drop and/or their cocks achieve full cum-spewing capabilities. Pretty much everyone said I was beautiful and that I remained so, even when I had long since come to prefer they'd say "handsome." Definitely, undeniably, there *was* a consensus!

I mean, surely not everyone would lie, 24/7, would they? Okay, maybe, they would, but I've seen enough of my pictures, from babyhood to manhood, including a few nude ones, to know that I looked pretty damned good, the whole damned way. And, I, after all, have become quite the authority on genuinely attractive young men, having written over 180 published books that always included at least one, sometimes more than one (well, maybe not in my *THE GLUTEN-FREE WAY: MY WAY*, or in my *CATALYTIC QUOTES: SOME HEARD THROUGH A TIME WARP*), but there are always exceptions to every rule, aren't there?

PSEUDONYM and TITLE INDEX

(All references are to item numbers)

John Anderson (1 book)

12 Inches, #89A

Don Baxter (1 book)

Island Meat, #72A

Stu Chadwick (2 books)

Brother to Brother, #67A
Making the Team, #75A

Christopher Dane (2 books)

The Galactic Arena, #109
Riders of the Dragon, #111

Adriana deBolt (3 books)

The Alien Within, #97
The Crystal of Power, #96
Voyage of the Trigon, #108

Cort Forbes (2 books)

Enlisted Man, #88
Young Cruisers: An Anthology, #137

Adam Hayes (1 book)

Hot Greek Summer, #77A

Joey (1 book)

Diary of a Hustler, #136

Karl Klyne (2 books)

Jason and the Astronauts, #113
The Last Galaxy Game, #95

Anna Lambert (3 books)

House of the Brave Bulls, #94
Love's Courage, #81
Vanessa in White Marble, #93

Billy Lambert (1 book)

Dog on a Surfboard (and the Rest of the Adventure), #145

W. Lambert III (5 books)

Assignment: Grey Area, #115
Encores in Fade, #112
Michael: The Master, #114
The Brentridge Gold: The Pleiades Portals Series, #143
The Sex Lab, #10

Willa Lambert (8 books)

Africa: Spice Island Love: Book #1 of the Seven Continent Series, #174
Emerald-Silk Intrigue, #133
From this Beloved Hour, #125
Heart on Fire: A Romance, #154
Jungle Quest Intrigue, #134
Love's Emerald Flame, #92
Love's Golden Spell, #132
Moon-Stone Intrigue, #135

William J. Lambert (1 book)

Valley of the Damned, #16

William J. Lambert III (14 books)

Adonis, #1
Adonis at Actum, #2
Adonis at Bomasa, #3
Bob, Carl, Ted and Alan, #15
Demon's Coronation, #13
Demon's Stalk, #6
Five Roads to Tlen, #4
Gaius Maximus, #34
The Gods of Tlen, #5
Male Sex Idol, #26
The Maneaters of Malibu, #12
Pop 'n' Swap, #11
Their Husbands are at War, #17
The Young Master, #8

Wm. J. Lambert III (2 books)

Master Black, #14
The Sixty-Niners, #9

Raymond C. Lang (1 book)

In the Hole, #54

Raymond R. Lang (2 books)

Cockring, #52
The Secret of the Phallic Stone, #53

Raymond Lange (2 books)

The Boy of Thira, #77
Young Men of the Night, #70

L. Linehan (1 book)

Bohack: Symbiotic Worlds, #110

William Maltese (48 books)

Anal Cousins: Case Studies in Variant Sexual Practices, #156
Ardennian Boy (with Wayne Gunn), #153
Back of the Boat Gourmet Cooking: Afloat—Pool-side—Backyard
　(with Bonnie Clark), #175
Beyond Machu, #151
Blood-Red Resolution: Being Excerpts from the Crypto-Coded Files
　of the United Courier Service: A Novel of Adventure, #160
Bond-Shattering, #150
California Creamin' & Other Stories: An Erotic Anthology, #139
Catalytic Quotes: (Some Heard Through a Time Warp): One Music-
　History- Literary- and Trivia-Buff's Pure Conjecture on the
　Seemingly Sometimes Idiosyncratic Transmigration of the Crea-
　tive Muse, #163
circuSex: A One-Hand Read®, #148
A Conspiracy of Ravens: A One-Hand Read®, #147
Dare to Love in Oz, #172
Diary of a Hustler (Told by Joey), #136A
Draqualian Silk: A Collector's & Bibliographical Guide to the
　Books of William Maltese, 1969-2010, #180
Emerald-Silk Intrigue, #133A
The Fag Is Not for Burning: A Mystery Novel, #157
From This Beloved Hour, #125A
Gerun, the Heretic: Being Excerpts from the Clan-Missionary
　Chronicles: A Science Fiction Novel, #158
The Gluten-Free Way: My Way (with Adrienne Z. Milligan), #171
Goldsands, #159
The Gomorrha Conjurations, #152
Grit (with Jardonn Smith), #179
The "Happy" Hustler, #178
Heart on Fire: A Romance, #154
I, Debauchee: Book #1 of the William Maltese "I" Series, #173
Jungle Quest Intrigue, #134A
Love Hurts, #161
Love's Emerald Flame, #92A
Love's Golden Spell, #132A
Moon-Stone Intrigue, #135A
Moonstone Murders: The Movie Script, #162
Murder by Meteorite: A Play in Three Acts, #169
Ride the Man Down: #1 in the New World Shaman Series, #168
Slaves, #138A
A Slip to Die for: A Stud Draqual Mystery, #141

Slovakian Boy, #149
Snakes, #166
SS & M: Being Excerpts from the Nazi Death-Head Files, #155
SS Mann Hunt, #144
Sucks!: Book #1 of the Draqual Vampyre Chronicles, #164
Summer Sweat: An Erotic Anthology, #140
Thai Died: A Stud Draqual Mystery, #146
Total Meltdown: A Tripler and Clarke Adventure (with Raymond
    Gaynor), #170
Tusks, #165
Wet Skin: Wet & Wild First-Time Stories (with Laura Baumbach),
    #167
When Summer Comes, #142
*William Maltese's Flicker: #1 Book of Answers: First Book of the
    Flicker Series*, #176
*William Maltese's Wine Taster's Diary: Spokane and Pullman,
    Washington*, #177
Young Cruisers: An Anthology, #137A

Alex Mann (1 book)

Big Foot, #89

Doug Mason (2 books)

Daddy's Big Boy, #65B
Pumping Jocks, #71A

Wilhelm Mauser (5 books)

Abducted Daughter, #62
An Incestuous Stepmother, #64
Incestuous Summer, #59
Lessons for Mother, #61
The Gang-Ravished Teacher, #63

Norm Peters (1 book)

"YM" Weekend, #87A

Kyle Reich (6 books)

Black Sun, #72

Gay Collection Series, Book #5, #65A
Macho Brother, #76
Night of the Animals, #79
Stocks & Bonds, #65
Teacher in Chains, #91

Mark Richards (1 book)

G.I. Jock, by Mark Richards, #88A

Mitch Stone (1 book)

Ty's Mission, #35A

Chad Stuart (23 books)

Animal Man, #58
Beat the Man Down, #36
Big Guns, #24
Black Room Terror, #57
Blackballed, #27
Buck, #42
E-Mission, #35
The Erection, #28
Flight into Sodomy, #66
G.I. Jock, #33
Greek Row, #75
Gusher Comin', #56
Joint Hunger, #30
K-YMCA, #87
Making the Jock, #31
The Meat Eaters, #41
Men in Heat, #73
Montana Bound, #68
Mountain Men, #29
A Presidential Affair, #43
Shaft Man, #32
The Siegfried Mating, #55
Up on the Floor, #80

Rick Taylor (1 book)

Deep Load, #90A

Bryant Tyler (1 book)

Shaft, #90

Alex von Mann (1 book)

Slaves, #138

Ernst Webber (1 book)

The Incestuous Stepfather, #60

Scott Weyburn (1 book)

The President's Men, #43A

Lambert Wilhelm (55 books)

Abort Project K!, #116
B&D Boys, #44
B&D Buddies, #106
B&D Hustlers, #122
Balling Brothers, #107
Black Room Buddies, #131
Bodybuilding Buddies, #117
Bondage Boy, #47
Boy in Bondage, #49
Brother in Bondage, #46
Brothers in the End, #82
Bugger Boy, #38
Call Boy Brothers, #105
College Buddies, #100
Cop Out, #69
Cop Sucker, #50
Country Studs, #127
Cruising Cops, #99
The Doctor's Unorthodox Practice, #20
Dog Collar Boys, #22
Faculty Wife, #19
Fun House Buddies, #102
Golden Shower Slave, #130
The Gray Flannel Swap, #7
Hazards of Hustling, #121

Heavy Cruisers, #126
Homecoming Buddies, #98
Hotel Hustlers, #51
Hung Father, #83
Hunter Stud, #124
In Stocks and Bondage, #128
Into Leather, into Bondage, #118
Jamaican Traders, #21
Jock Stud, #39
Leather Bound, #45
Masters and Slaves, #129
Meat, #74
Midnight Hustler, #120
Oil Rig Boys, #84
Raped Stud, #85
Richard's Brother, #67
Sex Intrigue, #25
Snowbound Studs, #101
Son Loving Father, #86
Starship Intercourse, #18
Strung and Hung, #48
Stud Maker, #37
Stud on the Rings, #123
The Sweat Game, #71
Tied Up Ranch Hands, #103
Too Beautiful, #23
Trucker Sucker, #40
Two Brothers, #78
Well-Hung Hustlers, #119
White Water Buddies, #104

Mike Woodward (2 books)

Brothers All the Way, #78A
Hard Packer, #74A

PUBLISHER, TITLE, and AUTHOR INDEX

(All references are to item numbers)

Arena Publications (37 books)

(Imprints: Driveshaft Library, Golden Boy Books, and Power Force Series)

12 Inches, by John Anderson, #89A
Big Foot, by Alex Mann, #89
Black Sun, by Kyle Reich, #72
The Boy of Thira, by Raymond Lange, #77
Brother to Brother, by Stu Chadwick, #67A
Brothers All the Way, by Mike Woodward, #78A
Brothers in the End, by Lambert Wilhelm, #82
Cop Out, by Lambert Wilhelm, #69
Daddy's Big Boy, by Doug Mason, #65B
Deep Load, by Rick Taylor, #90A
Enlisted Man, by Cort Forbes, #88
Flight into Sodomy, by Chad Stuart, #66
G.I. Jock, by Mark Richards, #88A
Greek Row, by Chad Stuart, #75
Hard Packer, by Mike Woodward, #74A
Hot Greek Summer, by Adam Hayes, #77A
Island Meat, by Don Baxter, #72A
K-YMCA, by Chad Stuart, #87
Macho Brother, Kyle Reich, #76
Making the Team, by Stu Chadwick, #75A
Meat, by Lambert Wilhelm, #74
Men in Heat, by Chad Stuart, #73
Montana Bound, by Chad Stuart, #68
Night of the Animals, by Kyle Reich, #79
The President's Men, by Scott Weyburn, #43A
Pumping Jocks, by Doug Mason, #71A

Richard's Brother, by Lambert Wilhelm, #67
Shaft, by Bryant Tyler, #90
Stocks & Bonds, by Kyle Reich, #65
The Sweat Game, by Lambert Wilhelm, #71
Teacher in Chains, by Kyle Reich, #91
Two Brothers, by Lambert Wilhelm, #78
Ty's Mission, by Mitch Stone, #35A
Up on the Floor, by Chad Stuart, #80
"YM" Weekend, by Norm Peters, #87A
Young Men of the Night, by Raymond Lange, #70

Bee-Line Books (3 books)

(Imprints, Bee-Line Books and An Orpheus Original)

Pop 'n' Swap, by William J. Lambert III, #11
The Sex Lab, by W. Lambert III, #10
The Sixty-Niners, by William J. Lambert III, #9

The Blueboy Library (4 books)

Cockring, by Raymond R. Lang, #52
In the Hole, by Raymond C. Lang, #54
The Secret of the Phallic Stone, by Raymond R. Lang, #53
The Siegfried Mating, by Chad Stuart, #55

The Borgo Press Imprint of Wildside Press (27 books)

Anal Cousins: Case Studies in Variant Sexual Practices, by William
     Maltese, #156
Back of the Boat Gourmet Cooking: Afloat—Pool-side—Backyard,
     by Bonnie Clark and William Maltese, #175
*Blood-Red Resolution: Being Excerpts from the Crypto-Coded Files
     of the United Courier Service: A Novel of Adventure*, by William
     Maltese, #160
*Catalytic Quotes: (Some Heard Through a Time Warp): One Music-
     History- Literary- and Trivia-Buff's Pure Conjecture on the
     Seemingly Sometimes Idiosyncratic Transmigration of the Crea-
     tive Muse*, by William Maltese, #163
*Draqualian Silk: A Collector's & Bibliographical Guide to the
     Books of William Maltese, 1969-2010*, by William Maltese, #180
Emerald-Silk Intrigue, by William Maltese Writing as Willa Lam-
     bert, #133A

The Fag Is Not for Burning: A Mystery Novel, by William Maltese, #157

From This Beloved Hour, by William Maltese Writing as Willa Lambert, #125A

Gerun, the Heretic: Being Excerpts from the Clan-Missionary Chronicles: A Science Fiction Novel, by William Maltese, #158

The Gluten-Free Way: My Way, by Adrienne Z. Milligan and William Maltese, #171

The Gomorrha Conjurations, by William Maltese, #152

The "Happy" Hustler, by William Maltese, #178

Heart on Fire: A Romance, by William Maltese Writing by "Willa Lambert," #154

Jungle Quest Intrigue, by William Maltese Writing as Willa Lambert, #134A

Love's Emerald Flame, by William Maltese Writing as Willa Lambert, #92A

Love's Golden Spell, by William Maltese Writing as Willa Lambert, #132A

Moon-Stone Intrigue, by William Maltese Writing as Willa Lambert, #135A

Moonstone Murders: The Movie Script, by William Maltese, #162

Murder by Meteorite: A Play in Three Acts, by William Maltese, #169

Slaves, by William Maltese, #138A

A Slip to Die For: A Stud Draqual Mystery, by William Maltese, #141A

SS & M: Being Excerpts from the Nazi Death-Head Files, by William Maltese, #155

Summer Sweat: An Erotic Anthology, by William Maltese, #140A

Total Meltdown: A Tripler and Clarke Adventure, by Raymond Gaynor and William Maltese, #170

When Summer Comes, by William Maltese, #142A

William Maltese's Wine Taster's Diary: Spokane and Pullman, Washington, by William Maltese, #177

Young Cruisers: An Anthology, by William Maltese, #137A

Carousel Books (American Art Enterprises) (15 books)

Abort Project K!, by Lambert Wilhelm, #116
The Alien Within, by as Adriana deBolt, #97
Assignment: Grey Area, by W. Lambert III, #115
Bohack: Symbiotic Worlds, by L. Linehan, #110
The Crystal of Power, by Adriana deBolt, #96

Encores in Fade, by W. Lambert III, #112
The Galactic Arena, by Christopher Dane, #109
House of the Brave Bulls, by Anna Lambert, #94
Jason and the Astronauts, by Karl Klyne, #113
The Last Galaxy Game, by Karl Klyne, #95
Love's Courage, by Anna Lambert, #81
Michael: The Master, by W. Lambert III, #114
Riders of the Dragon, by Christopher Dane, #111
Vanessa in White Marble, by Anna Lambert, #93
Voyage of the Trigon, by Adriana deBolt, #108

Green Candy Press (2 books)

Slovakian Boy, by William Maltese, #149
Thai Died: A Stud Draqual Mystery, by William Maltese, #146

Greenleaf Classics (66 books)

(Imprints: Adonis Classics, Adult Book, Adult Reading/ Gay Novel, Candid Reader, Companion Book, Greenleaf Classics, Nitime Swapbook, Pleasure Reader)

Adonis, by William J. Lambert III, #1
Adonis at Actum, by William J. Lambert III, #2
Adonis at Bomasa, by William J. Lambert III, #3
B&D Boys, by Lambert Wilhelm, #44
B&D Buddies, by Lambert Wilhelm, #106
B&D Hustlers, by Lambert Wilhelm, #122
Balling Brothers, by Lambert Wilhelm, #107
Beat the Man Down, by Chad Stuart, #36
Big Guns, by Chad Stuart, #24
Black Room Buddies, by Lambert Wilhelm, #131
Blackballed, by Chad Stuart, #27
Bob, Carl, Ted and Alan, William J. Lambert III, #15
Bodybuilding Buddies, by Lambert Wilhelm, #117
Bondage Boy, by Lambert Wilhelm, #47
Boy in Bondage, by Lambert Wilhelm, #49
Brother in Bondage, by Lambert Wilhelm, #46
Bugger Boy, by Lambert Wilhelm, #38
Call Boy Brothers, by Lambert Wilhelm, #105
College Buddies, by Lambert Wilhelm, #100
Cop Sucker, by Lambert Wilhelm, #50
Country Studs, by Lambert Wilhelm, #127

Cruising Cops, by Lambert Wilhelm, #99
Demon's Coronation, William J. Lambert III, #13
Demon's Stalk, by William J. Lambert III, #6
The Doctor's Unorthodox Practice, by Lambert Wilhelm, #20
The Erection, by Chad Stuart, #28
Faculty Wife, by Lambert Wilhelm, #19
Five Roads to Tlen, by William J. Lambert III, #4
Fun House Buddies, by Lambert Wilhelm, #102
The Gods of Tlen, by William J. Lambert III, #5
G.I. Jock, by Chad Stuart, #33
Golden Shower Slave, by Lambert Wilhelm, #130
The Gray Flannel Swap, by Lambert Wilhelm, #7
Hazards of Hustling, by Lambert Wilhelm, #121
Heavy Cruisers, by Lambert Wilhelm, #126
Homecoming Buddies, by Lambert Wilhelm, #98
Hotel Hustlers, by Lambert Wilhelm, #51
Hung Father, by Lambert Wilhelm, #83
Hunter Stud, by Lambert Wilhelm, #124
In Stocks and Bondage, by Lambert Wilhelm, #128
Into Leather, into Bondage, by Lambert Wilhelm, #118
Jamaican Traders, by Lambert Wilhelm, #21
Jock Stud, by Lambert Wilhelm, #39
Joint Hunger, by Chad Stuart, #30
Leather Bound, by Lambert Wilhelm, #45
Making the Jock, by Chad Stuart, #31
Master Black, Wm. J. Lambert III, #14
Masters and Slaves, by Lambert Wilhelm, #129
Midnight Hustler, by Lambert Wilhelm, #120
Mountain Men, Chad Stuart, #29
The Maneaters of Malibu, William J. Lambert III, #12
Oil Rig Boys, by Lambert Wilhelm, #84
Raped Stud, by Lambert Wilhelm, #85
Shaft Man, by Chad Stuart, #32
Snowbound Studs, by Lambert Wilhelm, #101
Son Loving Father, by Lambert Wilhelm, #86
Starship Intercourse, by Lambert Wilhelm, #18
Strung and Hung, by Lambert Wilhelm, #48
Stud Maker, by Lambert Wilhelm, #37
Stud on the Rings, by Lambert Wilhelm, #123
Tied Up Ranch Hands, by Lambert Wilhelm, #103
Trucker Sucker, by Lambert Wilhelm, #40
Valley of the Damned, William J. Lambert, #16
Well-Hung Hustlers, Lambert Wilhelm, #119

White Water Buddies, by Lambert Wilhelm, #104
The Young Master, by William J. Lambert III, #8

Hard Trade Specials (Surree House) (3 books)

Animal Man, by Chad Stuart, #58
Black Room Terror, by Chad Stuart, #57
Gusher Comin', by Chad Stuart, #56

Harlequin Romances (3 books)

From this Beloved Hour, by Willa Lambert, #125
Love's Emerald Flame, by Willa Lambert, #92
Love's Golden Spell, by Willa Lambert, #132

Heritage House Books (Moonspinner Press) (3 books)

Emerald-Silk Intrigue, by Willa Lambert, #133
Jungle Quest Intrigue, by Willa Lambert, #134
Moon-Stone Intrigue, by Willa Lambert, #135

iUniverse (2 books)

A Conspiracy of Ravens: A One-Hand Read®, by William Maltese, #147
circuSex: A One-Hand Read®, by William Maltese, #148

MLR Press (16 books)

(Imprints: MLR Press, Passion in Print Press)

Africa: Spice Island Love: Book #1 of the Seven Continent Series, by Willa Lambert, #174
Ardennian Boy, by William Maltese and Wayne Gunn, #153
Beyond Machu, by William Maltese, #151
Bond-Shattering, by William Maltese, #150
California Creamin' and Other Stories, by William Maltese, #139B
circuSex: A One-Hand Read®, by William Maltese, #148A
Diary of a Hustler, by William Maltese (Told by Joey), #136A
Goldsands, by William Maltese, #159
Grit, by William Maltese and Jardonn Smith, #179
I, Debauchee: Book #1 of the William Maltese "I" Series, by William Maltese, #173

Love Hurts, by William Maltese, #161
Ride the Man Down: #1 in the New World Shaman Series, by William Maltese, #168
Snakes, by William Maltese, #166
Sucks!: Book #1 of the Draqual Vampyre Chronicles, by William Maltese, #164
Tusks, by William Maltese, #165
Wet Skin: Wet & Wild First-Time Stories, by Laura Baumbach and William Maltese, #167

Nightwares Books (1 book)

Bond-Shattering, by William Maltese, #150

Parisian Press (4 books)

Dog Collar Boys, by Lambert Wilhelm, #22
Male Sex Idol, by William J. Lambert III, #26
Sex Intrigue, by Lambert Wilhelm, #25
Too Beautiful, by Lambert Wilhelm, #23

Prowler Books (7 books)

California Creamin' & Other Stories: An Erotic Anthology, by William Maltese, #139
California Creamin' and Other Stories: An Erotic Anthology, by William Maltese, #139A
Diary of a Hustler, by Joey, #136
Slaves, by Alex von Mann, #138
A Slip to Die for: A Stud Draqual Mystery, by William Maltese, #141
Summer Sweat: An Erotic Anthology, by William Maltese, #140
When Summer Comes, by William Maltese, #142
Young Cruisers, by Cort Forbes, #137

Publisher's Consultants (6 books)

(Imprints: Captive Women Series, Family Series Books, and Monterey Library Press)

Abducted Daughter, by Wilhelm Mauser, #62
The Gang-Ravished Teacher, by Wilhelm Mauser, #63
Gay Collection Series, Book #5, two novels by Marvin Page (not

William Maltese) and Kyle Reich (Maltese), #65A
An Incestuous Stepmother, by Wilhelm Mauser, #64
The Incestuous Stepfather, by Ernst Webber, #60
Incestuous Summer, by Wilhelm Mauser, #59
Lessons for Mother, by Wilhelm Mauser, #61

RAM-10 (Hamilton House Publishing) (4 books)

Buck, by Chad Stuart, #42
E-Mission, by Chad Stuart, #35
The Meat Eaters, by Chad Stuart, #41
A Presidential Affair, by Chad Stuart, #43

Savant Books (2 books)

Dare to Love in Oz, by William Maltese, #172
*William Maltese's Flicker: #1 Book of Answers: First Book of the
    Flicker Series*, by William Maltese, #176

Southern Tier Editions (1 book)

Beyond Machu, by William Maltese, #151

Trojan Classics (1 book)

Gaius Maximus, by William J. Lambert III, #34

Venice Books (Venice Publishing) (1 book)

Their Husbands Are at War, by William J. Lambert III, #17

Writers Club Press (3 books)

The Brentridge Gold: The Pleiades Portals Series, by W. Lambert
    III, #143
Dog on a Surfboard (and the Rest of the Adventure), by Billy Lam-
    bert, #145
SS Mann Hunt, by William Maltese, #144

TITLE and PSEUDONYM INDEX

(All references are to item numbers;
short stories in collections are listed in quotation marks)

12 Inches, by John Anderson, #89A
Abducted Daughter, by Wilhelm Mauser, #62
Abort Project K!, by Lambert Wilhelm, #116
"Abracadacus," by William Maltese, #140
Adonis, by William J. Lambert III, #1
Adonis at Actum, by William J. Lambert III, #2
Adonis at Bomasa, by William J. Lambert III, #3
Africa: Spice Island Love: Book #1 of the Seven Continent Series, by
    Willa Lambert, #174
The Alien Within, by Adriana deBolt, #97
Anal Cousins: Case Studies in Variant Sexual Practices, by William
    Maltese, #156
"Anasazi Medicine Bag," by William Maltese, #161
Animal Man, by Chad Stuart, #58
Ardennian Boy, by William Maltese and Wayne Gunn, #153
Assignment: Grey Area, by W. Lambert III, #115
B&D Boys, by Lambert Wilhelm, #44
B&D Buddies, by Lambert Wilhelm, #106
B&D Hustlers, by Lambert Wilhelm, #122
Back of the Boat Gourmet Cooking: Afloat—Pool-side—Backyard,
    by Bonnie Clark and William Maltese, #175
Balling Brothers, by Lambert Wilhelm, #107
Beat the Man Down, by Chad Stuart, #36
"Been There, Done That," by Cort Forbes, #137
"Been There, Done That," by William Maltese, #137A
Beyond Machu, by William Maltese, #151
Big Foot, by Alex Mann, #89
Big Guns, by Chad Stuart, #24
"Black and Blue," by Cort Forbes, #137
"Black and Blue," by William Maltese, #137A

Black Room Buddies, by Lambert Wilhelm, #131
Black Room Terror, by Chad Stuart, #57
Black Sun, by Kyle Reich, #72
Blackballed, by Chad Stuart, #27
Blood-Red Resolution: Being Excerpts from the Crypto-Coded Files of the United Courier Service: A Novel of Adventure, by William Maltese, #160
Bob, Carl, Ted and Alan, by William J. Lambert III, #15
Bodybuilding Buddies, by Lambert Wilhelm, #117
Bohack: Symbiotic Worlds, by L. Linehan, #110
Bond-Shattering, by William Maltese, #150
Bondage Boy, by Lambert Wilhelm, #47
Boy in Bondage, by Lambert Wilhelm, #49
The Boy of Thira, by Raymond Lange, #77
The Brentridge Gold: The Pleiades Portals Series, by W. Lambert III, #143
Brother in Bondage, by Lambert Wilhelm, #46
Brother to Brother, by Stu Chadwick, #67A
Brothers All the Way, by Mike Woodward, #78A
Brothers in the End, by Lambert Wilhelm, #82
Buck, by Chad Stuart, #42
Bugger Boy, by Lambert Wilhelm, #38
"California Creamin'," by William Maltese, #139
California Creamin' & Other Stories: An Erotic Anthology, by William Maltese, #139
California Creamin' and Other Stories, by William Maltese, #139B
California Creamin' and Other Stories: An Erotic Anthology, by William Maltese, #139A
Call Boy Brothers, by Lambert Wilhelm, #105
"Catalyst," by William Maltese, #161
Catalytic Quotes: (Some Heard Through a Time Warp): One Music-History- Literary- and Trivia-Buff's Pure Conjecture on the Seemingly Sometimes Idiosyncratic Transmigration of the Creative Muse, by William Maltese, #163
"Cataracts," by William Maltese, #167
"Changing of the Guard," by William Maltese, #140
circuSex: A One-Hand Read®, by William Maltese, #148
"Closet Case," by William Maltese, #161
Cockring, by Raymond R. Lang, #52
College Buddies, by Lambert Wilhelm, #100
"Comes a Naked Stranger," by William Maltese, #140
A Conspiracy of Ravens: A One-Hand Read®, by William Maltese, #147

Cop Out, by Lambert Wilhelm, #69
"Cop Out," by William Maltese, #140
Cop Sucker, by Lambert Wilhelm, #50
"Counterfeit Cowboys," by William Maltese, #139
Country Studs, by Lambert Wilhelm, #127
"Cowboy Boots," by William Maltese, #139
"Crapshoots," by William Maltese, #140
Cruising Cops, by Lambert Wilhelm, #99
The Crystal of Power, by Adriana deBolt, #96
Daddy's Big Boy, by Doug Mason, #65B
Dare to Love in Oz, by William Maltese, #172
Deep Load, by Rick Taylor, #90A
Demon's Coronation, by William J. Lambert III, #13
Demon's Stalk, by William J. Lambert III, #6
Diary of a Hustler, by Joey, #136
Diary of a Hustler, by William Maltese (Told by Joey), #136A
The Doctor's Unorthodox Practice, by Lambert Wilhelm, #20
Dog Collar Boys, by Lambert Wilhelm, #22
Dog on a Surfboard (and the Rest of the Adventure), by Billy Lambert, #145
"Doppelmörder," by William Maltese, #161
"Doubting Thomas," by William Maltese, #140
Draqualian Silk: A Collector's & Bibliographical Guide to the Books of William Maltese, 1969-2010, by William Maltese, #180
E-Mission, by Chad Stuart, #35
"Eating Crow," by William Maltese, #140
Emerald-Silk Intrigue, by Willa Lambert, #133
Emerald-Silk Intrigue, by William Maltese, #133A
Encores in Fade, by W. Lambert III, #112
Enlisted Man, by Cort Forbes, #88
The Erection, by Chad Stuart, #28
Faculty Wife, by Lambert Wilhelm, #19
The Fag Is Not for Burning: A Mystery Novel, by William Maltese, #157
"Fetish," by William Maltese, #140
Five Roads to Tlen, by William J. Lambert III, #4
Flicker: #1 Book of Answers: First Book of the Flicker Series, by William Maltese, #176
Flight into Sodomy, by Chad Stuart, #66
"Food Chain," by William Maltese, #139
"Football," by William Maltese, #139
From This Beloved Hour, by Willa Lambert, #125
From This Beloved Hour, by William Maltese, #125A

"Fucking Drunk," by William Maltese, #139

Fun House Buddies, by Lambert Wilhelm, #102

Gaius Maximus, by William J. Lambert III, #34

The Galactic Arena, by Christopher Dane, #109

The Gang-Ravished Teacher, by Wilhelm Mauser, #63

Gay Collection Series, Book #5, by Kyle Reich, #65A

Gerun, the Heretic: Being Excerpts from the Clan-Missionary Chronicles: A Science Fiction Novel, by William Maltese, #158

G.I. Jock, by Mark Richards, #88A

G.I. Jock, by Chad Stuart, #33

The Gluten-Free Way: My Way, by Adrienne Z. Milligan and William Maltese, #171

The Gods of Tlen, by William J. Lambert III, #5

Golden Shower Slave, by Lambert Wilhelm, #130

Goldsands, by William Maltese, #159

The Gomorrha Conjurations, by William Maltese, #152

The Gray Flannel Swap, by Lambert Wilhelm, #7

Greek Row, by Chad Stuart, #75

Grit, by William Maltese and Jardonn Smith, #179

"Guess Who?" by William Maltese, #140

Gusher Comin', by Chad Stuart, #56

"Hand-Picked," by William Maltese, #161

The "Happy" Hustler, by William Maltese, #178

Hard Packer, by Mike Woodward, #74A

Hazards of Hustling, by Lambert Wilhelm, #121

Heart on Fire: A Romance, by William Maltese Writing by "Willa Lambert," #154

Heavy Cruisers, by Lambert Wilhelm, #126

"His Lord and Master," by William Maltese, #161

Homecoming Buddies, by Lambert Wilhelm, #98

Hot Greek Summer, by Adam Hayes, #77A

Hotel Hustlers, by Lambert Wilhelm, #51

House of the Brave Bulls, by Anna Lambert, #94

Hung Father, by Lambert Wilhelm, #83

Hunter Stud, by Lambert Wilhelm, #124

I, Debauchee: Book #1 of the William Maltese "I" Series, by William Maltese, #173

In Stocks and Bondage, by Lambert Wilhelm, #128

In the Hole, by Raymond C. Lang, #54

An Incestuous Stepmother, by Wilhelm Mauser, #64

The Incestuous Stepfather, by Ernst Webber, #60

Incestuous Summer, by Wilhelm Mauser, #59

Into Leather, into Bondage, by Lambert Wilhelm, #118

Island Meat, by Don Baxter, #72A
Jamaican Traders, by Lambert Wilhelm, #21
Jason and the Astronauts, by Karl Klyne, #113
Jock Stud, by Lambert Wilhelm, #39
Joint Hunger, by Chad Stuart, #30
Jungle Quest Intrigue, by Willa Lambert, #134
Jungle Quest Intrigue, by William Maltese, #134A
K-YMCA, by Chad Stuart, #87
"Lake Tahoe," by William Maltese, #161
"Lars of the Ring," by William Maltese, #161
The Last Galaxy Game, by Karl Klyne, #95
Leather Bound, by Lambert Wilhelm, #45
Lessons for Mother, by Wilhelm Mauser, #61
"Los Angeles," by William Maltese, #161
Love Hurts, by William Maltese, #161
Love's Courage, by Anna Lambert, #81
Love's Emerald Flame, by Willa Lambert, #92
Love's Emerald Flame, by William Maltese, #92A
Love's Golden Spell, by Willa Lambert, #132
Love's Golden Spell, by William Maltese, #132A
Macho Brother, by Kyle Reich, #76
Making the Jock, by Chad Stuart, #31
Making the Team, by Stu Chadwick, #75A
Male Sex Idol, by William J. Lambert III, #26
The Maneaters of Malibu, by William J. Lambert III, #12
Master Black, by Wm. J. Lambert III, #14
Masters and Slaves, by Lambert Wilhelm, #129
Meat, by Lambert Wilhelm, #74
The Meat Eaters, by Chad Stuart, #41
Men in Heat, by Chad Stuart, #73
"Mensur," by William Maltese, #139
Michael: The Master, by W. Lambert III, #114
Midnight Hustler, by Lambert Wilhelm, #120
Montana Bound, by Chad Stuart, #68
Moon-Stone Intrigue, by Willa Lambert, #135
Moon-Stone Intrigue, by William Maltese, #135A
Moonstone Murders: The Movie Script, by William Maltese, #162
Mountain Men, by Chad Stuart, #29
"Mt. Shasta," by William Maltese, #161
Murder by Meteorite: A Play in Three Acts, by William Maltese,
    #169
"The Music, Man," by William Maltese, #140
Night of the Animals, by Kyle Reich, #79

Oil Rig Boys, by Lambert Wilhelm, #84
"One…Two…Three…Out," by William Maltese, #140
"Open Fly-Fishing Season," by William Maltese, #139
"Pæan to Pain," by William Maltese, #161
"Performing Arts," by Cort Forbes, #137
"Performing Arts," by William Maltese, #137A
"Phantom Beach," by William Maltese, #161
"Play It Again, Sam," by Cort Forbes, #137
"Play It Again, Sam," by William Maltese, #137A
"Poet-Voyeur," by Cort Forbes, #137
"Poet-Voyeur," by William Maltese, #137A
"Poetic Defense of One-Hand Readers," by William Maltese, #139
Pop 'n' Swap, by William J. Lambert III, #11
A Presidential Affair, by Chad Stuart, #43
The President's Men, by Scott Weyburn, #43A
"Pumping Gas," by William Maltese, #139
Pumping Jocks, by Doug Mason, #71A
Raped Stud, by Lambert Wilhelm, #85
Richard's Brother, by Lambert Wilhelm, #67
Ride the Man Down: #1 in the New World Shaman Series, by William Maltese, #168
Riders of the Dragon, by Christopher Dane, #111
"Robinson Hole, Wyoming," by William Maltese, #139
The Secret of the Phallic Stone, by Raymond R. Lang, #53
Sex Intrigue, by Lambert Wilhelm, #25
The Sex Lab, by W. Lambert III, #10
Shaft, by Bryant Tyler, #90
Shaft Man, by Chad Stuart, #32
The Siegfried Mating, by Chad Stuart, #55
The Sixty-Niners, by William J. Lambert III, #9
Slaves, by Alex von Mann, #138
Slaves, by William Maltese, #138A
A Slip to Die for: A Stud Draqual Mystery, by William Maltese, #14
Slovakian Boy, by William Maltese, #149
Snakes, by William Maltese, #166
Snowbound Studs, by Lambert Wilhelm, #101
Son Loving Father, by Lambert Wilhelm, #86
SS & M: Being Excerpts from the Nazi Death-Head Files, by William Maltese, #155
SS Mann Hunt, by William Maltese, #144
Starship Intercourse, by Lambert Wilhelm, #18
Stocks & Bonds, by Kyle Reich, #65
Strung and Hung, by Lambert Wilhelm, #48

Stud Maker, by Lambert Wilhelm, #37

Stud on the Rings, by Lambert Wilhelm, #123

Sucks!: Book #1 of the Draqual Vampyre Chronicles, by William Maltese, #164

"Summer Sweat," by William Maltese, #140

Summer Sweat: An Erotic Anthology, by William Maltese, #140

The Sweat Game, by Lambert Wilhelm, #71

Teacher in Chains, by Kyle Reich, #91

Thai Died: A Stud Draqual Mystery, by William Maltese, #146

Their Husbands Are at War, by William J. Lambert III, #17

"Thou Shalt Not Covet Thy Neighbor's Torqring," by William Maltese, #161

Tied Up Ranch Hands, by Lambert Wilhelm, #103

Too Beautiful, by Lambert Wilhelm, #23

Total Meltdown: A Tripler and Clarke Adventure, by Raymond Gaynor and William Maltese, #170

"Trinity National Forest," by William Maltese, #161

Trucker Sucker, by Lambert Wilhelm, #40

Tusks, by William Maltese, #165

Two Brothers, by Lambert Wilhelm, #78

Ty's Mission, by Mitch Stone, #35A

"Uniform Sex," by William Maltese, #139

"Universal City," by William Maltese, #161

Up on the Floor, by Chad Stuart, #80

"Users," by William Maltese, #139

Valley of the Damned, by William J. Lambert, #16

Vanessa in White Marble, by Anna Lambert, #93

"Variations on a Tale of Two Cities," by William Maltese, #139

Voyage of the Trigon, by Adriana deBolt, #108

Well-Hung Hustlers, by Lambert Wilhelm, #119

Wet Skin: Wet & Wild First-Time Stories, by Laura Baumbach and William Maltese, #167

"What If...?" by William Maltese, #139

"When Opportunity Knocks," by Cort Forbes, #137

"When Opportunity Knocks," by William Maltese, #137A

When Summer Comes, by William Maltese, #142

White Water Buddies, by Lambert Wilhelm, #104

William Maltese's Flicker: #1 Book of Answers: First Book of the Flicker Series, by William Maltese, #176

William Maltese's Wine Taster's Diary: Spokane and Pullman, Washington, by William Maltese, #177

Wine Taster's Diary: Spokane and Pullman, Washington, by William Maltese, #177

"YM" Weekend, by Norm Peters, #87A
Young Cruisers: An Anthology, by Cort Forbes, #137
Young Cruisers: An Anthology, by William Maltese, #137A
The Young Master, by William J. Lambert III, #8
Young Men of the Night, by Raymond Lange, #70
"Zanzibar," by William Maltese, #161

ABOUT THE AUTHOR

WILLIAM MALTESE, the internationally bestselling author of novels, short story collections, and his popular Stud Draqual Mystery Series, has published (under various pseudonyms) close to two hundred books in genres including gay and straight erotica, sci-fi, science-fantasy, mystery, romance, western, adventure, espionage, cooking, wine, and children. With a Business/Advertising degree, Maltese enlisted in the U.S. Army, where he achieved and was honorably discharged at a Sergeant (E-5) rank. Presently, he divides his time between the Pacific Northwest and New York City. You can visit his websites at:

www.williammaltese.com
www.myspace.com/williammaltese
www.facebook.com/williammaltese